Garry Hogg was well-known as an author, journalist, reviewer, broadcaster and lecturer. He was a University Extension Lecturer for twelve years, and an officer of the National Book League (now Book Trust) from 1945 to 1948.

He published twenty-five books, the best known of which are his illustrated travel books, *Dutch Treat*, *Swiss Spring*, *Norwegian Journey* and *Portuguese Journey*.

CANNIBALISM
AND
HUMAN SACRIFICE

GARRY HOGG

ROBERT HALE · LONDON

Robert Hale Limited
Clerkenwell House
Clerkenwell Green
London EC1R 0HT

ISBN 0-7090-4243-4

Printed in Great Britain by
St Edmundsbury Press Limited, Bury St Edmunds, Suffolk
Bound by WBC Bookbinders Limited

CONTENTS

FOREWORD

IT MAY well be asked: What purpose is served by the writing of a book on such a subject as cannibalism? Indeed, this was my own reaction when my publisher invited me to undertake the task.

There is, however, a quite simple answer to the question: No book covering the subject generally exists in the English language. Inquiries from the Royal Anthropological Institute of Great Britain and Ireland elicited the reply: 'We know of no comprehensive work on cannibalism. The material on the subject is unfortunately scattered through many books and periodicals.'

Subsequent inquiries at the British Museum met with the same result: on the 80 miles of shelves in that incomparable library of 8,000,000 books, there is no single work in the English language that covers the immense field of cannibalism and human sacrifice. The Germans would appear to be the only people who have made any attempt to deal comprehensively with the subject on a large scale, and the work in question has not been translated into English.

To collect, check, classify, compare and contrast the enormous amount of material that is, as the Librarian of the Royal Anthropological Institute said, scattered through books and periodicals involved more time and energy than was at first anticipated. Material was forthcoming in the unlikeliest places—much of it in the form of diaries and letters written by missionaries in ink that would often seem to have been home made and on flimsy paper stained by damp, by sea-water, by rough handling from messengers on land and crews on the packet-boats that brought such missives back to England a hundred or a hundred-and-fifty years ago. Many of these were deeply moving: to read between the lines written with those spidery pens was a sobering experience. More than one of the writers had just seen their wives and children brutally massacred and worse, and well knew that a like fate probably awaited them too—perhaps before their letters were delivered at the London headquarters of their missions.

I take pleasure in here acknowledging a great deal of co-operation, all of it most willingly given.

First and foremost, that of Mr B. J. Kirkpatrick, Librarian of the Royal Anthropological Institute of Great Britain and Ireland, to whom I applied in the first instance for advice, and who responded with a list of potentially fruitful titles among the books in his and other libraries.

Secondly, that of the staff of the British Museum, who were relentless in their search for titles that might prove rewarding, and who bore patiently with my niggling persistence and demands for clarification on matters of detail; as always, no trouble was too great for them to take.

Thirdly, the librarians and archivists of the many Missionary Societies and similar bodies who placed desks and shelves at my disposal, spent many hours looking up possible material and making inquiries on my behalf from kindred organisations, and in some cases allowed me to take home with me irreplaceable volumes that, strictly, should not have passed outside the safety of their premises.

Of these, I would particularly like to thank by name the following:—Monsignor Shaw and Miss Margaret Walsh, of the Association for the Propagation of the Faith; the Rev. A. S. Clement, of the Baptist Missionary Society; Miss Joan Ferrier, of the Church Missionary Society; Mr C. D. Overton, Deputy Librarian of the Colonial Office Library; Miss Ruth Jones, Librarian at the International African Institute; Miss Irene Fletcher, of the London Missionary Society; Miss Mollie Allen, of the Melanesian Mission; Miss Joan Anderson, Archivist of the Methodist Missionary Society; Mr G. L. Keeble, Librarian at New Zealand House; Mr J. Skidmore, of the Society for Promoting Christian Knowledge; Mrs Margaret de Satgé, Archivist of the Society for the Propagation of the Gospel in Foreign Parts; Miss Aphra Ward, Librarian of the South American Missionary Society.

With these names should be coupled all those members of their staffs who, unknown to me, did so much spade-work in searching the remote shelves of libraries and other repositories of records on my behalf.

I should like, finally, to emphasise that wherever a theory is propounded or a conclusion drawn in the pages that follow, unless it is attributed to some specific authority it is my own. Not one of the individuals or organisations listed among these acknowledgements should be held in any way responsible for anything of the kind; the responsibility for any errors of statement or conclusion is mine alone.

G. H.

Groombridge, Sussex.

ACKNOWLEDGEMENTS

I AM grateful for permission to quote from the following:

W. H. Allen & Co., Ltd, for *In the Shadow of the Mau Mau*, by Ione Leigh; Angus & Robertson, Ltd, for *The Australian Aborigines*, by A. P. Elkin, and *Adam in Ochre*, by C. Simpson; The Royal Society, for *The Bagesu and Other Tribes of the Uganda Protectorate*, by J. Roscoe; Cassell & Co., Ltd, for *The Scourge of the Swastika*, by Lord Russell of Liverpool; André Deutsch Ltd, for *Easter Island*, by Alfred Métraux; Robert Hale, Ltd, for *Zanzabuku*, by Lewis Cotlow, and *Call of the Jungle*, by H. C. Engert; William Heinemann, Ltd, for *A Voice from the Congo*, by Edmund Ward; Hutchinson & Co., Ltd, for *Whispering Wind*, by Syd Kyle-Little; Michael Joseph, Ltd, for *The Last Cannibals*, by Jens Bjerre; Longmans Green & Co., Ltd, for *A Policeman's Lot*, by H. Söderman; Macmillan & Co., Ltd, for *Islands of Enchantment*, by F. Coombe, *Melanesians and Polynesians*, by G. Brown, and *Savage Life in Central Australia*, by G. Aiston and G. Horne; The Clarendon Press, Oxford, for *Orokaiva Society*, by F. E. Williams; Dr C. K. Meek and Routledge & Kegan Paul, Ltd, for *Tribal Studies in Northern Nigeria*; Dr C. K. Meek and The Clarendon Press, Oxford, for *The Northern Tribes of Nigeria*; G. P. Putnam's Sons for *In the Amazon Jungle*, by Algot Lange; Seeley Service & Co., Ltd, for *Among the Ibos of Nigeria*, by G. T. Basden, *A Church in the Wilds*, by W. B. Grubb, and *In the Isles of King Solomon*, by A. I. Hopkins; Edward Stanford, Ltd, for *South America*, by A. H. Keane; Whitcomb and Tombs, for *The Old Whaling Days*, by Robert McNab; H. F. & G. Witherby, Ltd, for *Wanderings Among South Sea Savages*, by H. W. Walker; Routledge & Kegan Paul, Ltd, for *The Melanesians of British New Guinea*, by C. G. Seligmann; The African Institute, for an article by E. E. Evans-Pritchard in vol. 26 of *Africa*.

INTRODUCTION

Fundamentally, man is a carnivorous animal: he eats flesh. By instinct, tradition and indeed choice, the overwhelming majority of the world's population of 2,500,000,000 are flesh eaters. In a way this is surprising; for the supply of flesh at any one time is vastly exceeded by the total amount of vegetable foodstuffs—vegetables, roots, herbage, and so on—available to him. And what is more, few vegetables have the power to resist capture and consumption that most animals possess.

There are very few types of living creature on the face of the earth that Man has not sampled. He eats beefsteak, mutton chops, lamb cutlets, calves' brains, ox tongue, bacon and ham, besides countless cuts from animals less familiar: kangaroo, wallaby, monkey and bear. Like Rudyard Kipling's 'Noble and Generous Cetacean', he eats 'the starfish and the garfish, and the crab and the dab, and the plaice and the dace, and the skate and his mate, and the mackereel and the really truly twirly-whirly eel'. During and immediately after the Second World War, indeed, he became reconciled to the sight, if not the taste, of the whale itself. And of course in various latitudes and longitudes he has eaten octopus and squid and, perhaps without even knowing it, the 200,000,000-year-old coelacanth itself.

There are few species of bird that he has not snared or shot and then cooked and devoured, from the ostrich and emu to the skylark and the humming-bird. Indeed, such is Man's greed for flesh that he has explored the possibilities of smaller creatures than these—and found himself in a territory whose inhabitants, in variety alone, pass the resource of man to compute.

Everyone knows that John the Baptist survived in the desert on a menu of locusts and wild honey. He was, however, only one man out of untold millions who, down the ages, have looked upon the locust as food. By some it has been regarded as a *spécialité de la maison*. Seventy years ago, Queen Ranavalona of Madagascar employed a band of servants whose sole duty it was to search the fields so that she and her guests at her

Tananarive palace might glut themselves on locusts. Three thousand years earlier, in his palace at Nineveh, King Asurbanipal had locusts served on sticks so that his guests could eat them much as we eat chipolata sausages and other titbits at our own parties today.

For the great majority of people fortunate (if that is the word) enough to live in countries where the locust occurs, this insect is a staple of their diet still. In Tanganyika, locusts have their wings and legs removed and are then roasted or fried in butter; alternatively, they are dried and used for flavouring porridge. More sophisticated connoisseurs, in North Africa, season locusts with nutmeg, pepper and salt, and boil them as soup; alternatively, they are allowed to go cold, then pounded with fried breadcrumbs or rice *purée*, and put in a saucepan to thicken into a broth. The taste of cooked locust has been compared with that of shrimps, boiled egg-yolk, hazel-nuts, crayfish-bisque, and even caviare!

Nor is the locust the most surprising species of food that Man has discovered in this vast territory. In the Belgian Congo, fried termites are sold in basketfuls. A distinguished British traveller recently reported that termites, fried with butter, make a delicious meal. An earlier traveller described how the natives dry the termites in iron pots in the same way as coffee is roasted. They consider them a delectable food, with or without sauce, eaten by the handful. And, as though to emphasise his point, he added: "I have eaten them this way several times and think them delicate, nourishing and wholesome; they are sweeter than, but not so cloying as, the maggot of the *Rynchophorus palmarum*, which is served up at all the luxurious tables of West India."

Ants, too, are widely appreciated; especially the so-called 'sugar-ant' found in Central Australia. These ants select from among their numbers certain individuals whom they forcibly feed until their stomachs swell to the size of gooseberries. The contents of their stomachs consist of the exudations of certain plants and the honey-dew of certain insects. When they come across these ants, the Australians grip them one at a time by the head, squeeze the stomach between their front teeth and suck it dry. They will tell you that the taste is one of strong contrast—and all the better for that: first the sharp sting of the formic acid, and then, as the taut membrane bursts, the sweetness and fragrance of pure honey.

In Indonesia, Malaya, Madagascar, the Belgian Congo and elsewhere, the palm-worm is considered a delicacy. The creature lives in the heart of the palm-tree, and, says a French gourmet, "may be compared with a lump of fat from a capon, wrapped in a very tender, transparent pellicle". These palm-worms, half an inch thick and perhaps two inches long, are heated gently over the fire. When they are sufficiently warmed, they are sprinkled with breadcrumbs, pepper and muscat. Alternatively they may be boiled and then served with a sprinkling of orange or lemon juice. Some connoisseurs prefer to eat them raw; others again prefer them fried alive in oil.

To locusts, termites, ants and palm-worms may be added caterpillars and spiders, moths and dragonflies, beetles and butterflies; and even then only the fringe of the vast insect kingdom's resources have been hinted at. Aphides and wasp grubs may be added to the list, and a researcher some seventy years ago offered an interesting menu for the host who cared to entertain his guests with dishes they might not have sampled previously. The menu included woodlouse sauce with the fried sole, wireworm sauce with the mutton, curried cockchafers, cauliflower garnished with caterpillars, and ended with moths on toast. Sir Hugh Casson, only the other day, reported that fried wasp appeared regularly on the lunch menus of sophisticated New York restaurants!

One type of dish, however, occupied a category distinct from all those hitherto mentioned; indeed, distinct from all those others which would have to be listed to make the curious catalogue of meat-dishes complete: human flesh.

There is abundant evidence that from the remotest periods of pre-history Man has eaten the flesh of his fellows. In 1927, in the Chinese village of Choukoutien, some forty miles southwest of Pekin, a single tooth was discovered which enabled the anatomist Davidson Black to identify a creature closely related to *Pithecanthropus erectus*, the Javan Ape-man already discovered by a Dutch anatomist. Later excavations brought to light the bones and skulls of some forty contemporaries of Black's *Pithecanthropus Pekinensis*, together with a number of their weapons and implements. Charred remains of bones lying on their hearths gave an insight into this primitive man's cooking habits, and there was clear evidence in some curiously broken-up skulls that the brains had been extracted, and cooked. If Pekin Man was, as this evidence strongly suggests, an eater of human flesh, he was also something of an epicure in this respect. And Pekin Man, like Java Man, lived some 500,000 years ago!

Neanderthal Man, living some 220,000 years ago in Central Europe, was almost certainly a cannibal; there is evidence for this in the caves and rock shelters of the Dordogne, particularly at le Moustier, from which comes the term 'Mousterian' culture, and from skeletal remains in a Mousterian settlement at Krapina, in Croatia. Cro-Magnon Man, living some 75,000 years ago and called for the first time *Homo sapiens*, was an eater at times of the flesh of his fellows, if one is to judge by evidence found in the caves of Aurignac, near Toulouse, from which the term 'Aurignacian' derives.

Mesolithic and Neolithic Man, between 10,000 and 2,000 years B.C., maintained the traditions of their ancestors in this respect: there is evidence of this in Switzerland and elsewhere. And in the later Bronze Age, when Man first began working metal, he was still on occasion an eater of human flesh. Austria, among other European countries, offers evidence of this.

The Greek historian Herodotus, writing about 450 B.C., described cannibalistic practices among the Issedones and the nomadic Scythian Massagetae, including the deliberate killing and devouring of old people of their tribes. It was Herodotus who reported also the custom of using dead men's skulls as drinking-cups. Strabo, another Greek historian writing in the last years before Christ, declared positively that the eating of human flesh was a common practice in Ireland, and St Jerome himself, nearly four hundred years later, reported the existence of this practice in Scotland, where the Moss-troopers skirmishing on the Border were also alleged to drink the blood of their defeated enemies.

It is a known fact that during the fighting between the Spaniards and the Arabs in the ninth century, the women of Elvira cut up and ate the body of Sauwar, an Arab chief responsible for the massacre of their menfolk. At the end of the thirteenth century young Marco Polo, then only a seventeen-year-old boy, set off on what was to prove a twenty-four-

years' absence from Venice, during which time he travelled
in the Far East, notably Tartary and China. He, and other
travellers after him, confirmed that many Chinese and Tibetan
tribes ate the flesh of their fellows.

In the year of Shakespeare's birth, 1564, the Polish hero
Wisniowiecki was defeated by the Turks, who then tore out
his heart and devoured it. In the sixteenth century it was the
prerogative of the executioners in many European countries to
retain as their perquisite the blood and certain parts of the body
of the persons they had executed, to make what use of them they
would. The Zingaris of Bohemia, according to a 'rajah' of
their tribe, were in the habit of eating human flesh in the eighteenth century, the most delicate morsels of raw or roasted
flesh being apparently the ears, the palms of the hands, the
soles of the feet, the calves and the cheeks. 'Rajahs' had the
privilege of cutting off the heads of prisoners and drinking the
still warm blood escaping from their veins and arteries. In the
nineteenth century it was not unusual for a Chinese executioner
to eat the heart or the brains of his victims.

These examples are of course for the most part gleaned from
the older historians, from travellers who brought home tales
from foreign parts, from soldiers who had campaigned in distant lands. To them may be added a great number of cases of
the eating of human flesh caused by extreme hunger in times of
siege or famine or shipwreck. Such examples may be multiplied indefinitely, and the majority of them can be easily
authenticated. But it was not until comparatively recent times
that the anthropologist began to make a study of the subject, to
correlate and analyse the evidence and formulate theories in
connection with it.

In many cases he was a traveller himself. But he relied also
on the information from travellers coming from all over the
world; from missionaries in widely scattered fields; from explorers in 'Darkest' Africa, the South American jungles, the
savage islands of Polynesia and Melanesia; from students of
folk-lore who took the trouble to learn the language and then
record the stories and legends of primitive peoples, like the
Kwakiuti Indians, for instance, on the North Pacific Coast.

The amount of information that was thus collected in the
nineteenth and early twentieth centuries was enormous; and

the variety of authenticated detail was perhaps even more remarkable. The practice of eating human flesh was noted in almost every part of the world, except Europe, as a recognised ingredient of the accepted social order.

In the Congo, slaves were deliberately fattened for sale as food in the markets. In Nigeria, victims' bodies were cut up ceremonially and devoured at native shrines. Fijian chiefs used to have a meal of human flesh when they had their hair cut. Young mothers of the Chavantes tribe in Uruguay habitually ate certain of their infants. Dardistan tribesmen drank the blood and ate the hearts of human beings. In West Africa a sect called the Leopard Society dressed in leopard-skins and hunted human beings in the forests, to devour them ceremonially when they had run them down and torn their throats out.

In certain parts of Australia the practice was to smoke-dry the bodies of the victims and then devour those portions of the bodies that had been reduced to liquor or grease by the heat. Elsewhere, the practice was to allow bodies to rot, and then swallow the products of the putrefying processes as they escaped from the corpses. Certain South American tribes reduced the corpses to ashes, mixed the ashes with liquid, and swallowed the mixture. Some African tribes sold the corpses of their dead for food among tribes where food was scarce. A South American tribe actually bred children by their captive women to ensure a regular supply of human flesh when need arose. The variations are endless.

The practice of eating human flesh, in fact, was found to be prevalent in greater or less degree over most of the world. From the South Seas to Vancouver, from the West Indies to the East Indies, in Polynesia, Melanesia, Australia and New Zealand, in North, West, East and Central Africa, in North and South America, there was abundant evidence of current indulgence in the practice; or at least there were the state-ments of men still living who remembered having indulged in such practices, or witnessed them, as younger men.

The older anthropologists used the term 'anthropophagy' to describe the practice, forming the word from the Greek *anthropos* (man) and *phagein* (to eat). The better-known word, of course, is cannibalism. This is a corruption of the word

Carib, the name of a West Indian tribe among whom the practice was first noticed by the Spanish conquistadors. Under that heading, during the past hundred years or so, an enormous amount has been written by anthropologists, especially Americans; and it is presumably due to the wealth of strongly differentiated material that has been laid before them that their theories are so elaborate and often, it will be found, so conflicting; though always interesting.

For example, the American anthropologist Dr Spier wrote:

Primitive people so frequently aligned men and animals in their thinking that it is possible that human flesh was not considered significantly different from other foodstuffs. There is *probably no instinctive aversion* to eating it; the horror shown by civilised, and by many primitive, peoples was developed by convention, parallel to their aversion to eating other foods considered unorthodox, unclean, or unfit for human consumption, much as the pig and the dog are unclean for all Semitic peoples. The abhorrence of such foods is an extraordinarily deep emotion, not dictated by biological necessity.

Dr Eric Miller, on the other hand, writing with no less authority, took an almost diametrically opposite view.

Whether (he wrote) the custom arose in a particular area through famine conditions, or through occasional dietetic necessity, some additional ideological or emotional stimulus is required to overcome *instinctive repugnance* to cannibalism and to confirm it into a regular practice.

But Dr Miller had already made the point that, except in cases of famine, where cannibalism may be said to result from a single motive, there are nearly always two, or even three, interwoven motives—dietetic, magical, pietistic—to account for the practice.

Broadly speaking, however, anthropologists are agreed that where cannibalism exists as a long-established feature of the social life of a community, in whatever part of the world that community may be found, it originated in one or other of several distinct forms. It may be connected with religious ceremonial; it may have magical significance; it may be the ultimate result of a temporary and unwelcome farinaceous diet which led to experimenting with human flesh as food. This last would be a catastrophic form of experiment, for it has been

widely found that when the taste for human flesh is once indulged, such taste quickly develops into a fierce and eventually
unappeasable lust for flesh which no mere animal flesh can ever
satisfy; thus the stages of degradation in gluttony succeed one
another inexorably.

The first two of these motives for cannibalism are of course
closely interwoven; for religion, magic and superstition are
virtually interchangeable terms among primitives. But the
link between these and the crudest motive—that of mere lust
for human flesh—is close, too; for once give a religious, or
magical, or pietistic excuse for the devouring of fellow human
beings, and the demand inevitably grows and grows; and
supply must follow demand.

It is extraordinarily interesting—once one has succeeded in
accepting the morbid aspect of the subject—to note the variations among the motives prompting different peoples to indulge
in cannibalism. For example, certain African and Australian
tribes devoured their dead kinsfolk in the belief that this was the
most flattering method of 'burying' them. A group of tribes
on the North Pacific seaboard ate human flesh as part of an
elaborate ceremonial designed to establish good relations with
their tribal gods. The Ovimbundu tribesmen of South-west
Africa made a banquet off human flesh as a means of ensuring
good luck for a caravan about to start out on a long trek.

The Bagesu of the Uganda Protectorate held cannibal feasts
in order to honour their recent dead, and at these feasts it was a
regular practice to eat the corpses of their fellow-tribesmen.
As an act of revenge, of course, the eating of human flesh was
very widespread indeed. It is easy to see how the mere act of
eating an enemy produced the maximum degree of satisfaction
among the victors. In Africa, in South America, among the
Hallenga and the Fangs of Gaboon, in much of cannibal
Melanesia, part or all of the body of an enemy would be devoured as a final gesture of contempt. In some cases the victim would be methodically dismembered, an arm or a leg at a
time, and the limbs would be cooked and eaten in front of him,
as a supreme gesture of scorn.

Cannibalism was practised by the Bataks as a severe form of
punishment—meted out only to men whose crime was treason
or, what was looked upon as much the same thing, adultery

with a Batak chief's wife. A curious echo of the phrase 'to rub salt into a wound' is seen in this instance: the close relatives of the offender were obliged by tribal law to provide salt and lime for dressing the victim's body before the feast could begin, and must also be present at the feast. This was in all probability a subtle means of preventing the development of a feud between the family of the victim and the family which had feasted off his corpse. Another aspect was that, by devouring the body they would have made it impossible for the victim's ghost to return and inhabit it again and so perhaps exact his own revenge.

More complex, and much more interesting in their very complexity, are the religious, pietistic or magical motives for cannibalism, which have gathered about themselves an extraordinarily detailed and lively body of legend, amounting in some cases almost to a mythology.

Perhaps the most fundamental, as well as the most universal, of these religio-magical beliefs is that a man who eats part of another man's body will immediately come to possess some of the qualities that belonged to him when he was still alive. This was the transference of the 'soul-stuff', or 'life-principle' (there are many other words and phrases to describe this essential ingredient that could, so primitive man thought, be transferred thus from the dead to the living). For a man to eat the heart of a man he had slain in battle meant that he acquired that amount of extra courage; it was all the better if he had been fortunate enough to slay a doughty warrior. The child of an Australian tribesman might be encouraged to eat some part of his dead father's flesh, so that when he grew up he would resemble his father in his courage, or skill as a tracker, or powers of leadership.

There were many variants of this method of transferring the 'soul-stuff' from the dead man to the living man. Sometimes the blood of the dead man would be swallowed, preferably while it was yet warm. Less primitive, or more highly developed, tribes contented themselves with licking the blood off the spear that had killed the enemy; or even, as an ultimate refinement, eating the first meal after the battle without first cleansing the hands of any blood that had been splashed on to them. One habit of the Maori—and one with a very obvious twofold explanation—was to eat the eyes of the men they had slain in battle.

The acquisition of an enemy's 'life-principle' was believed to strengthen greatly the procreative powers, and among many tribes a pre-requisite of marriage was a successful solo head-hunting expedition. Indeed, the all-important question of fertility, whether in the procreation of children or in the growth of crops, was closely associated with blood and this 'life-principle', and it was customary among many tribes to shower a triumphant warrior with grain when he returned from battle or a head-hunting expedition, and while he swallowed his victim's blood, in order to ensure the fertility of both man and seed. On a less 'spiritual' basis, it was the practice in many regions to eat a certain part of a healthy man's corpse in order to cure the corresponding part that was diseased in a living man.

The Jumana and Kobena tribes of the Amazon Basin, like the Bihor tribes of India, reverently ate the corpses of their own more honoured dead kinsmen in the hope that the better qualities they had possessed in life might thus be transmitted to them. In Mexico, sacramental rites probably reached a higher degree of complexity than anywhere else. Human flesh was considered the only food likely to be acceptable to the principal gods who had to be propitiated. Therefore human beings, carefully selected, were looked upon as representations of such gods as Quetzalcoatl and Tetzcatlipoca and, with most elaborate ceremonial rites, were eventually sacrificed to those gods whom they in fact represented, the onlookers being invited to share portions of the flesh in order thus to identify themselves with the gods to whom sacrifice had been made.

Inevitably, when there is such elaboration of ceremonial, the texture of tabu becomes increasingly close-knit. Ceremonial regulations breed more and yet more regulations; tabu prompts tabu. Among some tribes, after a successful foray to capture victims for tribal feasts or other purposes, the nearest relatives of the victorious hunters are prohibited from taking any part in the feasting; among other tribes, it is the killer and his family who have absolute priority. Sometimes only the actual killer is debarred from the feast; sometimes women and children only are debarred; sometimes distinctions are drawn between inter-married clans and others. Curiously, there are cases where, if a man has been killed as an act of revenge, the family for whom the act of revenge has been carried out must absent themselves from the feast. Indeed, there is no limit to the tortuosities of the mental processes of the so-called 'simple savage'. In the pages that follow, representative examples of these will be examined, compared and contrasted.

CHAPTER ONE

CANNIBALISM AMONG THE FIJI ISLANDERS

In the heart of the South Pacific Ocean, between the Equator and the Tropic of Capricorn, and extending roughly the same distance east and west of the International Date Line, there lie a number of groups of islands, some containing a mere handful, others consisting of several hundred, large and small. These islands are generally referred to as the South Sea Islands and, as such, have come to be associated with romance and voluptuous ease, 'lotus-eating' and the simple life beneath a hot sun. There are other aspects than these to be considered.

The ethnographer, primarily concerned with the physical characteristics and the distribution of the various races of mankind, has divided the main body of these groups of islands according to the dominant physical characteristic of the races inhabiting them. The majority of the inhabitants of the islands lying to the east, such as the Marquesas, Samoa, Tonga Island, the Society Islands, Tahiti, and others less popularly known, have light brown skin and generally wavy hair. Ethnographers refer to the region they inhabit as Polynesia—'Many islands'.

West of the International Date Line there is another group of islands, on the whole larger than those of Polynesia. They include the Solomon Islands, the New Hebrides, New Caledonia, the Ellice Islands and many others less familiar. Because the majority of the inhabitants of these islands are darker skinned, and have crinkly hair, the islands are known as Melanesia—'Black islands'.

Lying literally astride of the International Date Line is a group of islands numbering in all not far short of three hundred and known generically as Fiji. The ambiguous position of this group of islands, in the easternmost fringe of Melanesia and the westernmost fringe of Polynesia, has led anthropologists to refer to them sometimes as Melanesian, sometimes as Polynesian. The true ethnographer, however, makes no mistake: he recognises among the vast majority of the islanders the darker skin, the crinkled hair, of the true Melanesian; and as such he describes him.

It is in Melanesia that cannibalism was longest in dying. The islands already mentioned, like the vastly larger island to the west of them, New Guinea, just to the north of Australia, are peopled by inhabitants who clung obstinately to their ancient tradition of devouring human flesh long after the tradition had begun to fade, or had even been wholly stamped out, elsewhere. Indeed, it is likely that, away from the coastline, in the fastnesses of the mountains, cannibalism is still practised at the present day. For this reason, among others, it will be as well, perhaps, to examine the practice of cannibalism as reported and described by travellers who, within the last generation or two, have been familiar with this region of the South Pacific either as traders or as missionaries or skippers of coasting craft, or as travellers with some training in anthropology.

These are very numerous, and their reports can nearly always be substantiated or corroborated by comparison with those received from other sources which tally in regard to place and date. Among the countless reports that accumulated during the nineteenth century, the least suspect, of course, were those from missionaries in the field. Few missionaries anywhere in the world can have had to face greater horrors than those workers of the Methodist Missionary Society who established their missions in the Fiji Islands rather more than a hundred years ago.

On November 22nd, 1836, a pioneer in this noble organisation sent back to England—

AN APPEAL TO THE SYMPATHY OF THE CHRISTIAN PUBLIC
ON BEHALF OF THE CANNIBAL FEEGEEANS

Men and Brethren (it began), To your sympathy this Appeal is made, and your help is implored on behalf of a most interesting but deeply depraved people, the inhabitants of the group of islands called FEEGEE, little known to the civilised world except for the extreme danger to which vessels touching at them are exposed, from the murderous propensities of the islanders, and for the horrid CANNIBALISM to which they are addicted, in which abomination they exceed the New Zealanders themselves.

In FEEGEE, cannibalism is not an occasional, but a constant

practice; not indulged in from a species of horrid revenge, but from an absolute preference for human flesh over all other food.

It is on behalf of this cannibal race that we appeal to you. Let all the horrors of a CANNIBAL FEAST be present to your minds while you read. We appeal to you on behalf of FEEGEEAN widows, strangled when their husbands die, and on behalf of the FEE-GEEANS enslaved by vices too horrible for minute description. Pity CANNIBAL FEEGEE, and do so quickly. Come, then, ye Christians, and teach the poor, idolatrous, war-loving, man-devouring FEEGEEANS better things. . . .

We spare you the details of a cannibal feast (the writer goes on to say, rather surprisingly in view of the customary reticence of these missionaries, when it comes to lurid detail): the previous murders, the mode of *cooking* human beings, the assembled crowd of all ranks, all ages, both sexes, Chiefs and people, men, women and *children*, anticipating the feast with horrid glee. The actual feast. The attendants bringing into the circle BAKED HUMAN BEINGS—not one, nor two, nor ten, but twenty, thirty, forty, fifty at a single feast! We have heard on credible authority of 200 human beings having been thus devoured on one of these occasions. The writer of this APPEAL has himself conversed with persons who have seen forty and fifty eaten at a single sitting—eaten without anything like disgust; eaten indeed with a high relish!

To gratify this unnatural propensity, they make war, assassinate, kidnap, and absolutely rob the graves of their inhabitants. I have myself known FEEGEEANS to be guilty of the latter abomination; and such is the indomitable appetite of the FEEGEEANS for human flesh, that individuals have been known to act thus towards their own deceased children. . . .

This complete lack of parental affection, of any love, however primitive, within the Fijian family, has been noted by an American anthropologist, A. P. Rice, who in a learned paper read before an American Anthropologists' Association, had this to say:

Within the Fiji Islands group, Cannibalism is one of the established institutions; it is one of the elements of the Fijians' social structure, and is regarded as a refinement which should, and indeed must, be cultivated to become a 'gentleman'. Flesh-eating is a definite part of the Fijians' religion, but they delight in human flesh for its own sake. For example, there is a record of a man living in Ruwai who actually killed his wife, with whom he had been living contentedly, and who even before their marriage had been of his own social standing; and ate her. He agreed that his act was the result of his extreme fondness for human flesh.

The appeal for support in the missionary field in Fiji was successful, and the successive volumes of the Methodist Society's *Missionary Notices* reveal the fervour and courage and indomitable persistence in the face of appalling hazard that the Society's missionaries displayed. Among them were such eminent Christians as Cross and Cargill and John Hunt, whose letters and reports from their mission stations back to their London headquarters make vivid and impressive, though all too often very uncomfortable, reading.

Some of the circumstances connected with the immolation of human victims (wrote the Rev. David Cargill in 1838) are most revolting and diabolical. The passions of the people during the performance of these horrible rites seem inflamed by a fiendish ferocity which is not exceeded by anything we have ever heard of in the annals of human depravity.

When about to offer a human sacrifice, the victim is selected from among the inhabitants of a distant territory, or is procured by negotiation from a tribe which is not related to the persons about to sacrifice. The victim is kept for some time, and supplied with abundance of food, that he may become fat.

When about to be immolated, he is made to sit on the ground with his feet under his thighs and his hands placed before him. He is then bound so that he cannot move a limb or a joint. In this posture he is placed on stones heated for the occasion (and some of them are red-hot), and then covered with leaves and earth, to be roasted alive. When cooked, he is taken out of the oven and, his face and other parts being painted black, that he may resemble a living man ornamented for a feast or for war, he is carried to the temple of the gods and, being still retained in a sitting posture, is offered as a propitiatory sacrifice.

These ceremonies being concluded, the body is carried beyond the precincts of the consecrated ground, cut into quarters, and distributed among the people; and they who were the cruel sacrificers of its life are also the beastly devourers of its flesh. . . .

The unnatural propensity to eat human flesh exists among them in its most savage forms. The Feegeeans eat human flesh, not merely from a principle of revenge, nor from necessity, but from choice. Captives and strangers are frequently killed and eaten. The natives of Thakanndrove kidnap men, women and children to glut their appetite for human flesh; it is said that, as if they were human hyenas, they disinter dead bodies, even after they have been two or three days beneath the ground; and that, having washed them in the sea, they roast and devour them. The flesh of women is preferred to that of men, and when they have a plentiful supply the head is not eaten. In some cases the heart is preserved for months. The bones of those persons whose bodies have been eaten are never buried, but are thrown about as the bones of beasts, and the smaller ones are formed into needles. Recently a boat's crew from the vessel *Active* was attacked by the natives in the expectation of obtaining their clothing and belongings. The four unhappy men were cooked and eaten, and *their* bones have now been formed into needles for making sails.

One of the great names among the Methodist Missionary Society's workers in Fiji is that of the Rev. John Hunt. He had established his mission base at Rewa, and reported back at some length to his head office in June of the year following David Cargill's letter:

Having given you some account of our comfortable—(in the conditions prevailing this is surely a quite extraordinary word to use!)—circumstances, I shall now give some account of the difficulties which we meet with in the great work in which we are engaged. As we are come to Feegee to Christianise, and thus to civilise the people, I shall mention a few features in their character which appear to me calculated to retard the progress of Christianity.

The first which I shall mention is their *cruelty*. Cruelty is so natural to the Feegeeans that it has lost every part of its own hideous form, and appears more lovely than hateful to the minds of those who are truly without natural affection. I know but little of their religious cruelty. It is very uncertain whether the numerous murders which are perpetrated at the building of canoes, and god-houses, are connected with their religion, or with their politics. Whatever may be their motives, their horrid acts of barbarity, and cannibalism, on the finishing of canoes and god-houses, are as shocking to humanity as they are unparalleled in history. Rome produced its monsters of iniquity, as Caligula, Domitian, Nero and Commodus; Grecian history furnishes examples, in the characters of Olympias and others, and English history in the acts of Henry and Mary. But cruelty in Greece, and Rome, and England bears its own name, and wears its own form; it is called a monster, and every man hates it, and dreads to be underneath the influence of those who are governed by its principles.

But in Feegee, some of those who are most esteemed, are esteemed partly on account of their obedience to the dictates of this monster; and not only Chiefs but the common people delight in treacherously murdering, and feasting on the bodies of their neighbours, as well as on their enemies. We have heard the most shocking things of Namusi Matua, the Chief of Rewa, who has lately embraced Christianity. If the whole were told, I should think his history would be unparalleled in the history of human depravity.

It is said that when he built a canoe, he used to make a point of killing a man for every plank. Sometimes he would do his work by wholesale, and kill a whole settlement for a feast for his canoe builders. Being an adept at this kind of business, he was often employed by Tanoa, another Chieftain, in this inhuman work. So it would be impossible to imagine the number of victims that this man has killed; not in times of war but merely to satisfy the cravings of cannibal appetites. . . .

John Hunt was not content, as his colleague in the field, David Cargill, was, in the letter quoted above, merely to describe what happened; he analysed to the best of his ability and evolved some sort of a theory. And having speculated, he ended his report from the mission field in Fiji on a more hopeful note:

The case would be far different if they were led on to these acts of barbarity by religious motives or persuasions. But this, I believe, is not the reason for the sacrifices they make. All the answer I can get from my inquiries on this subject is: 'That is our custom'. But this custom disappears where the Light of the Gospel shines, and where its influence is felt, even in a small degree. We know of *no instance* of cannibalism having happened in Rewa, since the Gospel came to Rewa. The Chief has had a new god-house built, and many new canoes, but we do not know that a single man has been killed, either from malice or for cannibal purposes.

The Rev. John Hunt's letter, ending on such a note of optimism, carried the date June 29th, 1839. Like many missionaries in many fields, he was too sanguine. Having effected a conversion, he persuaded himself that the conversion was permanent. It is possible, of course, that so far as this one individual chief was concerned, the conversion was total, and lasting. But it is very clear from a report written by David Cargill only four months later that the conversion was by no means general.

The report forms part of a day-to-day record, or diary, that he was able to maintain for a considerable period, in spite of the appalling conditions in which he was obliged to live. He writes much as journalists had to write when reporting back the scenes they witnessed in war-torn Europe both during and after the war. And the story he tells is a horror story that may well have been matched only by the tales of atrocities of recent times:

October 31st, 1839, Thursday. This morning we witnessed a shocking spectacle. Twenty (20) dead bodies of men, women and children were brought to Rewa as a present from Tanoa. They were distributed among the people to be cooked and eaten. They were dragged about in the water and on the beach. The children amused themselves by sporting with and mutilating the body of a little girl. A crowd of men and women maltreated the body of a grey-haired old man and that of a young woman. Human entrails were floating down the river in front of the mission premises. Mutilated limbs, heads and trunks of the bodies of human beings have been floating about, and scenes of disgust and horror have been presented to our view in every direction. How true it is that the dark places of the earth are full of the habitations of cruelty.

November 1st, Friday. This morning a little after break of day I was surprised to hear the voices of several persons who were talking very loudly near the front fence of the mission premises. On going out to ascertain the cause of the noise, I found a human head in our garden. This was the head of the old man whose body had been abused on the beach. The arm of the body had been broken by a bullet which passed through the bone near the shoulder, and the upper part of the skull had been knocked off with a club. The head had been thrown into our garden during the night, with the intention, no doubt, of annoying us and shocking our feelings.

These poor victims of war were brought from Verata, and were killed by the Bau people. 260 human beings were killed and brought away by the victors to be roasted and eaten. Many women and children were taken alive to be kept for slaves. About 30 *living* children were hoisted up to the mastheads as flags of triumph. The motion of the canoes while sailing soon killed the helpless creatures and silenced their piercing cries. Other children were taken, alive, to Bau that the boys there might learn the art of Feegeean warfare by firing arrows at them and beating them with clubs. For days they have been tearing and devouring like wolves and hyenas.

This entry in David Cargill's diary was followed not long afterwards by another, briefer but no less horrible in its content:

February 2nd, 1840. Immediately after our English Class at the Mission we were called to witness one of the most horrid scenes that our eyes have yet beheld in this land. Eleven dead bodies were dragged to the front of the old king's house, but a few paces from our own door, from the adjoining island of Lauthala, having been slain together with the people of one whole village on the morning of the Sabbath by order of Tuiilaila, the young king. The reason assigned was their having killed one of the Bau people living in this land.

The execution of the bloody massacre was committed to the people of a village situated nearer to the island of Lauthala than this. They fell upon them by break of day, while they were still asleep, and spared neither age nor sex. As far as we can learn, about 40 of them were slain, or very near that number, and among the rest the principal chief of that isle. The bodies, being all brought into the presence of the two principal chiefs and their people, were quickly given out one by one, to be roasted and eaten, and were severally dragged away on the ground like logs of wood by their respective owners. After a while the chiefs and people dispersed to their disgusting feast. The offensiveness of the bodies evidently diminished not their zest. Two bodies were dressed at a fire but a few paces from our fence.

The cold-blooded cruelty of the Fijians heightens the horror implicit in their cannibal practices. It is one thing, one might say, in the heat of battle to slay a man and, having returned in triumph, to roast and share him with one's companions in the successful foray. It is quite another—if it is permissible to look on this as a matter of degrees—to act as the Fijians seem consistently to have done. This is obviously the thought dominating the mind of another Methodist missionary, named Jaggar, reporting back to London in 1844, and by yet another of the courageous and unhappy workers in the field, the Rev. John Watsford, a couple of years later. Jaggar wrote:

One of the servants of the king a few months ago ran away. She was soon, however, brought back to the king's house. There, at the request of the queen, her arm was cut off below the elbow and cooked for the king, who ate it *in her presence*, and then ordered that her body be burnt in different parts. The girl, now a woman, is still living.

Two men that were taken alive in the war at Viwa were removed from thence to Kamba, to be killed. The Bau chief told his brother—who had been converted by our Mission—the manner in which he intended them to be killed. His brother said to him: "That will be very cruel. If you will allow the men to live, I will give you a canoe." The Bau chief answered: "Keep your canoe. I want to eat men." His brother then left the village that he might not witness the horrible sight.

The cruel deed was then perpetrated. The men doomed to death were made to dig a hole in the earth for the purpose of making a native oven, and were then required to cut firewood *to roast their own bodies*. They were then directed to go and wash, and afterwards to make a cup of a banana-leaf. This, from opening a vein in each man, was soon filled with blood. This blood was then drunk, *in the presence of the sufferers*, by the Kamba people.

Seru, the Bau chief, then had their arms and legs cut off, cooked and eaten, some of the flesh being presented to them. He then ordered a fish-hook to be put into their tongues, which were then drawn out as far as possible before being cut off. These were roasted and eaten, to the taunts of "We are eating your tongues!" As life in the victims was still not extinct, an incision was made in the side of each man, and his bowels taken out. This soon terminated their sufferings in this world.

The father of the present king was one of the greatest cannibals ever known. He used to say, when vegetables were set before him: "What is there to eat with these?" If they answered "Pig", he would then say: "No, that will not do." Fish, too, he would refuse, asking: "Have you not got an *ikalevu*?" This is the Feegeeans' word for 'great fish', but when used it always means a *dead human body*.

A variant on this sinister euphemism is reported, not by a missionary, this time, but by a well-known and intrepid traveller, Alfred St Johnston, who seems to have had a predilection for making his temporary home among the fiercest primitive tribes he could locate. Obviously he survived his experiences, for at the end of the nineteenth century he published his memoirs under the pleasantly alliterative title, *Camping Among Cannibals*. In this book he wrote: "The expression 'long pig' is not a phrase invented by Europeans but is one frequently used by the Fijians, who looked upon a corpse as ordinary butcher's meat. They call a human body *puaka balava*—'long pig'—in contradistinction to *puaka dina*—'real pig'."

The missionary, Jaggar, completed his grim report of cannibalistic practices among the Bau tribes of his island:

The Bau Chief used to feel his victims. If they were fat, he would say, "Your fat is good. I shall eat you." If they were lean, he would send them away to be fattened. He preferred human flesh to all else, especially in the morning, and if his sons did not eat the flesh with him he would beat them.

Another chief ran away in battle but was captured in a tree, from which he was brought into the presence of Chief Tanoa, who was actually related to him. His hands were tied and he was made to sit before Tanoa, who *kissed* him while, *with his own hands*, he cut off one of his arms. Having drunk some of the blood that had been spilled, he then threw the arm upon the fire to roast, and afterwards ate it *in his presence*.

The captured chief said to him: "Do not do this to me. Like you, I am a chief." Tanoa then cut off the other arm, and also both his legs; also as much of his tongue as he could. Then he divided up the trunk, leaving the parts to dry in the sun.

Two years later, the Rev. John Watsford wrote from Ono to announce that the war between Bau and Rewa had at last come to an end. He does not say what it was that brought hostilities to a close, and it is unlikely that it was as the result of any influence brought to bear upon the combatants by the Mission workers, for all their courage and perseverance. For there is continuous evidence throughout these reports that not only fighting but cannibal practices took place on the very threshold of the Mission. Thankfully reporting the cessation of these hostilities, Watsford wrote on November 6th, 1846:

We cannot tell you how many have been slain. Hundreds of wretched human beings have been sent to their account, with all their sins upon their heads. Dead bodies were thrown upon the beach at Vewa, having drifted from Bau, where they were thrown into the sea, there being *too many* at Bau to be eaten. Bau literally stank for many days, human flesh having been cooked in every hut and the entrails having been thrown outside as food for pigs, or left to putrefy in the sun.

The Somosomo people were fed with human flesh during their stay at Bau, they being on a visit at the time. Some of the chiefs of other tribes, when bringing their food, carried a cooked human being on one shoulder and a pig on the other; but they always preferred the 'long pig', as they call a man, when baked. One woman who had been clubbed was left upon the beach in front of our house at Vewa. The poor creature's head was smashed to pieces and the body quite naked. Whether it was done by the heathen *to insult us*, or not, we do not know.

One Christian man was clubbed at Rewa, and part of his body was eaten by the Vewa heathen and his bones then thrown near our door. My lad gathered them up and buried them, and afterwards learned that they were the bones of one of his friends. After Rewa was destroyed, heaps of dead bodies lay in all directions; their bones still lie bleaching in the sun.

We do not, and we cannot, tell you all that we know of Feegeean cruelty and crime. Every fresh act seems to rise above the last. A chief at Rakeraki had a box in which he kept human flesh. Legs and arms were salted for him and thus preserved in this box.

If he saw anyone, even if of his friends, who was fatter than the rest, he had him—or her—killed at once, and part roasted and part preserved. His people declare that he eats human flesh every day.

At Bau, the people preserve human flesh and chew it as some chew tobacco. They carry it about with them, and use it in the same way as tobacco. I heard of an instance of cruelty the other day that surpasses everything I have before heard of the kind. A canoe was wrecked near Natawar, and many of the occupants succeeded in swimming to shore. They were taken by the Natawar people and ovens were at once prepared in which to roast them. The poor wretches were bound ready for the ovens and their enemies were waiting anxiously to devour them. They did not club them, lest any of their blood should be lost. Some, however, could not wait until the ovens were sufficiently heated, but pulled the ears off the wretched creatures and ate them raw.

When the ovens were ready, they cut their victims up very carefully, placing dishes under every part to catch the blood. If a drop fell, they licked it up off the ground with the greatest greediness. While the poor wretches were being cut in pieces, they pleaded hard for life; but all was of no avail: all were devoured.

It is curious how a small detail, in this case a comparison between a familiar habit such as chewing tobacco and the hideous practice of tearing off a victim's ears and chewing them, can prove more impressive, somehow, than an elaborate account of massacre followed by wholesale consumption of human flesh. The detail typifies, crystallises, an attitude. A Professor of Botany at Trinity College, Dublin, Dr W. H. Harvey, who had been doing research in the neighbouring Tonga, or Friendly Isles, confirmed this practice: "Sometimes the Fijians cook a man whole (which they call 'long pig'), then put him in a sitting posture, with a fan in his hand and ornamented as if alive; and thus they carry him in state, as a grand head-dish for the feast. The tribesmen chew little bits of raw human flesh as sailors chew tobacco, and then put them in their children's mouths."

Alfred St Johnston, incidentally, confirms this practice of ornamenting a victim before consigning him to the oven, and stresses, too, this aspect of scorn which the primitive will show on these occasions: "If a man was to be cooked whole, they would paint and decorate his face as though he were alive, and one of the chief persons of the place would stand by the body, which was placed in a sitting position, and talk in a mocking strain to it for some time, when it would be handed over to the cooks, who prepared it and placed it in the oven."

Being a mere traveller, as opposed to being a missionary, St Johnston had an entirely different attitude towards what he saw. He was writing many years later than the various Methodist missionaries already quoted, and he was writing with wonder, rather than with the deep spiritual horror that animated Cargill, Jaggar, Hunt and Watsford and their brethren in the mission fields of Fiji. He was observant, quick to accumulate cross-references from the skippers of the trading-vessels whom he encountered, and to collate the varied material that thus came his way. He evolved theories, some of which are substantiated by later anthropologists working in the same area.

> The Fijians (he wrote in 1883) loved human flesh for its own sake, and did not merely eat a slain enemy out of revenge. Probably the absence of any animal they could eat gave rise to the custom. . . .

This theory is supported by the American anthropologist, A. P. Rice, who wrote: "In Fiji there are no indigenous animals (the pig was introduced only in the eighteenth century) with the exception of the rat. Thus cannibalism is more understandable—even 'excusable'—here."

> The crew of every boat that was wrecked upon these shores (St Johnston continued) was killed and eaten in some parts. Often a man would order to be clubbed some man or woman that he considered would be good for cooking, his plea being that his "black tooth was aching" and only human flesh could cure it. Such was the absolute right of a man over his wife that he could kill and eat her, if he wished; which has been not rarely done.
>
> Such inordinate gluttons were some of these chiefs that they would reserve the whole *bakolo*, as a human body to be eaten was called, for their own eating, having the flesh slightly cooked time after time to keep it from going putrid. As a rule a Fijian will touch nothing that has become tainted, but sooner than lose any part of a human roast, they would eat it when the flesh would hardly hang together.
>
> So great was their craving for this strange flesh that when a man had been killed in one of their many bruits and quarrels, and his relations had buried his body, the Fijians frequently enacted the part of ghouls and, digging the body up from the grave, cooked it and feasted thereon. So customary was this that the

relations of a buried man who had *not* died from natural causes
watched his grave until the body had probably become too
loathsome for even a Fijian's appetite.

The flesh was either baked whole in the ovens, or cut up and
stewed in the large earthenware pots they use for cooking.   Certain herbs were nearly always cooked with the flesh, either to
prevent indigestion or as a sort of savoury stuffing—I know not
which.   The cooks who prepared it and placed it in the oven
filled the inside of the body with hot stones so that it would be well
cooked all through.

After a battle, the victors would cook and eat many of the slain
at once, but generally some of the bodies were borne home to the
victors' village, where they were dragged by ropes tied round
their necks through the open place to the temple.   There they
were offered to the gods, and afterwards cooked and divided
among the men, the priests always coming in for a large share.
By the side of the temples great heaps of human bones lay whitening in the sun—a sign of how many bodies had been thus offered
to the gods.   Women, however, were not allowed to take part in
the awful banquet, yet women's bodies were considered better for
cooking than men, and the thighs and arms were looked upon as
the favourite portions.   So delicious was human flesh held to be,
that the highest praise that could be given to other food was to
say: "It is as good as *bakolo*".

Some of the most famous of the great cannibals have eaten an
enormous number of human beings, many of them in their time
having consumed hundreds of bodies. . . .

A. P. Rice confirms this with authority.   He quotes the case
of a Fijian chieftain who boasted of having in his lengthy lifetime devoured the tastier and more desirable portions of the
bodies of over nine hundred human beings.   This particular
chieftain was said, by those who knew him well, to be by no
means a naturally bloodthirsty man—and the epithet here
takes on a somewhat grisly connotation.   In fact, he was considered, generally speaking, a particularly friendly individual
and noted for his hospitality to strangers visiting his island.
Possibly the 'hospitality' was on the lines of the hospitality
practised by the legendary Procrustes in Attica.   He, it will be
recalled, offered shelter to travellers passing his way.   But he
had the inhospitable habit of cutting off the legs of any of his
guests who were too long for his beds, or alternatively stretching
them if they were not long enough to fill them.   Theseus,
happily, put an end to these malpractices so reprehensible in a
host!

Rice also records the case of Chichia, a Fijian chieftain who captured some men from Bau:

> On the following day he called a great war dance among his tribesmen to celebrate the victory and prepare for the feast to follow it. The dancers appeared with their faces and bodies hideously painted, and carrying clubs and spears. Their dance, which lasted for many hours, consisted of a series of poses in war-like, threatening and boastful attitudes. After the dancing, drinks were served, and the feast was announced.
>
> And such a feast! It consisted of 200 human bodies, 200 hogs, and 200 baskets of yams. The preparation of the human bodies and of the hogs was identical, and every member of the tribe had of course to partake of the two main dishes—he was not allowed to select one *or* the other. This was to ensure that the men did not glut themselves on the human bodies to such an extent that there was insufficient human flesh and others would therefore have to content themselves with mere hog flesh.
>
> Some of the men did, in fact, attempt to concentrate their attention on the human flesh alone, but they were discovered and sternly forced to practise a less obvious form of greed. In fact, there was no evidence of a shortage of either commodity, but by the time the feast came to an end there was little remaining but bone.

The traveller, Alfred St Johnston, continued his observations of cannibal practices among the Fiji Islanders:

> No important business could be commenced without the slaying of one or two human beings as a fitting inauguration. Was a canoe to be built, then a man must be slain for the laying of its keel; if the man for whom the canoe was being built was a very great chief, then a fresh man was killed for *every new timber that was added*. More men were used at its launching—as *rollers* to aid its passage to the sea. Others again were slain to wash its deck in blood and to furnish the feast of human flesh considered so desirable on such occasions. After the canoe was afloat still more victims were required at the first taking down of the mast.
>
> At Bau there used to be a regular display of slaughter, in a sort of arena, round which were raised stone seats for the onlookers. In this space was a large 'braining-stone', which was used thus: two strong natives seized the victim, each taking hold of an arm and leg, and, lifting him from the ground, they ran with him head foremost—at their utmost speed against the stones—dashing out his brains; which was fine sport for the spectators.

Alfred St Johnston, it may have been noticed, seems to have taken an unhealthy pleasure in the recording of detail of this kind. Most references to cannibalism, made by civilised

persons, are touched with more than a hint of horror. You do
not need to have the missionary's constitutional and ingrained
loathing of all that is non-Christian in practice, to feel a deep
sense of horror when confronted by such phenomena: the very
idea of devouring the flesh and blood of one's fellow-men is so
alien to one's whole conception of what is right and what is
wrong that one shrinks from even a hint of the subject. There
is horror beneath Coleridge's lines, when he makes his Ancient
Mariner say, "I bit my arm, I sucked the blood, And cried:
'A sail! A sail!'" And he, be it noted, is drinking his *own*
blood.

Yet St Johnston concludes his chapter on the subject of
cannibalism in Fiji with a paragraph that, as it were, smites one
between the eyes:

> This subject of cannibalism has a terrible sort of fascination for
> me. Although the ghastly tales, told to me by a skipper who
> sailed these waters and saw these things when they took place,
> made me shudder, *I have enjoyed them thoroughly*. I have no wish
> to appear singular when I say that I should have gloried in the
> rush and struggle of old Fijian times—with my hand against
> everybody, and everybody against me; and the fierce madness of
> unchecked passion and rage with which they went to battle, and
> the clubbing of my foes. And—*I am sure I should have enjoyed the
> eating of them afterwards*.

The use of the word 'singular' in such a context strikes one
as being a superlative example of under-statement!

Another traveller among the Fijian Islands in the nineteenth
century, and rather before St Johnston's time, was Felix
Maynard. He was a French surgeon who attached himself to a
small whaling fleet operating in the South Pacific and later produced a book on the subject, written, curiously enough, in
collaboration with Alexandre Dumas. He had the powers of
observation and analysis that one would associate with a
medical man, but was very definitely not as cold-blooded in his
descriptive writing as doctors sometimes are; and there is more
compassion in a single sentence of his than in the whole of St
Johnston's book.

> Captain Morell (he writes), the American skipper of whom I have
> already spoken, came near to being the victim of an ambush in the
> Fiji Islands. He lost fourteen of his companions. After regain-
> ing his ship, he said, he saw the savages cutting up the members

of his poor sailors while they were still alive, and more than one of them saw his own arm or leg roasted and devoured before his death.

In Naclear Bay, in the Fijis, a Captain Dillon came near to losing his life. While searching for sandal-wood trees with eighteen or twenty of his men, he found himself separated from the majority of his party and surrounded by a large number of the natives. It was impossible to regain the sea, so he and four others took refuge on a steep rock. "We were," said Dillon later, "five refugees on a rock, and the ground below was covered with several thousand savages. They lit fires at the foot of the rock and heated hearths upon which to roast the limbs of my unfortunate companions. The corpses of these," he continued, "as well as those of two chiefs of a neighbouring island, were brought before the fires in the following manner: two natives from Naclear constructed a kind of stretcher with branches of trees, which they placed upon their shoulders. The corpses of their victims were put crosswise upon this structure, so that the head hung down on one side and the legs on the other. Thus they were carried in triumph to the fires, where they were placed on the grass in a sitting position.

"The savages sang and danced around them with demonstrations of the most ferocious joy. They fired several bullets at the inanimate bodies, using for this posthumous execution the guns which had fallen into their hands. When this ceremony was finished, the priests commenced to cut up the corpses before our eyes, and the fragments were placed upon the hearths. Meanwhile we ourselves were surrounded upon every side save that where a thicket of mangroves bordered the river."

Two of Dillon's companions (Maynard continues), one named Savage and the other a Chinese, abandoned their captain, foolishly believing the promises of the barbarians that they would come to no harm. "Savage," Dillon said, "was soon in their midst. They surrounded him, appearing to congratulate him. Suddenly, however, they uttered a great cry, seizing Savage at the same time by the legs. Six men held him suspended head downwards and plunged him into a hole full of water, where he was speedily suffocated. Meanwhile, a native approached the Chinese from behind, and dashed out his brains with a blow of his club. Thereupon the two unfortunate fellows were cut up and placed on the hearth with their companions."

Fortunately for Dillon, Maynard records, a boat's crew from another vessel that heard the outcry made a determined assault from the sea and succeeded in rescuing the captain and his two remaining companions in the nick of time.

Missionaries' tales; travellers' tales: the reports of men who were there, who, from their own volition or through force of circumstances, found themselves often uncomfortably, alarmingly, close to a way of life that was frightening in the extreme. They were not, however, anthropologists—though they may have unconsciously picked up more than a smattering of the knowledge that is ordinarily the perquisite of the researcher in anthropology. Except as a chance remark, thrown in as a parenthesis, they offer no interpretation or explanation of what they see.

A. P. Rice, the American anthropologist, in his learned paper bracketed together all the South Sea Islands, whether to the east or to the west of the International Date Line, ignoring the differences of pigment in the skin and the quality of the hair which the ethnographer uses to distinguish between Polynesians and Melanesians. For him, all these islanders were to be found inhabiting a scattering of islands so numerous as to deserve the one name, Polynesia. He writes, thus, in one long paper of the Marquesans, the Society Islanders, the Hawaiians and Tahitians, the Tongans, the Papuans, the New Caledonians and New Hebrideans, the Samoans, and the Maori of New Zealand. And also, as we have already seen, of the Fijians.

> Cannibalism (he writes) is a custom which has not been confined exclusively to any particular part of the world. The Greek classics refer to it; the Ancient Irish ate their dead; the Saxons had a word in their language that stood for all that is horrible (he does not give us that word, however); in Mexico and Peru, before the Spanish Conquest, the lust for human flesh was so great that wars were declared in order that victims for these feasts might be procured.

Writing of cannibalism in Fiji—the group of islanders who, he says, may well have been the progenitors of this cult of cannibalism, and from whom the practice spread by degrees into the adjacent islands east and west of the Fiji group—he is quick to note the religious aspect. Though, as he has already remarked, the Fijians may well have been cannibals because until comparatively recent times there was no indigenous animal on their islands, save the rat, and in this sense their cannibalism may be 'excusable', he goes on to show that the Fijians genuinely believed that their tribal gods demanded human flesh by way of sacrifice. "The heads of the victims," he emphasises, "are turned over to the tribal priests in order that the priests may use them in religious ceremonies."

Subsequently, he goes into this aspect of the matter more fully:

> When bodies of enemies were procured for the oven, the event was always publicised by the peculiar beating of the tribal drums. Once heard, it is said by those who have been within earshot, it is a sound and a rhythm that can never be mistaken—and never be forgotten. The bodies taken in warfare or forays to adjacent islands were brought back to the beach in canoes. When the canoes had been beached, the bodies were thrown into the sea for cleansing and purification. . . .

(This belief in the cleansing and purifying qualities of sea water was widely held, and we shall see other and more elaborate rituals in this connection among other cannibalistic tribes.)

> Lest the corpses should drift away on the tides and be lost (Rice continues), they were fastened by the left wrist to vine stems.   In due course they are brought ashore, during which time the men of the tribe execute an elaborate and protracted war-dance on the beach, and at the same time the women of the tribe participate in a very different and highly suggestive variant of the dance. The bodies are then dragged, face downwards, up the beach to the village, where they are deposited at the feet of the chief.   He immediately invites the tribal priests to offer the bodies to their God of War.
>
> In the larger islands of the group, where the villages are often some distance from the beach, the bodies are not dragged along the ground, since over a long journey too much of their valuable flesh would thus be scraped away; instead, they are lashed to strong poles and carried like ghastly litters on men's shoulders. The picture inevitably evokes images of the carrying on poles of ' stuck pig' and other semi-wild prey of the hunter on safari.
>
> After the religious ceremony has ended, the bodies are brought back to the beach again, still face downwards, there to be carved up by skilled men with knives of split bamboo—which, carefully fashioned, can be given a razor-like edge and are perfectly effective for this gross surgery.   The chief carver first cuts off the four limbs, joint by joint.   These are taken by his assistants, folded individually in plantain leaves and placed carefully in the ovens—suitably sized holes in the ground, floored and lined with stones.

Bodies (Rice continues, and here he seems to challenge some of the missionaries' and travellers' reports already quoted) were in no case eaten raw.

The heart, the thighs and the arms above the elbows were considered by epicures to be the most palatable portions.   *Vakatotoga* is a name given to a terrible form of torture to which many victims were subjected. Their arms and legs were cut off while they were still alive—though it may be hoped that the majority of them died fairly soon from loss of blood. These limbs were then baked over the fires and eaten in the victims' presence. Children and adults were habitually kidnapped for a special gesture to a distinguished individual, and no distinction was made in regard either to sex or to age. In Valebpsarus the trunk of the body was always eaten first, for the very practical reason that this was the portion of a corpse that would not 'keep' in a tropical climate. . . .

In this connection it is interesting to note that, as other anthropologists have reported, certain cannibal tribes in other parts of the world used to store the flesh and bones of their human victims in north-facing parts of their huts, or, if they were fortunate enough to live near the sea or a lake, in pits carefully dug to a point below water level.

When (Rice concludes) for one reason or another there was a surplus of corpses and the supply of human flesh thus exceeded current demand, the torsos were thrown away and only the limbs devoured. There is a record of a particularly lavish feast where there was an unprecedented surfeit of corpses and everyone could afford to ignore the torsos and take his pick of the more succulent portions of the thighs and upper arms.

This anthropologist repeats over and over again his contention that the origin at least of cannibalism in Polynesia— and particularly among the Fiji Islanders—was what the thoughtless would call an 'unnatural' appetite for flesh, but what he, more reasonably, calls "a most natural appetite for good red meat. Natural man," he emphasises, "is carnivorous. Meat is his natural food. The cannibals whom we in our childhood used to regard with such horror when tales about them were read to us, should in fact—many races of them at least—have been represented to us as unfortunate dwellers in an unhappily situated, or at any rate inadequately stocked, locality; and not as mere savages who wilfully did their utmost to disobey the laws of the so-called civilised nations."

That is the objective utterance of the dispassionate observer; and as such, if less colourful and spectacular than, say, the astonishing last paragraph of Alfred St Johnston, is a fairer assessment of a situation which, as he emphasises, is happily today a matter of past history.

CHAPTER TWO

HUMAN SACRIFICE AMONG THE AZTECS

THERE IS a very great deal more to be said about the variations in practice among the other Polynesian and Melanesian tribes, but perhaps it will be found more palatable if, before examining these, we turn to a very different part of the world; to a race of people among whom the physical detail of cannibalism is less prominent and the mythological or religio-magical element dominates the picture.

It has been seen that, so far as the Fijians at any rate are concerned, the element of religion enters only very perfunctorily into their cannibalism. It is rather as though, with a deep-rooted and hardly admitted, or even perhaps recognised, awareness that the eating of human flesh was in some way *wrong*, they sought to protect themselves from the potential consequences of wrong-doing by appeasing their tribal gods. But the gesture of appeasement, as we have seen, was slight; the gods were identified with the tribal chiefs, to whom the best portions of the flesh were automatically rendered—which suggests the obvious underlying emotion of fear. And indeed, it is difficult if not impossible to separate fear from religio-superstition; and this may be seen even today, and without the necessity for travelling very far from home.

Obviously, however, among the Fijians the main thing was the consumption of the flesh; the gesture to the tribal god, by way of the tribal priest, was perfunctory; if the victim became available on the field of battle, then was it, they clearly asked themselves, worth while waiting till their return home before indulging in a victors' feast? And, like Pilate in another context, they stayed not for an answer.

In most, if not all, primitive tribal customs there is a close link between sacrifice and cannibalism, even if in some cases (as in the ones already considered) the link is exiguous in the extreme. Sacrifice, of course, was a gesture: the supreme gesture, if you

will.   There is no part of the world, however remote, in which
sacrifice in one form or another has not played an essential part
in the way of life of the people.   The Old Testament is full of
references to it; history, legend, myth and story, from remotest
recorded times until the day before yesterday, is alive with it.
Sir James Frazer's monumental anthropological work, *The
Golden Bough*, the twelve volumes of which occupied him for a
quarter of a century and followed half a lifetime of research, is
an exhaustive (and completely fascinating) survey of the whole
field of the beliefs of mankind as revealed in their customs and
practices.   It began with an examination of the rules of the
priesthood and 'sacred kingship' of the Grove of Nemi, the
first rule of which was that the new candidate for the priesthood
must first slay the existing priest; after which he himself would
in due course be slain by his successor.   And his worldwide
studies revealed that sacrifice, and as often as not human sacrifice, was an integral part of the priestly rites, and that immolation was very extensively associated with the consuming of
human flesh.

Frazer, in common with other anthropologists, states positively that the practice of cannibalism, as such, is almost certainly less of an established institution than human sacrifice,
or immolation.   Nevertheless, except in the case of the Fijians,
and certain other Melanesian tribes to whom we shall revert in
due course, among whom the sheer lust for human flesh seems
to have predominated over all other considerations, the basic
ritualistic motive is virtually identical.   Both in the sacrificing
of human beings, and in the partaking of portions of their flesh
before or after the sacrifice, there is always the underlying
principle of the transfer of 'soul-substance'.

The ancient people of Mexico probably afford as interesting
an example of this aspect of sacrifice-cum-cannibalistic practice
as any whose traditions and customs have been examined by
anthropologists.   Mexico, and the Mexicans, have excited
interest and speculation for many years past, and it is interesting
to note the number of books that have been published in comparatively recent times dealing with Mexico Today and
Yesterday.

It is the Mexico of Yesterday that we are concerned with at
this moment: the Mexico which came under the sway of that

strange people, the Maya, who flooded into its fertile valleys by
way of Oaxaca, and who in their turn were absorbed by the
Toltecs.   The Toltec civilisation probably attained its peak in
the eleventh century A.D.—at about the same time as William
the Conqueror brought a Norman civilising influence across the
Channel to our own shores.

But the Toltecs, too, had to give way to a further wave of
invaders: the Aztecs. It was the Aztecs who dominated
Southern Mexico longest, under such leaders as Montezuma,
who was a contemporary of Christopher Columbus. We
know more about the way of life established and maintained
by these Aztecs than about that in any previous period—
though only enough is known about them to whet our curiosity
for more. The Spanish Conquistadors came, and saw, and
mercilessly overthrew the Aztec regime in the early part of the
sixteenth century, when they were at the height of their power
and achievement. The picture has been painted in brilliant
new colours by Jean Descola in his book, *The Conquistadors*.

Human sacrifice was an essential element in the Aztec culture
and to a large extent explains the almost continuous wars that
the Aztecs waged with neighbouring peoples between the
Caribbean and the Pacific: a regular and unbroken supply of
victims was essential to the priests if the sun was to be kept in
constant and beneficent motion across the Aztec sky, bringing
fertility to crops and men alike.

It is curious to trace the development of their 'religion'. At
first the Aztecs, who were originally a nomadic tribe known as
the Nahua, were impressed, not only by the settled way of life
of the Maya into whose territory they had irrupted, and by
their skill as agriculturists, but by the form of worship practised
by the Maya and the Toltecs. In course of time, however,
though they largely adopted, and improved upon, the agri-
cultural methods of the people they were superseding, they
preferred to maintain their own form of worship, and to bend
to it the priestly rites and rituals they had at first admired.

With them, the fertility of the land, and the prosperity of the
people who lived on it and lived only because of it, was wholly
identified with the life and the virility of their king, or chieftain.
For the Aztecs, their Warrior-god, Uitzilopochtli, was something more than a warrior or a god: he came to be virtually

identified with the sun itself—a Sun-god as well as a Warrior-god, whose virility must be maintained at its maximum by a perpetual supply of human victims' hearts.

In addition to the Warrior-god, or Sun-god, there were other deities, both male and female, in the Aztec hierarchy. Extremely important among these, and for obvious reasons, was Teteoinnan, the Earth-Mother. At the time of the harvest festival a female victim was flayed and her skin brought ceremonially to the temple, either of Teteoinnan or of Centeotl, the Goddess of Maize. The skin was worn by the officiating priest, who for the ritual assumed the identity of the goddess herself. This is but one of innumerable examples, in many parts of the world, in which the donning of a human skin enables a human being to identify himself with the god or goddess whom he (or she) serves: it is the elemental concept of the transfer of soul-stuff by close contact with flesh and blood.

The Aztec religious ceremonial became progressively more and more elaborate—as is the case with all religions ancient and modern. The Aztec year was divided into eighteen periods of twenty days each, and certain of these periods, coinciding as they did with the natural seasons of the year, were marked by special rituals and ceremonies.

In February, for example, young children were immolated to the gods of rain and water in order that the new year's crops might not wither from drought. At another festival, the blood of children who had been thus sacrificed was collected by the priest and kneaded into an image of the god, Uitzilopochtli, made of maize dough. The heart of the image was ceremonially cut out by the priest and given to the reigning Aztec king to consume, while the remainder of the image was distributed among the notables, a small portion to each.

Totec, the Moon-god, had to be propitiated in the period immediately preceding the first sowing of seed, and this entailed human sacrifice. This time it was not children who were involved, but a prisoner of war—and the more courageous he had proved himself in battle the better the prospects for the new crop. The ritual here was to fasten the prisoner to a frame of timber, with arms and legs spreadeagled. Arrows were then shot into him, so that he bled profusely, and his blood sacramentally fertilised the soil.

There were interesting and elaborate variants on this fundamental religio-magical practice. Sometimes, when the victim
had bled profusely but was yet alive, he was removed from his
wooden framework and sacrificed in the customary fashion, his
heart being cut from his living breast by a priest using an
obsidian knife. His skin would then be flayed from his body,
and donned by the priest representing the Earth-Mother,
symbolising the donning of a new mantle—that of a new and
full-eared maize crop. In order to emphasize the symbolism,
the priests assumed disguises resembling maize ears and maize
stalks, and indulged in an elaborate ritual dance before the
altars and within sight of the fields which had been recently
sown. Meanwhile, the flesh of the victim, or of the victims
where more than one had been sacrificed to the gods and
goddesses, was distributed among the warriors who had been
responsible for procuring the prisoners of war for the purpose
of the ceremony.

Among the Aztecs, the actual mechanics of sacrifice were
elaborated constantly, and there was hardly an aspect of the
ceremony which did not possess some deep and fundamental
symbolism.

The victim was first stripped of any ornaments he might be
wearing. He was then laid over a curved sacrificial altar, or
large stone, and his head, his legs and his arms would be taken
by five priests, one to each, and held rigid while the High
Priest, the sacrificial agent, who might often be identified with
the god or goddess he himself served, cut open the victim's
breast with his knife of obsidian—a form of volcanic rock which
was dark like bottle-glass and could be sharpened to a razor
edge.

The priest then tore out the victim's heart, often still
palpitating, and held it up to the sun that each might give
strength to the other. It was then put into a ceremonial basin
which had been placed in such a position as to collect the blood
that flowed from the wound. Then, mixed with the smoke of
incense, the smell of the blood was wafted upwards to the god in
whose honour the ceremony had just been enacted.

Bereft of its heart, and much of its blood, the body was of no
further service to the High Priest. It was therefore thrown
down the great flight of stone steps that characterised the

Aztec temples, from the altar at the summit to the people waiting in the courtyard below.   There it was seized by other priests and given to the warriors responsible for the original capture of the victim.   The skin was carefully removed, and donned by the chief of the warriors concerned, who believed that by wearing it he would gain something of the dead man's fertility and soul-stuff.   The body itself was then cut up and eaten by the warriors and their closest associates; but the feast at which this body was devoured was a solemn, a ceremonial occasion, very different from the cannibalistic orgies of the less 'civilised' Fijians already described.

The great Aztec feast, known as Toxcatl, was held on April 23rd, when the sun was at its zenith.   It was regarded as the greatest festival of the year, and not unnaturally the elaboration of the ceremony here reached its zenith too.   It was, in fact, virtually a sacrificing of the god himself to the god himself—a perversion of an originally straightforward practice which is to be found duplicated in many other parts of the world.

The ceremony may be said to have commenced a whole year before its climax, when a carefully selected victim, usually a prisoner captured in battle, was set apart from all others and prepared—one might almost say 'groomed'—for the part he was eventually to play.   He was established in the temple itself; he was regarded as something between a king and a god; he was waited upon hand and foot by notables of the community, under the constant supervision of the temple priests.   On the rare occasions when he was permitted to descend the stone steps of the temple and walk in the streets below, the people made holiday and he was regarded with awe, as a visitor, almost, from another planet.

For the three weeks of April preceding the Feast of Toxcatl he was attended day and night by four young and beautiful 'brides'.   These were known as the Goddess of Flowers, the Goddess of the Young Corn, the Goddess of Our Mother-among-the-Water, and the Goddess of Salt.   They were beautiful and ardent and—what is more—dedicated.   With them, for those blissful weeks, he lived a life of supreme voluptuousness.

On the day of the Feast of Toxcatl the young man was taken from the temple where he had lived for the past year and

brought to a hilltop near the great lake.   There he said farewell
to the four 'bride-goddesses'.   Then he walked on, alone, to a
special temple where the priests awaited him.   Immediately
his shadow crossed the temple threshold, the priests seized him
and the High Priest swiftly sacrificed him in the traditional
ceremonial manner.   A 'divine king' had been slain in homage
to the king-god whom he represented; and immediately the
heart ceased to palpitate, his successor was announced and the
long ritual process began all over again.   It was an ancient and
a grisly version of 'Le Roi est mort: Vive le Roi!'

Women, too, in the Aztec religious festivals, had their part to
play.   When the maize crop—the basic cereal crop of Mexico
—had come near to full ripeness, a goddess representing the
maize, Xilonen, was sacrificed as the climax to a long succession
of ceremonial dances in which the dancers carried lighted
symbolical torches.   The woman, or girl, was clad in the full
robes associated with the goddess with whom she was temporarily identified.   Her face was painted in yellow and red,
to represent the ripened grain, and her arms and legs were
adorned with bright red feathers.   She was equipped with a
shield and a brilliant red baton.

During the night before the festival she danced continuously
outside and inside the temple of Xilonen; on the day of the
festival she was seized by a priest and brought swiftly into the
presence of the goddess's High Priest himself.   The manner of
the sacrifice here differed from that which was usual for male
victims.   The priest who had seized her carried her on his
back, while the High Priest first cut off her head, and then tore
her heart from her breast.

The Aztec harvest festival also involved a woman victim.
A woman was selected with the greatest care to represent
Teteoinnan, the Earth-Mother.   At midnight on August 21st,
this woman was decapitated by the priests and flayed.   Her
skin was then donned by a young man, who identified himself
temporarily with the goddess.   But the skin of one of the
woman's thighs was removed separately from the rest, and was
taken ceremonially to another temple to be worn as a mask by
the High Priest serving Centeotl, the Maize Goddess.

There was still a further elaboration of this complex ceremony.   The young man who had donned the victim's skin and

was now impersonating the Earth-Mother, was taken to the altar of her temple and clothed in her symbolic apparel. There, he ritualistically sacrificed four selected victims, the object being the symbolic impregnation of the goddess—whose own fertility was so vital to the people's welfare. The last stage in this annual ceremony was twofold: the High Priest who had been wearing the mask made of a portion of the victim's thigh-skin, deposited his mask on some outlying frontier post of the Aztec territory; the young man who had been wearing the victim's skin save for that portion, and who had thus been identified with the goddess herself, was banished altogether!

The climax of the whole Aztec year was in January, when the festival of the God of Fire was celebrated. Oddly enough, though this was the climax of a series of festivals, all of which involved sacrifice, at this one the victims for three years out of every four were not human beings but animals. But they had to be animals captured by children or young persons, who brought them to the temples for the priests to sacrifice.

Every fourth year, however, the victims were human beings; and, what is more, human beings in couples. Young men and women, newly married, were selected on these special occasions. They were ceremonially attired in the robes associated with the Fire God, and instead of being sacrificed in the customary manner, by the High Priest with the obsidian knife, they were thrown in couples into the flames of the Fire God's altars. There they were watched with great attention, and just before they gave signs that they were about to expire among the flames, they were raked out by the High Priest's attendants and had their hearts torn from their charred flesh.

It is not easy to see why there should be this curious procedure, for on the surface of it nothing could be more apt than that pairs of young, healthy creatures, male and female, should feed the flames dedicated to a god. It is possible that this refinement of cruelty was designed to ensure that the Fire God should be fed first with the living bodies of his victims, and then have their hearts—the vital source of their energy— separately offered to him.

Anthropologists maintain that customs such as these which have just been described reached their apotheosis among the Aztec communities in the fifteenth century. Furthermore,

such was the power and influence of the Aztecs that similar
religious customs were traced among other tribes of Central
and Southern America—notably among the Incas of Peru and
the scattered tribes in Ecuador. Even after the Spaniards'
arrival and occupation of so much of this territory it seems that
these practices survived. Maize was the basic foodstuff of these
peoples; and maize crops needed adequate sun and adequate
rain if they were to meet the demands of the people. Without
a constant supply of sacrificial victims, the Earth-Mother
would lose the co-operation of her fellow-gods, and swift and
certain starvation would ensue.

It is known that these practices, if in modified form, survived
not merely the arrival of the Spaniards but for some centuries
thereafter. April 22nd/23rd was an important date also for
the Pawnee Indians; among them as recently as 1838 there was
a case of human sacrifice which has close parallels with the
elaborate ritual of the Aztecs in their heyday.

A girl in her earliest teens was selected for sacrifice. For a
period—not of months, as with the Aztecs, but of days—she was
conducted through the village, from wigwam to wigwam, in
a procession headed by the chiefs and warriors. At each
stopping-place she received a gift. When the last one had
been reached, she was painted red and black—an echo of the
Aztec painting to represent the colours of the maize crop—and
then placed over an open fire and slowly roasted to death,
while tribesmen shot arrows at her body to spill her blood.

At the appointed moment the chief sacrificer tore out her
heart and ate it. The remainder of her body was then ceremonially cut up into small portions, which were placed in
baskets and taken out to the maize fields. The next stage in
the ceremonial was to take the pieces of flesh, one at a time,
from the baskets and carefully squeeze drops of the warm blood
on the newly planted grain. By this process, they believed, the
seeds would be vitalised. The fragments of flesh, squeezed
almost dry of blood, were then made into a sort of paste which
was carefully rubbed over root vegetables such as potatoes to
bring them safely to maturity.

It will be seen from this example, horrible as it is, that the
element of cannibalism is reduced here to an absolute minimum: the ritual devouring of the heart of the child by the

sacrificing priest. The gesture, obviously, is to identify the priest, as representative of the god, with the child-victim whose blood will later vitalise the planted grain. The underlying belief is a widespread one, and need not necessarily involve the consumption of human flesh, though the flesh is indeed devoured symbolically.

In Bengal, for example, a Dravidian tribe known as the Khonds used regularly to sacrifice a victim they referred to as Meriah, in order to guarantee good crops in their locality. The victim in this case was not a girl but a young man, and a young man who must come from a pious home. He was treated with the utmost reverence during the period preceding the sacrifice, and on the day of the sacrifice was brought in solemn procession to the sacred grove where the priests officiated.

The Khond priests appear to have been conscious of the 'guilt' attached to such sacrifice, and went to great lengths to exonerate themselves before carrying out their sacrificial deed. The method of sacrifice did not, in their case, involve fire. Usually the victim was strangled, or squeezed to death; alternatively he was strapped to a wooden image of an elephant, which curiously enough represented the Earth Goddess. Thus strapped to the elephant, he was cut to pieces while still alive: a method of despatch which echoes the Aztec practice of decapitating a woman victim while held on the back of a priest of the temple.

When the victim had eventually died as a result of this piecemeal carving up by the priest's knife, his flesh was divided into two main portions. One of these was buried in the ground as an oblation to the Earth Goddess; the other was distributed in carefully proportioned shares among the heads of families. These portions were ceremonially wrapped in leaves and then interred in the most important and deserving fields, or even suspended from a pole over a stream whose waters irrigated the fields. The head, bones and intestines were burned and the ashes then scattered over the other fields, the granaries and store-houses; and the surplus, if any, sprinkled over the first corn to be gathered in.

The Aztecs, then, though they practised cannibalism, did so only because the consumption of human flesh had come to be an integral part—and a small part at that—of an elaborate system of sacrificial ceremonial that was aimed primarily at the propitiating of one or other of their gods or goddesses. The general impression that one gains, from examining the evidence, is that their attitude towards the whole matter was diametrically opposed to that of the Fijian Islanders, and of the other Melanesian tribes whose practices have still to be considered. They were, of course, a far more highly developed race than the Fijians ever were, or are ever likely to become; there is thought —deep thought—behind their actions: thought amounting almost to a philosophy. Amounting certainly to what passes for a religion. But, unaccountably, the Aztecs do not appear to have evolved a mythology of their own: not, at any rate, a mythology comparable with that, say, of the ancient Greeks, of the Scandinavians; or even of the North American Indians. We turn to them next.

CHAPTER THREE

CUSTOM AND MYTH AMONG THE KWAKIUTL INDIANS

Many of us were brought up on Fenimore Cooper's *Last of the Mohicans*; on stories of Redskins and Cowboys, and films based on these stories; or on Longfellow's *Song of Hiawatha*. We used to be, and perhaps still are—if we remain sufficiently young in heart—addicted to these stories, these never-to-be-completed sagas. We may know that the richest store of all, and the most romantic, is to be found in the long, rambling poem that tells of Gitche Manitou the Mighty, of Ishkoodah the Comet, of Mudjekeewis with his belt of wampum, of Chibiabos the Musician, and the Very Strong One, Kwasind, and tells at great (but for many of us never too great) length the story of Hiawatha and Minnehaha, 'Laughing Water'.

These stories are the mythology of the Delawares and Mohawks, the Choctaws and Camanches, the Shoshonies and Blackfeet, the Hurons and Ojibways, and many other tribes whom, for convenience, Longfellow grouped about the Wisconsin shore of Lake Superior, the true home of the Ojibways, "in the region", as he says, "between the Pictured Rocks and the Grand Sable". And what better situation for them could be found than near the 'Picture Rocks', when the saga of their lives is one vast, crowded, colourful canvas?

He did not, however, include among the tribes whose stories he told a tribe of North American Indians whose home was some two thousand miles to the west of Lake Superior, on the American–Canadian frontier where it abandons its die-straight, arbitrary line and hooks down through Juan de Fuca Strait to take in the southern extremity of Vancouver Island. These are the Kwakiutl Indians.

The Kwakiutl Indians for the most part occupied a strip of territory along the North-east Pacific coastline which includes Rivers Inlet and Cape Mudge. They were hunters, of course— as all North-American Indians were and remain; hunters and trappers. But also, because of their situation, fishers too. The hills and forests of British Columbia formed their hinterland; the cold Pacific their frontier. The mighty wall of the northern Rocky Mountains was the backcloth to their lives: a backcloth through which they had no desire to penetrate, for they were a self-contained community of many tribes, and clans within their tribes; a community close knit and with peculiarly close ties with the great gods, good and evil, and the Guardian and other Spirits of their tribes.

Like all communities that are more than ordinarily isolated, by some geographical or other feature, they tended to turn in upon themselves. Their legends, stories and—so far as the word is apt in this context—history are more concerned with their inter-tribal relationships, and their relationships with their tribal gods and Guardian Spirits, than with other peoples living beyond the fringe of their territories. It is therefore not surprising that a tribal mythology has evolved among the Kwakiutl Indians that is not easy to parallel anywhere else in the world.

They claim their origin variously: the tribe's mythical ancestor was one who either descended into their territory from heaven, or arose from the underworld, or emerged from the depths of the ocean itself. How long ago this was, they have no means of computing; but it is evident from the enormous body of legend—amounting to a saga that makes Longfellow's *Song of Hiawatha* look like a shorthand jotting in a small notebook—that it was a long while ago. For every tribe has its own tutelary deities; every tribe has its covey of Spirits, some good, some evil, who must be propitiated, flattered or warily guarded against. It is this abnormally close and, as it were, personal relationship between tribes and clans and tribal gods and spirits which accounts for the wealth of fascinating detail, the fantastic variety of story and picture, that is the common property of the Kwakiutls, and has been over a period of years collected, recorded and collated. With them, far more than with the Aztecs, religion and the life of the tribe, collectively and individually, was a highly personal affair that called for constant watchfulness and presence of mind, enterprise, courage and acceptance.

One of the complications in their lives was the disconcerting knowledge that the supernatural powers—the gods and spirits—

which were favourably disposed to the tribal ancestors might not continue generation after generation to be well disposed towards their descendants. Fortunately, however, they believed that there were other spirits which of their own volition remained in contact with the Indians and were prepared, for a consideration, to endow them with something at any rate of their own supernatural powers. The problem was always to ascertain who was who, and which was which. A false step could prove disastrous.

The first step which a Kwakiutl Indian takes is, not unnaturally, to obtain the favourable regard, and thence the protection, of one of the tribal spirits. His choice is reasonably wide, but he will act to a large extent on the advice of the elders of his clan, allowing his own inclination to temper their advice within moderation. By obtaining the protection of this spirit he will, the Kwakiutl believes, become imbued with some at any rate of the main characteristics of the spirit, and thus become superior in some respects (if still inferior in others) to many of his fellow tribesmen.

He may choose, for example, to seek the sponsorship of Winalagilis, a warrior whose home is in the distant north of the territory but who is rarely at home because he is a restless spirit whose pleasure it is to rove the whole earth waging individual wars where he will and when he will, except that it must always be against some people whom he can reach without leaving his canoe. Sponsorship by Winalagilis will endow the Kwakiutl youth with any one of three characteristics, each of which should stand him in good stead throughout his life: he will be invulnerable; or he will have the power of command over the Disease Spirit, which was thought to be an invisible worm constantly gliding through the air and able to deal mortal blows at anyone to whom it was directed; or finally he may be capable of being wounded without either feeling pain or being in fact injured at all.

Again, he could seek the protection of Matem, a strange bird known to inhabit the summits of certain mountains, each in turn, and able to transmit to any Kwakiutl on whom it looked with favour the ability to fly.

Yet again—and here we have the most elaborate and certainly the most interesting, if the most horrific, of these notions—the youthful Kwakiutl could enlist the protection of the fearsome Baxbakualanuxsiwae. His mouthful of a name means 'He-who-is-First-to-eat-Man-at-the-mouth-of-the-River'. His home was known to be on the slopes of the great mountains. From the chimney of his house blood-red smoke rose in a continuous billowing cloud. He shared his house with his wife, Qominoqa, a terrifying female who was responsible for procuring his meals. She was assisted by a female slave, Kinqalalala, who had the job of rounding up the victims and collecting corpses.

At the door of this malodorous house perched another slave, a raven named Qoaxqoaxualanuxsiwae, whose specific privilege was to eat the eyes from the bodies discarded by his master when his appetite was glutted. A companion at the threshold to this house was Hoxhok, a fabulous bird of no known species, with a formidable beak used for picking out the brains from skulls which it had first cracked with one well-aimed blow. There was also, as attendant on the owner of the house and his motley companions, a grizzly bear, Haialikilal.

The Kwakiutl youth who decides to seek the patronage of Baxbakualanuxsiwae will, if he is successful, join that *corps d'élite* in the tribe known as the Hamatsas. These held a special position in the tribe, and a very privileged one: they were at liberty to eat human flesh—whether the victim was an enemy slain in battle or captured on a foray, or a fellow member of the tribe. The Hamatsas were, in a word, licenced cannibals, whose privilege, and even duty, was to maintain an affinity with Baxbakualanuxsiwae by sharing his passion for human flesh. But, as we shall see, this privilege was wrapped about by an extraordinary cocoon of duty and tabu.

Since this particular tribal spirit was such a fierce and voracious character, it is natural that the legends that were evolved concerning him were more elaborate, more terrifying in their detail, than those which were recounted concerning such relatively mild-mannered individuals as, say, Winalagilis or Matem. There are infinite variations, for example, in the legend the Kwakiutls tell of how their ancestors, 'in the dark backward and abysm of time', first made contact with the spirit who became such a dangerous acquisition to their tribe.

Nanwaqawe (one of the legends runs), a Chief of the Kwakiutls in their earliest days, had four sons who occupied all their time in hunting the mountain-goat. In those days members of the Kwakiutl tribe were constantly disappearing, one after another, in the most mysterious fashion. Soon, the women of the tribe lamented, we shall no more have husbands, brothers or sons—for it was the menfolk who most often disappeared.

At last a day came when the chief knew he must find out what was happening to the men of his tribe. He, and only he, knew of the existence of a spirit in the mountains powerful enough to cause these men to disappear. And he knew that in allowing his four beloved sons to range the mountains for goats he was allowing them also to risk their lives. Nevertheless, as chief of his tribe, he knew that it was his duty to solve the mystery. So, the day came when he called his four sons, Tawixamaye, his eldest son, Qoaqoasililagilis, his second son, Yaqois, his third son, and his youngest son, Nulilokue, and bade them listen carefully to his words.

"Go into the mountains, my sons," he said solemnly, "and when you come near to a house on the mountainside the smoke of which looks red like blood, do not enter it, or you will never return home. It is the house of Baxbakualanuxsiwae. Do not enter, either, the house on the mountainside the smoke of which is grey on one side; for that is the house of the grizzly bear, Haialikilal. Harm will befall you, if you enter that house. But now go, my very dear sons, and keep wide open your eyes as you go, or you will not return."

Early the next morning the four young men left their father's house, and by noon they had come within sight of the house on the mountainside from which grey smoke rose into the sky. Then the eldest son said to his brothers: "This is the house of the grizzly bear that perhaps has eaten our fellows. Let us see if our father's warning is good."

As they approached, the grizzly bear came out, crossing his own threshold, and blood and flesh dripped from his yellow fangs.

"That," cried the eldest brother, "must be the blood of a Kwakiutl! Come, let us slay this bear."

All the rest of the day the four brothers fought with the grizzly bear, Haialikilal, whose great yellow teeth were bared to seize their flesh. But as darkness fell, the eldest brother struck a shrewd blow and broke the bear's skull, and at last he dropped lifeless at their feet. They looked inside the grizzly bear's house, and saw that the beaten floor was strewn with human bones and skulls.

"Come," said the eldest brother, "our journey into the mountains is not yet completed."

Though night had begun to fall, they walked on and on, until at last the youngest brother, Nulilokue, dropped exhausted to the ground unable to go any further. So they all lay down close to him, and slept until daybreak.

Next morning they walked on, climbing steadily up the mountainside, till they saw in the distance a great pillar of smoke, red like blood, rising into the heavens, and they knew they were looking at the house of Baxbakualanuxsiwae.

"Come, my dear brothers," said the eldest son, "let us go and see if our father's warning is good."

They continued on their way, walking more rapidly now, and came at length to the threshold of the house on the mountain-side from which the great plume of blood-red smoke rose to the heavens, making the sky murky overhead. The eldest brother hammered upon the closed door; but there was no reply, no sound at all from within. He hammered again, and yet again; and because there was still no sound from within, at length he opened the door and the four of them went into the darkness beyond the threshold.

Then, from the murky, smoke-filled darkness a woman's voice spoke to them: "Help me!" it cried. "I am rooted to the floor. Help me! Then I may help you—whom I have long awaited."

"What must we do to help you?" asked the eldest brother.

"Exactly what I tell you," answered the woman's voice, coming to them from the smoky darkness through which they could as yet see nothing at all. "Do not take any notice of anything you may see when the smoke clears. But dig a deep hole in the floor. Then place stones in this fire, and afterwards, when they are red-hot, throw them into the hole that you have dug in the floor."

When the four brothers had done as she bade them, she said: "Now, cover the hole with boards. As soon as Baxbakuala-nuxsiwae returns from hunting—for this is his house—he will put his mask over his face and begin to dance."

Hardly had the woman spoken these words than the four

brothers quickly laid boards over the hole into which they had
thrown the red-hot stones. And hardly had they done this
than they heard a fierce whistling sound beyond the threshold.
Then the doorway was darkened and the sunlight blotted out,
as the great form of Baxbakualanuxsiwae filled it. In he came,
and stood a moment just inside the doorway and called out his
terrible cry: "Hap! Hap! Hap! Hap!"—"Eat! Eat!
Eat! Eat!" And as he did so, the Hoxhok, with its great
beak, as long as a man's hand and as hard as stone, and
Qoaxqoaxualanuxsiwae, the eyeball-eating raven, began also
to cry out: "Hap! Hap! Hap! Hap!"

Then Baxbakualanuxsiwae lay down on the beaten earth
floor and the four brothers, the youngest one cowering behind
the older ones, saw that his whole body was covered all over
with gaping, blood-stained mouths. The monster then rose
from the floor and began prowling round in the murky, smoke-
filled darkness, continuously crying out "Hap! Hap! Hap!
Hap!" in a voice of increasing excitement. The raven, meanwhile, whose feathers covered him from his head down to his
waist, danced wildly in front of him, in front of the fire, from
which the blood-red smoke ascended to a hole in the roof.
Then the bird with the great stone beak came in, and it too
danced in front of the fire, and all three of them cried out continuously: "Hap! Hap! Hap! Hap!" their cries becoming fiercer and fiercer all the time. And as they cried their
terrible cry, they danced ever more wildly in front of the fire.

Then, from a room in the back of the house, there came first
Qominoqa, the spirit's wife, and danced and sang and cried in
a great voice: "Hoip!" and "Hai! Hai! Hai! Hai!"
And after her came Kinqalalala, the female slave, and she too
danced and cried "Hoip!" and "Hai! Hai! Hai! Hai!"

At last Baxbakualanuxsiwae's great feet came close to the
edge of the pit which the four brothers had dug in the floor.
Waiting his opportunity, the eldest brother suddenly snatched
away the boards they had laid over the pit, and Baxbakualanuxsiwae, still dancing and crying out "Hap! Hap! Hap!
Hap!" plunged to the bottom of the pit among the red-hot
stones that glowed there in the murky darkness.

"Now—quick! Bury him!" shrieked the woman who had
bidden them dig the hole in the floor. And, quick as lightning,

the four brothers threw into the hole more stones and sods and earth till the hole was almost filled.

And now, Baxbakualanuxsiwae was dying. His flesh steamed and hissed on the red-hot stones, and the smoke of it rose to join the blood-red smoke that poured out through the hole in the roof of his house. And then he died. And at the moment when he died, his wife and his female slave died too; and the two grisly birds vanished.

"Now take Baxbakualanuxsiwae's ornaments of red cedar bark," said the woman, "and his masks and whistles and his totem-pole, which is the Hamatsa Pole. But before you go, you shall learn from me the Song of Baxbakualanuxsiwae."

But the eldest son replied: "First we will go home and tell our dear father all that we have seen and heard and done since we left him. Then may be we will return, bringing him with us that he may see for himself." And with that, they left the house and went swiftly back down the mountainside to their father's house by the great river, where they told him all that had befallen them.

"I will come with you and see this wonder for myself," said the chieftain, who was their father, and at dawn they set out once again up the mountainside.

When they had come to the house, from the roof of which a little blood-red smoke still ascended into the heavens, the woman who was rooted to the floor offered them food and said to them: "Now you shall dance, and possess among you the cannibal mask—the mask of the Hamatsa—and the mask also of the raven and the mask of the Hoxhok, and besides that, all the red cedar bark. And also the whistles of Baxbakualanuxsiwae. But before that, I will teach you the secret songs."

When the woman who was rooted to the floor had ended her songs, the chief asked her: "Now, tell me who you are?"

And the woman laughed a terrible laugh and replied: "So you do not know who I am? I am—your own long-lost daughter, whom Baxbakualanuxsiwae the Cannibal would not devour but preferred to keep rooted to the floor of his house, so that he might scorn me to the end of time."

And her father said: "I rejoice. And these your four brothers rejoice with me that we have found you at last. Now, let us all return to our home together and feast there."

But the woman wept, and answered: "Alas, it is impossible that I should go with you to your house, dear father, with these my four new-found brothers, for I am rooted to the ground and am unable to move from this spot where I stand."

"Then we will dig you out," said her father, and bade the four brothers set to work at once.

This they did with a will; but the further down they dug, the thicker became the root, and at last they knew that they could never succeed in uprooting her.

"If you cut the root," said the woman, sorrowfully, "I must surely die. So now you must all return home, without me. And as soon as you reach your home on the great river, you must give a Winter Dance. Let my eldest brother, Tawixamaye, disappear, and he shall afterwards become Hamatsa, the Cannibal. Then, four days later, let Qoaqoasililagilis disappear also; and he shall become Qominoqa and set about finding food for the Hamatsa. And thenceforward let the Hamatsa do no work whatsoever, or else he will die early."

And so, sorrowfully, the chieftain and his four sons went home as they were bidden to do by the woman rooted to the floor of the house. And there they made a great feast, accompanied by much ceremonial dancing, as the woman had instructed them. And immediately after the feast Tawixamaye disappeared, and in due course became the tribe's first Hamatsa, exactly as the woman had foretold, and his brother served him as he had been bidden he must do.

Now, these dances were an essential part of the life of the Kwakiutls. They had a fundamental purpose, for they reveal that the dancer is impersonating the spirit. Just as Baxbakualanuxsiwae had danced on the floor of his house before plunging to his grisly death on the red-hot stones in the pit that the brothers had dug for him, so the *protégé* of the spirit, the young Kwakiutl who has sought his patronage, must dance. He wears the fearsome mask, and carries with him various of the spirits' possessions as further evidence that he and the spirit are one. The dance is a dramatic presentation of that part of the myth relating to the transfer of the spirit to the Kwakiutl youth. The dance is the youth's way—or one of his ways—of proving to his fellow tribesmen that he has been accepted by the spirit.

But, as the superstitions of the Kwakiutls developed and

became more complex, and at the same time more gripping, the ceremonial dance came to assume another function. The youth who had fled—as his ancestor, Tawixamaye had done—to live for a while with his patron and imbibe his skill and knowledge and ways, must be brought back to the tribe. And, having been brought back to the tribe, must have some part of the 'devil' in him exorcised, or he would be too dangerous to have as a member of the tribe. The ceremonial dances came, therefore, to play some part in this purgation. They would first attract him, so that he came flying back from the deep forests into which he had penetrated to find his guardian spirit; and having brought him back, would give him an opportunity to shed some at any rate of the rage with which he had been filled.

The would-be Hamatsa, the youth who proposes to identify himself with the tribal spirit, Baxbakualanuẍsiwae, departs into the forest alone, and is expected to remain there, alone save for the company of the spirit he has gone to seek, for three months or more. Part way through that period, however, he returns to the outskirts of his native village, uttering the piercing whistling sound, and the dreadful cry, "Hap! Hap! Hap! Hap!" which he has now learned from the spirit in the forest.

Next, he calls loudly for his Kinqalalala, who is always a close female relation, and demands that she procure flesh for him. Having made this demand, the youth then charges into the village among his fellow tribesmen and savagely bites pieces out of their arms and chests.

As soon as he has started doing this, a group of men known as the Heliga run towards him, shaking ceremonial rattles which are supposed to pacify the budding Hamatsa. There are always six of these 'healers', whose office in the tribe is hereditary, and four of them must always accompany the Hamatsa when he is in one of his 'holy rages', or ecstasies. Their duty is to stay near him and so far as is possible direct his savage attacks on his fellows so that he makes no mistakes—at once restraining and advising him. Their cry is a challenge to his: "Hoip! Hoip! Hoip! Hoip!" The rattles they carry are always either skulls, or wood carved in the shape of a skull, which commonsense would suggest is more likely to inflame the youth's passions than to calm them!

A few days before the newly-created Hamatsa returns finally
to his village, at the end of his sojourn in the forest, the veteran
Hamatsas of the village are summoned. They leave their
village and take a track through the trees that leads to the hut
which the young Hamatsa has built for himself. When they
arrive, they find that he is already provided with a supply of
human flesh for immediate consumption, and his first greeting
to them is to say: "These are my travelling provisions, which
Baxbakualanuxsiwae himself has given to me."

Where, in fact, has this human flesh come from? The
answer is evidence of a curious practice peculiar to the Kwakiutl tribes, known as 'Tree Burial'.

Corpses destined for consumption by the Hamatsa were
frequently put into wooden chests and the chests carried up to
the upper branches of trees, as high up as was practicable.
There, they were exposed to the breezes as well as to the sun,
and the result was that in many cases they reached a stage of
natural mummification.

When a corpse was required for ceremonial consumption, it
was taken down from the tree and first of all carefully soaked in
salt water. Then one of the Heliga would take some hemlock
twigs, remove the leaves, and push the twigs with great care
beneath the skin of the corpse. Eventually he succeeded in
that way in removing the decayed part of the flesh. The
corpse was then laid on the roof of the small hut in the forest in
which the new Hamatsa was spending the last part of his
voluntary exile from his village. The hands of the corpse were
made to dangle over the eaves; the belly was slit open and
spread wide on a framework of sticks, much as a sheep's carcass
is spread in a butcher's shop; and the Hamatsa lit a fire beneath
it in order to smoke the corpse.

Having first greeted the veteran Hamatsas, he would take
down the smoked corpse and lay it on a clean mat in front of his
hut. Each Hamatsa then, in strict order of tribal seniority,
was invited to select the portion of the corpse that he would like
to eat.

The Kinqalalala then bent down and picked up the corpse and
proceeded to walk slowly backwards, with the corpse laid across
her outstretched arms, facing the Hamatsa all the time. She
would pass the fire over which the corpse had been smoked,

followed closely by the Hamatsa. They entered the hut and passed through to the rear of it, where the corpse was laid ceremonially across a tribal drum. That was the signal for the veteran Hamatsas to come rushing in through the hut in a state of frenzy and dance round the corpse on the drum, impatient to begin their feast.

But there was one more piece of ritual before they could begin. The Kinqalalala had first to eat four mouthfuls of the corpse herself. Each bite as she took it was carefully observed and counted by all present. After that, each veteran Hamatsa in turn took his portion, and every bite was carefully watched by the others. It was laid down by tribal law—and the reason for this will be seen in due course—that each mouthful must be swallowed whole; there must be no chewing of the flesh first. And between each mouthful and the next, the Hamatsa must drink salt water.

When this ceremony was over, the Heliga seized a Hamatsa each and ran with them swiftly down to the nearest salt water. The Hamatsas were made to wade into the water until it reached the level of their chests. Then, facing the sunrise, each Hamatsa dipped four times beneath the water, each time repeating the terrible cry of Baxbakualanuxsiwae: "Hap! Hap! Hap! Hap!" The dipping into the salt water was believed to dispel the frenzied excitement of the Hamatsas—for the time being, at any rate.

It was then time for the newly-initiated Hamatsa to return to his village, having been accepted by the veterans of his tribe. His return was marked by prolonged ceremonial dancing—dancing in which every motion, every gesture, every grimace, had a symbolic meaning; and it was of course the dancing of the Hamatsa which was of greatest importance.

He danced to begin with in a squatting position, which was to indicate that he was in a state of tremendous, hardly controlled, excitement: that of a man looking for human flesh to devour. He trembled violently, extending first one arm and then the other, while he danced first on one foot and then on the other. As he circulated through the dancing-hut, his eyes were cast upwards, symbolising the search for a corpse laid on the roof above him, and he uttered the terrible cry of the Cannibal Spirit: "Hap! Hap! Hap! Hap!"

Then he changed to an erect posture, dancing in great leaps forward and from side to side, hurling himself into all parts of the dancing-hut, but still trembling violently all the time. It was then that his Kinqalalala joined in the dance. Repeating the ritual of the forest hut, when the veteran Hamatsas had come from their share of flesh, she danced backwards, holding her arms outstretched towards the young Hamatsa to indicate that a corpse still lay across them, waiting to be devoured.

As she did that, the Hamatsa became more and more excited, lunging out towards her to grasp the invisible corpse she was pretending to carry.

During the dancing, the Hamatsa wore a number of symbolical ornaments, though for the most part he danced naked till, in the final stages, a blanket would be thrown over his shoulders. He would wear a head-ring, a neck-ring, a waist-ring, wrist- and ankle-rings, and these were often constructed from hemlock twigs such as those which had been ceremonially used to remove the decaying flesh from the corpse devoured by the Hamatsas in the forest hut. His face would be painted, nearly always black. But it carried two curved lines painted bright red, running from the corners of his mouth to each ear. There was symbolism even in these red lines: they represented the parts of the newly initiated Hamatsa which had been torn from him during the period of his sojourn in the forest lair of Baxbakualanuxsiwae. And it was a clear-cut pronouncement that this Hamatsa was proposing to live in future off human flesh, as his tribal spirit had always done, and those of his own ancestors who had identified themselves with it.

By now, the Hamatsa had been fully recognised and accepted. He had still, however, to be fitted into the life and customs of his tribe, or clan, and these appear to have become progressively more and more complex with every succeeding generation.

During the first four days after his return and the ceremonial dancing he was allowed a great deal of latitude. He might run amok and bite flesh from anyone he chose. But after this brief period of untrammelled activity, the first of the complex tabus settled upon him. The Hamatsa and his attendant Kinqalalala had to enter in turn four individual huts, and there eat without question whatever was laid before them. Each of these meals was repeated four times.

There were conditions attached to his devouring of human flesh, whether that of some victim expressly killed for his benefit, or that of some corpse taken down from a Burial Tree. For example, immediately the last mouthful of flesh had passed his lips, he had to drink a quantity of salt water sufficient to bring about a violent fit of vomiting. In his vomiting it was essential that the gobbets of flesh he had swallowed—it will be remembered that he was not allowed to chew, or tear to pieces, any morsel of flesh that entered his mouth—must all be brought up. They had to be carefully counted by his attendants. If the number of gobbets failed to tally with the number he had swallowed, then his excrement must be carefully examined, in order to ensure that the human flesh which had passed his lips had been disposed of through one channel or the other.

The bones of any corpse whose flesh has been eaten by the Hamatsa had to be carefully collected, and preserved for a period of four lunar months. They were kept first for a short period in a part of the hut that faced north, away from the sun; then for a similar period in a cavity dug beneath rocks over which salt water flowed. Every four days their hiding-place was changed about, until the end of the fourth lunar month, when the bones were finally put into a canoe, taken out to deep water, and ceremonially jettisoned there.

It is easy to see, in such ritual detail as this, the lurking sense of guilt: the Hamatsa was permitted to do as the tribal spirit Baxbakualanuxsiwae had always done, and the Hamatsa's own ancestors remote and near; but he must at the same time cleanse himself of the evil he was permitted to practise. One of the cleansing agents was salt sea-water.

There were other, smaller, more trivial-seeming tabus. Even the most personal and intimate of the Hamatsa's daily movements and actions must be scrutinised. For example, when he had occasion to defecate, he must always be accompanied by several other Hamatsas, veterans. He must leave his hut by the rear door. He, and his companions, must carry a small stick of a certain wood. They must seat themselves together, and rise together, ceremonially. When they returned to their huts they must cross the threshold with their right feet foremost, and never look back over their shoulders until they were inside.

For the first four months after his initiation, the Hamatsa had to wear on his person a piece of soiled cedar bark. (It will be remembered that cedar bark was one of the possessions that were taken from the hut on the mountainside in which Baxbakualanuxsiwae had lived.) He had to live quite alone, and a Hamatsa representing the 'Grizzly Bear' was stationed at the door of his hut to ensure that he had no visitors. He had to eat from a bowl that had not been touched by any other member of his clan, and the spoon he used must not have been touched either. At the end of this period of four months both spoon and bowl had to be thrown away where no one else would ever find them.

When he wished to drink, the Hamatsa had to dip his bowl three times into the stream, and must not ever swallow more than four mouthfuls of water at any one time. He had to carry with him the wing-bone of an eagle and drink through it, so that there was no risk that his lips—over which human flesh had passed—would touch it. He must carry with him a bone with which to scratch his head for lice and nits, instead of using his own finger-nails.

For a period of sixteen days after eating human flesh he must not partake of any warm food, nor blow on warmed food to cool it. During this period, and sometimes for even longer, he was not allowed to do any work. Nor was he permitted to have intercourse with any woman. He may well have found this second tabu more difficult to observe, and much less welcome, than the first! With so many restrictions and tribal tabus, surely the Hamatsa must often have wondered whether his privileges were not heavily outweighed by his prohibitions.

The Kwakiutl Indians have asserted, when interrogated, that the practice of cannibalism only became general about a hundred years ago. White men who travelled in their territory were able to witness many of their ceremonial dances, and two of them, Hunt and Moffat, brought back first-hand information about their customs. They say that sometimes slaves were killed for the benefit of the Hamatsas, and that at other times the Hamatsas contented themselves with snatching mouthfuls of flesh from their own tribesmen—usually from the chests and upper arms of well-fleshed individuals.

They vouch for an example of ritual cannibalism which took

place near Fort Rupert. A Kwakiutl shot and wounded a slave, who ran away and collapsed on the beach at the water's edge. He was pursued by the tribesmen, including a group of the 'Bear Dancers' and Hamatsas. The slave's body was cut to pieces with knives while the Hamatsas squatted in a circle round them crying out their terrible cry: "Hap! Hap! Hap! Hap!"

Helpless to intervene, Moffat and Hunt watched the Bear Dancers snatch up the flesh, warm and quivering, and, growling like the Grizzly they represented, offer it to the Hamatsas in order of seniority.

The wife of the dead slave was at the time in Fort Rupert, and, like Hunt and Moffat, witnessed the slaughter of her husband, helpless to avert it. But she had a weapon that the white men did not possess: she could throw a curse over the Hamatsas.

"I will give you five years to live," she shrieked at them from the walls of Fort Rupert. "The Spirit of your Dancing is strong, but my spirit is stronger still. You have killed my husband with knives; I shall kill you with the point of my tongue."

Within five years of this episode, the white men report, every member of the tribe who had taken part in the killing of this slave was dead. In memory of the grim episode, a rock on the beach where the ritual feast took place was carved into the likeness of the Baxbakualanuxsiwae mask.

The tradition died hard. A Hamatsa demanded that another slave—this time a female—should dance for him. She stood a moment looking at him in terror, and said: "I will dance. But do not get hungry. Do not eat me!" She had hardly finished speaking when her master, a fellow member of the tribe, split her skull open with an axe, and the Hamatsa thereupon began to eat her flesh. This actual Hamatsa was still alive towards the end of the nineteenth century, and on interrogation remarked, among other things, that it is very much harder to consume fresh human flesh than the dried flesh of corpses that have been left to mummify in the trees and then brought down to appease the Hamatsa's hunger. He also said that it was a common practice to swallow hot water after a mouthful of flesh taken from a living body, as it was believed that this would cause the inflammation of the wound made by the teeth.   All cannibal tribes, of course, file their teeth to sharp points in order to deal more effectively with their food.

There was a variant of the practice whereby the returning Hamatsa ran riot among the members of his tribe, biting flesh from them.   Sometimes he brought a corpse with him—that of a slave or some victim captured and killed for the purpose.   He ate part of this corpse after his ceremonial dance was completed, but because this was the first corpse to be devoured by him since his initiation, it was prepared with extra elaborate care.   One of the most important details was the removal of the skin at the wrists and ankles, for the Kwakiutls believed that to eat of either hand or foot would result in almost immediate death.   This is one of many examples of the divergencies of custom in this respect: to the Kwakiutls, hands and feet were tabu; but among the Mangeromas of the Amazon jungles, whose customs we shall be examining in due course, the palms of the hands, and the soles of the feet, were looked upon as the greatest delicacies, and were reserved for those of the tribe who for one reason or another demanded priority.

Most recently, that is to say at the very end of the nineteenth century, it seems that the barbarous practices among the Kwakiutls had become modified to a very great extent: the ceremonial was retained, but symbolism played a larger and larger part in the ceremonial, replacing the physical act.   For example, the late-nineteenth-century Hamatsa did not necessarily bite a mouthful of flesh from the chest or the arm.   Instead, he caught a piece of skin between his teeth and sucked at it hard, to extract the taste of blood.   Then, with a sharp knife, he would snip off a piece of the skin and pretend to swallow it.   However, instead of swallowing it in fact, he put it into his hair behind his ear, to lie there until the ceremonial dancing was over.   Then, it was returned to the owner, who was thus assured that a piece of his own skin would not eventually be used to his harm in some piece of witchcraft.

It was, as it were, the beginning of the end.   From the horrors of that house on the mountainside in which Baxbaku-alanuxsiwae and his hideous attendants practised their fiendish rites, the customs of the Kwakiutls have been refined to a ritual dance with gestures hardly more dangerous than mime.

CHAPTER FOUR

CANNIBALS IN THE AMAZON BASIN

BEFORE LEAVING the vast continent of America, with its cannibal Aztecs in the centre and its cannibal Kwakiutls on its north-westernmost frontier, we should turn to see what South America has to offer.

The central regions of South America are so vast, so inaccessible, so ridden with disease and danger from man and beast and insect, that comparatively few white men, explorers or traders, have got further than the fringe. Whole expeditions—that of Colonel Fawcett, to name only one of the many—have plunged into these impenetrable jungles, with their crocodile-filled rivers, never to return.

The Amazon Basin, an area of nearly three million square miles, drained by a four-thousand-mile-long multiple river which itself is fed by tributaries too numerous to count, let alone name, is one of these formidable areas. Another is the Matto Grosso, another region of Brazil, further to the south, and having its own dangers. Yet a third is the Gran Chaco, on the Argentine–Paraguay frontier: fifty thousand square miles of almost impenetrable jungle, swamp and interlaced waterways. Regions such as these in South America have defied the efforts of geographers to chart them; defied the inroads of explorers seeking to probe their mysteries; swallowed up the great majority of the men intrepid enough to attempt to unravel their secrets. It may well be that, somewhere beyond those barriers of swamp and river and close-set, foetid jungle, there are tribes still living almost exactly as Prehistoric Man lived. Nothing —however astonishing or terrifying—should really be unexpected in Central South America.

Thus, the information that has been extracted from these dark and terrible regions is more fragmentary than that which has emerged from regions as forbidding even as, say, the Congo Basin, parts of Nigeria, or the darker corners of East Africa. Few mission stations, for instance, have ever been established in these regions; and of the very few which intrepid missionaries have tried to establish, none have survived. A few naturalists, like H. W. Bates, succeeded in surveying a small stretch of the Amazon and returning to write up notes like *The Naturalist on the Amazons*. Ten years earlier, another and less well-known naturalist, Russel Wallace, who has been described as 'the co-discoverer with Charles Darwin of the Principle of Natural Selection', published a small book which he called *Travels on the Amazon*. This was all of a hundred years ago; and though there have been more recent surveys in the past hundred years, by expeditions better equipped, there remains an aura of mystery and cruelty that hangs, like a miasma or an exhalation from the swamps and foetid undergrowth itself, over the limitless square miles of these regions.

A. H. Keane, a Fellow of the Royal Geographical Society, wrote, some fifty years ago, and without mincing his words, of a region less impenetrable than those just mentioned, the eastern part of Peru, where the River Ucayali follows fairly closely the frontier with Brazil, to flow eventually (as it seems practically every northern river must do) into the Amazon:

> The Amajuacas of the Ucayali, near the old Peruvian frontier, have been over and over again converted to Christianity, each time relapsing and murdering the evangelists. The Cashibos, also of the Ucayali, eat their aged parents, but perhaps more from religious sentiment than from cruelty. But religion certainly has nothing to do with their habit of imitating the cry of game, to decoy and then devour hunters in the forests.
>
> Before their conversion, it was the practice of the Cocomas of the Hualaga, but now removed to the Ucayali, to eat their dead relations, and to swallow the ground-up bones in fermented drinks, on the plea that it was better to be inside a warm friend than buried in the cold earth. Worse things are related of the Tupinambas, and of the Tapuyás, and of the Botocudos.

It is when Keane comes to the southern end of Peru, where it touches both Brazil and Bolivia, that his condemnation of the region becomes most forceful:

> Beyond the narrow confines of the 'Iroquois of the South', as the Aucas just south of the Maule frontier on the southern limit of Peru were somewhat inaptly called, much of the land was wrapped in darkness and desolation: *homo homini lupus erat*—Man was as a wolf to his fellow-man. Head-hunting, cannibalism in exceedingly repulsive forms, brutal treatment of the women and

children, prevailed amongst the Amazonian and the Brazilian aborigines.

There is a certain Biblical, or evangelical, quality in his writing, and one would think, from his style, that he was writing about the same time as those courageous missionaries Hunt and Cargill and their fellows were writing home from Fiji. Yet his book appeared less than fifty years ago.

Russel Wallace, writing over a hundred years ago, wrote as an observant naturalist, and emotion is hardly even hinted at in this brief account of the customs of some Amazon tribes with whom he came in contact:

The dead are almost always buried in the houses, with their bracelets, tobacco-bag and other trinkets upon them. They are buried the same day they die; the parents and relations keeping up a continual mourning and lamentation over the body from the time of death to the time of interment. A few days afterwards, a great quantity of *caxiri* is made, and all friends and relations are invited to attend, to mourn for the dead and to dance, sing, and cry to his memory. Some of the larger houses have more than a hundred graves in them, but when the houses are small, and very full, the graves are dug outside.

The Tarianas and the Tucanos and some other tribes, about a month after the funeral, disinter the corpse, which is by then much decomposed, and put it in a great pan over the fire till all the volatile parts are driven off with a most horrible odour, leaving only a black, carbonaceous mass, which is then pounded into a fine powder and mixed in several large vats made out of hollowed trees, filled with *caxiri*. This is then drunk by the assembled company till all is finished. They believe that thus the virtues of the deceased will be transmitted to the drinkers.

The Cobeus, alone among the Vaupés, are real cannibals. They eat those of other tribes whom they kill in battle, and even make war for the express purpose of procuring human flesh for food. When they have amassed more than they can consume at once, they smoke-dry the flesh over the fire and thus preserve it for food for a long time. They burn their own dead, and drink the ashes in *caxiri* in the same way as the Tarianas and the Tucanos.

H. W. Bates, whose *The Naturalist on the Amazons* (he was one of the earliest to recognise that there was more than one main River Amazon; in modern maps the great river is named the Amazonas, and where it at last debouches into the Atlantic, exactly on the Equator, the map records it as 'Mouths of the Amazon') was published in 1863, writes of the Majerónas, whose territory, he says, embraces several hundred miles of the west bank of the River Jauari, which is one of the larger tributaries of the Amazon near the frontier of Venezuela:

They are a fierce, indomitable and hostile people, like the Aráras. They are also cannibals. Navigation on the Jauari is rendered impossible on account of the Majerónas lying in wait on its banks to intercept and murder all travellers—especially whites.

Four months before my arrival, two young half-castes (nearly white) of the village went to trade on the Jauari, the Majerónas having shown signs of abating their hostility a year or two previously. They had not been long gone, when their canoe returned with the news that the two young fellows had been shot with arrows, roasted, and eaten by the savages.

José Patricio, with his usual activity in the cause of law and order, despatched a party of armed men to make inquiries. When they reached the settlement of the horde who had eaten the two men, it was found evacuated, with the exception of one girl, who had been in the woods when the rest of her people had taken flight. The men brought her back with them.

It was gathered from her that the young men had brought their fate on themselves through improper conduct towards the Majerónas women. The girl was taken care of by Senhor José Patricio, baptised under the name of Maria, and taught Portuguese. I saw a good deal of her, for my friend sent her daily to my house to fill the water jars, make the fire, and so forth. I gained her goodwill by extracting the grub of an *oestrus* fly from her back, thus curing her of a painful tumour.

She was decidedly the best-humoured and, to all appearances, the kindest-hearted specimen of her race I had yet seen. Her ways were more like those of a careless, laughing country wench, such as might be met with any day among the labouring class in villages in our own country, than a cannibal. Yet I heard this artless maiden relate, in the coolest manner possible, how she ate a portion of the bodies of the young men whom her tribe had roasted.

What increased greatly the incongruity of the whole business is that the young widow of one of the victims, a neighbour of mine, happened to be present during the narrative, and showed her interest in it by *laughing* at the broken Portuguese in which the girl related her horrible story.

The South American Missionary Society did actually succeed in establishing, and maintaining for a short time, a mission in the hardly less hostile region known as El Gran Chaco. One of the society's missionaries was named W. Barbrooke Grubb, a Scottish lay missionary who was in fact something of a pioneer and explorer in that daunting country. Thirty years or so ago a book was published in which some of his experiences were related. There is a fine balance between credulity and incredulity in his reports, and he brings a considerable measure of the true scientist's clear-sightedness and sense of proportion into what he has to say.

Although cannibalism is not now practised in the Chaco (he wrote, in *A Church in the Wilds*), the people have many stories about it—which may be only invented or may be accounts which have reached them referring to some distant tribe. But it is quite possible that they are the result of a long-forgotten habit. These cannibals are supposed to be located in the far West, and in that direction, among the people of Guarani descent, such practices are evidently still in vogue.

One of their stories is as follows: Three venturesome Lenguas, curious to know what countries and people lay to the west of their own land, set out upon a long journey of discovery. After some months of journeying, they accidentally met two men, who greeted them in a very friendly manner. Although they could not understand each other's language, the Lenguas soon discovered that they would be welcome guests at the village of these men. In accordance with signs which were made to them, they followed them to their village.

On nearing it, and before they could see it, they smelt a peculiarly sickly odour, which surprised them greatly. On their arrival they were heartily welcomed by all, and were given food, some of which they had never tasted before, but which they say they found very palatable.

Although the people of the village seemed to be so friendly, there was something about the place which made them feel uncomfortable and suspicious. They could not tell what it was, but they had a feeling of insecurity. Just after dark, all the people—men, women and children—left the village: the men to bring in the heaps of firewood which they had previously cut, and the women and children to fetch water from the river near by.

The Lengua men had previously noticed several long earthenware pots cooking on the fires. Feeling curious, they took this opportunity of being alone to examine their contents. Approaching one pot, to their horror they discovered the fingers of a human hand protruding from a mass of boiling meat, and, stirring the contents with the end of their bows, they saw next a foot. In another pot, when turning over a large, round piece of meat, a human face was exposed. They were filled with horror, disgust and terror, and fled immediately into the woods, making all haste to their homes.

Barbrooke Grubb adds that although he had heard many tales connected with cannibalism, there was every reason to

believe that it was not practised by what he calls the Gran
Chaco peoples *proper*—an odd word, perhaps, to use in such a
context! He does assert, however, that cannibalism was
practised by the Chiriguano Indians, whose territories bordered
on the Chaco itself, and who were sufficiently well known to the
Chaco tribes for them to be able to report accurately about their
customs and habits.

The frontier between Brazil and Northern Peru where it
reaches its greatest width is exactly marked by the Javary River
(not to be confused with the Jauari River, many hundreds of
miles to the east and north, about which H. W. Bates has
already written). This river flows northwards into one of the
great branches of the Amazon, watering a river basin which has
been well described by F. S. Dellenbaugh:

> The region of the Javary River is one of the most formidable and
> least known portions of the South American continent. It
> abounds with obstacles to exploration of the most overwhelming
> kind. Low, swampy, with a heavy rainfall, it is inundated
> annually, like most of the Amazon Basin, and at time of high
> water the rivers know no limits. Lying, as it does, so near the
> Equator, the heat is intense and constant, oppressive even to the
> native. The forest growth—and it is forest wherever it is not
> river—is forced, as in a huge hot-house, and is so dense as to
> render progress through it extremely difficult. Not only are
> there obstructions in the way of tree trunks, underbrush and
> trailing vines and creepers like ropes, but the footing is nothing
> more than a mat of interlaced roots. The forest is sombre and
> gloomy.
>
> Disease is rampant, especially on the smaller branches of the
> rivers. The incurable beri-beri and a large assortment of fevers
> claim first place as death-dealers, smiting the traveller with fearful
> facility. Next come a myriad insects and reptiles—alligators,
> huge bird-eating spiders, and snakes of many varieties. Snakes,
> both the poisonous and the non-poisonous kinds, find here condi-
> tions precisely to their liking. The bush-master is met with in the
> more open places, and there are many that are venomous; but
> the most terrifying, though not a biting reptile, is the water-boa,
> or anaconda, the *sucuruju*. . . .

It was in this very region that, some fifty years ago, the
explorer Algot Lange decided to have a look round. He did
not enter the territory with his eyes closed: already there had
been expeditions into the region, mainly organised by the
rubber syndicates, for it was here that wild rubber was to be

found, and at the turn of the century it was still worth the while of the big firms to try further exploitation of the rubber in the Amazon Basin, though by then seeds from Brazilian rubber-trees had been taken to England, reared in the Kew glass-houses, and successfully planted in Malaya and Indonesia. Reports from members of these expeditions left no doubt in Algot Lange's mind as to what sort of conditions he was likely to experience. Nor, in the event, was he to be disappointed!

On impulse, Lange decided to join one of these expeditions, and he wrote a long account of the expedition, during which snake-bite, beri-beri, fever and other enemies had proved fatal to so many of his companions, and so very nearly fatal to himself. He was no prose stylist, but he had a toughness and resilience and imperviousness to impact, characteristic of the finest quality rubber itself. What follows is the tail-end of his experiences—told by him in an odd mixture of laconic report-age and melodramatic writing.

I had now only a few boxes of exposed plates (which I eventually succeeded in carrying all the way back to New York), and fifty-six bullets, the automatic revolver, and the machete. Last but not least, I had the hypodermic needle, and a few ampoules.

We had walked scarcely a quarter of a mile, when Jerome collapsed. He was beaten, and declared that it was no use to fight any more; he begged me to put a bullet through his brain. The prospect of another visitation of Death aroused me from my stupor. I got him to a dry spot, and found some dry leaves and branches with which I started a fire. Jerome was beyond recognising me. He lay by the fire, drawing long, wheezing breaths, and his face was horribly distorted, like that of a man in a violent fit. He babbled incessantly to himself, and occasionally stared at me and broke out into a shrill, dreadful laughter that made my flesh creep.

All this overwhelmed me and sapped the little energy I had left. I threw myself on the ground some distance from the fire, not caring if I ever rose again. How long it was before a penetrating, weird cry aroused me from this stupor I do not know; but when I raised my head I saw that the forest was growing darker as the fire burned low. I saw too that Jerome was trying to get on his feet, his eyes bulging from their sockets, his face crimson in colour. He was on one knee, when the thread of life snapped in him and he fell headlong into the fire. I saw this as though through a hazy veil, and almost instantly my senses left me again.

I have no clear knowledge of what happened after this. Throughout the rest of the night my madness mercifully left me insensible to the full appreciation of the situation and my future prospects. It was night once more before I was able to rouse myself from my collapse. The fire was out, the forest dark and still, except for the weird cry of the owl and the uncanny 'Mother-of-the-Moon'. Poor Jerome lay quiet among the embers. I did not have the courage, even if I had had the strength, to pull the body away, for there could be nothing left of his face by now. I looked at him once more, shuddering, and because I could not walk, without any object in mind—just kept moving—just crept on, like a sick, worthless dog.

It would seem that the state of stupor, or at least of hopeless confusion, overwhelmed him when he came to record this particular moment in print, for he has, up to this point, made no mention of leaving the fatal camp and beginning to walk on through the jungle. But shortly afterwards he picks up the narrative in more coherent style:

There was no shadow of hope for me, and I had long given up believing in miracles. For eight days I had scarcely had a mouthful to eat, except the broiled monkey shot by the young Indian some time before. The fever had me completely in its grasp. I was left alone, more than a hundred miles from other human beings, in absolute wilderness. I measured cynically the tenaciousness of life, the thread that yet held me among the numbers of the living, and I realised now what a fight between life and death meant to a man brought to bay. I had not the slightest doubt in my mind that this was the last of me.

All night long I crawled on and on and ever on, through the underbrush, with no sense of direction whatever, and still I am sure that I did not crawl in a circle but that I covered a considerable distance. For hours I moved along at the absolute mercy of any beast of the forest that might meet me. But the damp chill of the approaching morning usual in these regions came to me with a cooling touch and restored once more to some extent my sanity. My clothes were almost stripped from my body, my hands and face were smeared with mud and torn, and my knees were a mass of bruises.

Lange writes more in this vein, and then records how, in his state of near-insensibility, he became vaguely aware of the sound of dogs barking. He changed the direction of his interminable crawling progress through the undergrowth, heading for the unexpected sound. And then:

I saw in front of me a sight which had the same effect as a rescuing steamer on the shipwrecked. To my confused vision it seemed that I saw men and women and children, and a large, round house; I saw parrots fly across the open space in brilliant, flashing plumage, and heard their shrill screaming. I cried aloud, and fell forward. A little curly-haired dog jumped up and commenced licking my face. And then—I knew no more.

When I came to, I was lying in a comfortable hammock in a large, dark room. I heard the murmur of many voices, and presently a man came over and looked at me. I did not understand where I was, but thought I had finally gone mad. I fell asleep again. The next time I woke up I saw an old woman leaning over me and holding in her hand a gourd containing some chicken broth, which I swallowed slowly, not feeling the craving of hunger, in fact, not really knowing whether I was alive or dead. The old woman had a peculiar piece of wood through her lip, and looked very unreal to me, and I soon fell asleep again.

On the fifth day, so I learned later, I began to feel my senses return, my fever commenced to abate, and I was able to grasp the fact that I had crawled into the *maloca*, or communal village of the Mangeromas. I was as weak as a kitten, and indeed it has been a marvel to me ever since that I succeeded at all in coming out of the Shadow.

As soon as I could get out of my hammock, though I could not stand or walk without the aid of two women, I was taken over to a man whom I found later to be the chief of the tribe. He was well fed, and by his elaborate dress was distinguished from the rest of the men. He had a very pleasant, good-natured smile, and almost constantly displayed a row of white, *sharp-filed* teeth. His smile gave me confidence, but I very well knew now that I was living among cannibal Indians—whose reputation in this part of the Amazon Basin is anything but flattering.

Lange goes on to say, laconically, that he "prepared for this new ordeal without any special fear," adding that doubtless by that time his capacity for emotion of any kind must have become pretty well exhausted. He had already experienced so much terror that any new terror he might encounter was denuded in advance of much of its impact. To be able to remark that the cannibal chief's smile—revealing as it did the sharp, filed teeth which are the universal sign of cannibal practices—gave him 'confidence' is surely evidence of a blind spot somewhere in his make-up! So is his pleasant piece of under-statement to the effect that cannibals in this part of the Amazon Basin had a reputation that was 'anything but flattering'! He records that he was told in sign language that he was welcome to stay among these people for as long as he wished to do so, and he offers no hint that there might have been in the invitation an ulterior motive, such as that, for instance, which had been experienced by the Lenguas of whom Barbrooke Grubb recorded their terrifying experience. In return, he contrived to explain how it was that he found himself in that situation, and he added diplomatically that he considered himself "fortunate to have thus found his way to the Free Men of the Forest". His audience came to an end, and he was led back to his hammock to sleep and eat and sleep—and dream.

As my faculties slowly returned to their former activity (he continues), I looked at these tribesmen and found them very strange figures indeed. Every man had two feathers inserted in the cartilage of his nose; at some distance it appeared as if they wore moustaches. The chief himself had a sort of feather-dress, reaching down to his knees. The women wore no clothing whatever, their only ornamentation being the oval wooden piece in the lower lip and fancifully arranged designs on face, arms and body. The colours which they preferred were scarlet and black, and they procured these dyes from two plants. They would squeeze the pulp of these fruits and apply the richly-coloured juice with their fingers, forming one scarlet ring round each eye and finally two scarlet bands reaching from the temples to the chin.

I soon learned that it was impolite to refuse any dish that was put in front of me, no matter how repugnant. One day, the Chief ordered me to come over to his family triangle and have dinner with him. The meal consisted of some very tender fried fish, which were really delicious; then followed three broiled parrots, with fried bananas, which were equally good. But then came a soup which I could not swallow—the first mouthful almost choked me.

The meat which was one of the ingredients of the soup tasted and smelt as if it had been kept for weeks, and the herbs which were used were so bitter, and gave out such a rank odour, that my mouth puckered and the muscles of my throat refused to swallow. The Chief looked at me, and frowned—and I remembered the forest from which I had lately arrived, and the starvation and terrors. I closed my eyes and swallowed the dish, seeking what mental relief I could find in the so-called auto-suggestion. I had the greatest respect for the impulsive, unreasoning nature of these sons of the forest: easily insulted, as I was to find out, they are well-nigh implacable. The incident showed me on what a slender thread my life hung.

Lange goes on to describe life among the tribesmen, with whom he seems to have achieved an astonishing measure of understanding and acceptance. He learned to use their weapons, to track with them, to recognise the details of spoor and flora and fauna generally which are essential to their way of life. But, as he says:

> Within a comparatively short while I was to have evidence of what I already suspected: that the Mangeromas were cannibals still. Two Peruvian *caboclos*, or half-breeds, had been caught in one of the many ingenious and fatal traps this tribe is so expert at setting in the jungle. The bodies had been discovered by a tribal patrol and carried by them to the *maloca* for a feast that would be associated with an obscure religious rite.
>
> First, the hands and feet were cut off both corpses, and then audience was had with the Chief. He seemed to be well satisfied with what had taken place, spoke little, but nodded his head and smiled. Shortly after the audience was over, the community began to prepare for the feast. The tribal fires were rebuilt, the pots and jars were cleaned, and a procedure followed which, to me, was frightful. Indeed, I could only hasten to my hammock and simulate sleep, for I knew well, from that previous experience of the soup, that I would have to partake of the meal now in preparation: a horrible meal of human flesh. It was enough for me to see them strip the flesh from the palms of the hands and the soles of the feet, and clean these delicacies in the lard of the tapir.
>
> An awful thought coursed through my brain when I beheld the men bending eagerly over the pans to see if the meat were done: how long would it be, I said to myself, before they would forget themselves and place my own extremities in those same pots and pans?

With a sang-froid almost unbelievable in the circumstances, Algot Lange comforts himself with the reflection that when the hospitality of the tribe had been extended to him, the Mangeroma Chief had assured him that he should not be eaten—"*either fried or stewed*". He says that, with that assurance in mind, he slept in peace while the preparations were in full swing almost at the very entrance to the hut which had been put at his disposal!

Presumably he managed with a reasonably good grace to eat his share of the feast, for we next find him engaged with the Mangeromas in a punitive expedition against a settlement of Peruvian *caboclos*—their arch-enemies. After that, he is involved in the defence of the Mangeromas' own settlement, when the Peruvian half-breeds pay a retaliatory visit:

> These marauders came with murder and girl-robbery in their black hearts, while the Mangeromas were defending their homes

and families.   After the battle, the Mangeroma Indians cut off
the hands and feet of their dead or dying enemies and carried
these home.   The women and children received us with great
demonstrations of joy.   Soon the pots and pans were boiling inside the great house, and now the warriors, returned from battle,
prepared to feast upon the hands and feet of the slain, these portions having been distributed among the different families.

He crept into his hammock and lit his pipe, Lange continues
in a pleasantly reminiscent vein, and incidentally without
revealing whether or not he actually took part in the feast.
Had he been Alfred St Johnston, doubtless he would have
included some bloodthirsty reference to his delight in being
permitted to indulge as a Cannibal-White!   Then he watched.

All the men had laid aside their feather-dresses and squirrel-tails,
and were now moving about among the many fires on the floor of
the great hut.   Some were sitting in groups discussing the battle,
while women bent over the pots to examine the ghastly contents.
Here, a woman was engaged in stripping the flesh from the palm
of a hand and the sole of a foot; which operation finished, she
threw both into a large earthen pot to boil.   There, another
woman was applying a herb-poultice to her husband's wounds.
Over it all hung a thick, odoriferous smoke, gradually finding its
way out through the central opening in the thatched roof. . . .

Lange eventually recovered sufficiently to return home.
Rather to his surprise, the Mangeroma Chief permitted him to
do this.   A curious aspect of his book, *In the Amazon Jungle*, is
that, among the formal acknowledgements he makes to various
individuals and organisations that had facilitated his expedition
into this part of the Amazon Basin, he actually includes one to
the Cannibal Chief:

The generous high potentate of the tribe of Mangeroma cannibals
is the second to whom I wish to express my extreme gratitude,
although my obligations to him are of a slightly different character: in the first place, because he did not order me to be killed
and served up, well or medium done, to suit his fancy (which he
had a perfect right to do); and in the second place because he
took a great deal of interest in my personal welfare, and bestowed
all manner of strange favours upon me.

The macabre insertion—'well or medium done'—is characteristic of the man; the formal acknowledgement must surely
be unique, coming as it does from a potential dish of meat to a
potential consumer of that dish!

CHAPTER FIVE

CANNIBALISM AMONG NIGERIAN TRIBESMEN

THE EPITHET 'Darkest' has for long been automatically attributed to the continent of Africa. It is so still, today, in spite of the great numbers of highly intelligent and civilised individuals who have come to us from the various Protectorates and other groupings of tribes. This is no doubt, in part, because of the vastness of this continent, the area of which extends to little short of twelve million square miles, roughly equally divided north and south of the Equator, its eastern coast washed by the Indian Ocean, its western by the Atlantic.

It is small wonder, considering the continent's size, and the difficulties of communication, that many of its inhabitants, particularly in the remoter districts, have only very recently begun to extricate themselves from the superstition and religio-magical rites that went with the practice of cannibalism; or indeed that there should have existed until comparatively recent times tribes whose members habitually devoured human flesh not because of any religious significance at all, but because it was a satisfactory act of revenge. In fact it is not long since tribes could be found whose members ate human flesh for what was to them a good and sufficient reason: they liked it, and it was readily available to them.

Much anthropological work has been done in various regions of Africa: by C. K. Meek, P. A. Talbot and George Basden, for example, in Nigeria; by John Roscoe among the Bagesu of Uganda; by L. S. B. Leakey among the Kenya Mau Mau and Kikuyu; by E. W. Kapen and James Dennis and many others in what is perhaps the most backward region of all, the Congo Basin, which lies athwart the Equator and is likely in a very short while to equal if not surpass in importance all other parts of Africa because it is one of the world's two chief sources of supply of that vital commodity, uranium.

North and South Nigeria compose a British Protectorate

lying sandwiched between French West Africa and French Equatorial Africa, with the Gulf of Guinea as seaboard and the Equator not far to the south. Its area may not be far short of four hundred thousand square miles—even so, but a tiny fraction of the northern half of Africa when seen displayed on the map; its population hardly exceeds twenty million inhabitants. Growing towns like Lagos and Ibadan point to its steadily increasing development as an exporting country—tin and iron ore, bauxite, cocoa, palm-kernels and other substances in daily demand flowing from the quays and wharves at the mouths of the Niger.

But all this is of very recent development. It is but a flicker of time since, at any rate in the hinterland, among the mountains and mountainous plateaux such as the Mambila Plateau, which averages some 5,000 feet above sea level and is surrounded by mountains rising to nearly twice that height, with remote and isolated settlements on their steep and shaggy slopes, cannibal practices were almost universal.

This particular plateau has been well described by C. K. Meek:

> It is completely covered with soil, outcrops of granite occurring only at long intervals. The infertility of the soil forces the natives to use fertilising agents in the form of leguminous pigeon-pea plants specially cultivated for the purpose. But the plateau is eminently suitable for grazing cattle, and on this account, and also on account of the absence of noxious flies, is well patronised by cattle owners. It is covered with bracken, and there is a great variety of flowers, including orchids. There is a complete absence of trees except in the gullies, and the dearth of firewood entails great hardship on the inhabitants, who have not become accustomed yet to the use of clothing. The Mambila men wear a loin-covering of cloth; the women are completely nude.

Meek is writing between the two World Wars: his book was published only in 1931, so that what he reports—and he is a man who writes dispassionately, objectively—is little more than a quarter-century old. He turns next to an examination of the Mambilas, whom he takes as typical of the Nigerian hinterland tribes.

> The Mambila bury their dead in graves of the shaft and tunnel type. The body is buried naked, all ornaments being removed. It is laid on its side in a contracted position, with both hands hold-

ing the head. The face looks towards the west, for it is said by the Mambila that a man comes into the world from the east, and at death 'goes west'.

All the Mambila groups were cannibal until recently, and most of them would be cannibal still were it not for fear of the Administration. They ate the flesh of their enemies killed in war, and among their enemies might be members of a neighbouring village with whom they had intermarried when at peace. Thus it might happen that a man would kill and eat one of his own relatives. Instances have been reported of a man killing and eating his wife's brother during an affray between two villages. But it was stated that if a man killed and ate his *father-in-law*, he would fall ill and die. There is evidence, too, that these groups sometimes sold their own dead for food.

Religious ideas were not prominent in the cannibalism of the Mambila. Tribesmen who were willing to answer questions stated clearly that they ate human flesh purely as meat. When they killed an enemy, they cut pieces off his body and ate them raw, *in situ*, without any formalities. Pieces were taken home and given to the old men, who ate them from sheer lust of flesh. In such cases the flesh might be eaten raw or cooked. Even the intestines were eaten, being ripped up, cleaned and boiled.

On the other hand, it was stated that young men were compelled to eat, in order to become brave; the conception being, apparently, that by eating the flesh of a slain warrior they absorbed his courage. The skulls of enemies were preserved, and when the young men first went to war they were made to drink beer and a certain medicine from one of the skulls, with a view to making them fearless. Women, however, were not permitted to eat human flesh, and it was not permissible for married men to eat the flesh of women who had been killed during an attack on a village. But wifeless old men might eat the flesh of a woman with impunity.

The myths, or folk-lore, among these Nigerian tribes cannot be said to be as elaborate as that of, say, the Kwakiutls and indeed many tribes in other parts of the world. Or it may be that tribesmen were more reluctant to reveal them than was the case elsewhere. But it would seem from much of the available evidence of cannibalism in Nigeria that it was on the whole less of a religious ceremonial, and based on a cruder, more practical motive.

There is, however, one picturesque legend which has been used by apologists to account for the prevalence until comparatively recently of a practice now recognised as wrong.

They tell of a hawk that, a long time ago, was seen flying over the hut of a chief. It was grasping in its talons a piece of human flesh, and as it flew over the open place where the chief's meal was being prepared, the hawk happened to release its grip on the piece of flesh. It fell straight into the soup that was just then being prepared for the chief, but no one saw it.

When the chief began to eat his soup, he was so delighted with its taste that he called his cooks to his presence and asked them what they had put into it, and told them that in future all his soup was to have that same taste.

Naturally the cooks were unable to repeat the taste, as they had not seen what fell into it out of the sky. The chief, therefore, had his cooks slain, and appointed others in their place. But still no single one of them was able to reproduce the individual taste that had so pleased their chief. One after another, they tried portions of every animal known to them, from mountain tops and valleys and forests and open plains. They caught birds, and tried their flesh. They caught fish, and tried their flesh. They caught the greater insects, and tried them, too; but all without avail: not one single dish of soup ever repeated the luscious taste that had so captivated the chief.

Finally, in a rage of frustration, the chief picked up his club and slew his senior cook. "Cut him to pieces with your knives," he bade the others who were cowering round the pot in terror. "Cut him into small pieces, and throw them into the soup he cannot make!"

Too terrified to disobey, the other cooks drew their knives and did as they were told. Piece after piece of their fellowtribesman they threw into the steaming soup. And when it was ready, they served it to their chief, watching him in terror as he began to eat.

To their enormous relief, a great grin of contentment spread over his face, and they knew that the answer had been found at last: it was human flesh that had given that soup the delectable taste.

"Kill me a slave each day," their chief bade them, as they ceased their trembling and stood before him, "and cut him into small pieces and throw them into my soup."

The legend has a curious twist to it. So gluttonous for human flesh did the chief become that in time he had slain every member of his tribe who had not taken fright and fled from his territory.   At last the chief found himself alone.   But such was his passion, now, for human flesh that he at once began to tear from his body pieces of his own flesh.   At last little remained of him but bone and some of the flesh from those parts of his body which he could not reach.   And thus he died.

The legend, at once picturesque and macabre, also suggests a primitive consciousness, so slight as to be hardly recognisable among the tribes themselves, that the act of cannibalism was an evil thing, and must eventually bring retribution on those who practise it.

Anthropologists have collected much data about cannibal practices in various parts of this area of Africa.   The Ganawuri tribe, for instance, removed the flesh from the bodies of their fallen enemies, leaving only the intestines and the bones.   With the flesh spitted on their spear-heads, they rode home to hand over their booty to the tribal priests, whose task it was to divide it first among the old men.   The most important of the old men of the Ganawuri tribe would receive the flesh taken from the head.   The hair was first removed, then the flesh cut into strips and cooked and eaten at the sacred stone.   The other old men of the tribe cooked their own portions of the flesh in pots and ate it at a distance.   As far as was practicable, this feasting always took place on the night of the warriors' return; but however courageous the young men of the tribe might have shown themselves, they were rigidly debarred from partaking in the feast.

This tribe restricted themselves to the consumption of flesh from the bodies of enemies slain in battle.   They did not deliberately kill women of an enemy tribe, and if they did inadvertently kill them, they never ate their flesh.   A neighbouring tribe, however, the Ataka, did eat the flesh of enemy women, and another tribe, the Tangale, who were essentially head-hunters, specialised in the consumption of the flesh of enemy women's heads.   As among the Ganawuri, human flesh was given first to the old men of the tribe, and on rare occasions to the old women of the tribe.   They had the right, if they wished to exercise it, of giving small portions of the flesh to young men whom they specially favoured, but this was a right they seldom exercised.

The Rukuba cannibals also ate their enemies' and captives' flesh, but among them, too, it was the older men who were allowed to indulge before all others. The young men were occasionally smeared with the greasy soup that was left in the bottom and on the sides of the cooking-pots in which the flesh had been boiled. An even more self-sacrificing (if the term may be permitted in such a context!) practice existed among the Zumperi. They handed over the captured heads for the fathers of their tribe to eat, contenting themselves with licking off their spear-heads and clubs the congealed blood of their enemies, and swallowing it.

The Kaleri devoured as much as possible of the bodies of their victims, and were indeed so bloodthirsty that until very recent times they would kill and eat any stranger, black or white, presumptuous enough to cross the frontiers of their territory. The Yergum waited for two days to expire between the return of their warriors from battle and the beginning of their feasting. The heads were always boiled separately from the rest of the body, and no one in their tribe was permitted to eat flesh from the head unless he himself had actually killed an enemy in battle or foray. The remainder of the flesh, however, was of less significance, and might be consumed by any member of the tribe who could get hold of a piece—man, woman or even child. Among this tribe even the entrails, which were carefully separated from the bodies and discarded by such tribes as the Ganawuri, were consumed, after first being cleansed with a mixture of ash and running water.

The Jarawa cannibals used to separate the head from the rest of the body, but instead of boiling it in a pot, they coated the head with mud, then put the whole into the fire, when the mud dried and removed the hair complete, much as gipsies and others have cooked hedgehogs from time immemorial. The Hill Angas were careful never to eat the flesh either of young lads killed or captured, or of old men. They maintained that the young lads, if captured alive, were more profitably sold into slavery, and the flesh of old men, they thought, was too dried up and tough to be really palatable. The Sura cannibals, on the other hand, added salt and oil to the flesh of their victims when boiling them, and were thus well enough satisfied with a wider age-range in the selection of their menu. No women of their

tribe were permitted even to see the flesh, however, but boys
and young men, if by any chance they showed any reluctance
to eat of it, were forced to do so by their elders in order that
their courage might be increased thereby.

With such a wide variety of detail, it is not easy to distinguish
among the various motives for cannibalism which prevailed
until comparatively recently among these various tribes.
Some of them, obviously—like the Sura and the Hill Anga
tribes—believed that soul-stuff, or life-principle, was transferred from the victim to the man who devoured him, which is
why pressure was brought to bear on the immature to eat of the
flesh of the mature. The Hill Angas refrained from eating
young men and boys because it was thought that they might
well not have any virtues worth transferring; and old men
because any fine qualities they might have had in middle age,
such as courage, skill in tracking and so forth, would have begun
to deteriorate.

In cases where tribal law stipulated that only the old men
might eat the flesh, as among the Ganawuri, the argument was
probably that the old men needed an admixture of new blood
in their veins, whereas the young men of the tribe did not!

Certain of these tribes had evolved a fairly elaborate penal
code in connection with their cannibalistic practices. For
example, the Hill Angas would eat the flesh of a member of
their own tribe, if he had been convicted as a criminal and so
sentenced to death. The Sura would eat the flesh of a woman
of their own tribe whose crime was that of adultery. The
Warjawa were prepared to sacrifice any member of their own
tribe who had violated tribal law, and it is evident that such
punishment was accompanied by a fairly elaborate ritual. The
victim was not so much killed as sacrificed; his blood was
poured out as an oblation; only after this ceremonial was his
flesh made available for the other members of his or her tribe to
feast on it.

There was, among certain tribes, an element of something
less ignoble than mere lust for human flesh. There was the
superstition that by wholly destroying the victim's spirit—as
they believed they were doing by devouring his head as well as
his body and limbs—they were preventing him from seeking
any form of vengeance, or return from the after-world to harm

those who remained behind.   Though it was generally believed that the spirit resided in the head, it was also believed that the spirit was capable of transferring its abode at need from one part to another; hence the necessity for total destruction of the victim.

There was another belief more picturesque than this— indeed possessed of an almost charming quality.   The Hill Angas habitually devoured the old men of their own tribe that they might leave the present world while still in possession of the greater part of their faculties.   A certain squeamishness might be noticed in this connection, for often a family who had come to this decision would call upon someone from a different, and if possible distant, part of the settlement to carry out the deed, even offering payment for the service.   Then the old man's flesh would be ceremonially devoured, but his head would be carefully preserved in a pot, in front of which sacrifices would be made, and some sort of prayer spoken, at regular intervals afterwards.

It was among the Yergum and the Tangale tribes, for the most part, that the more primitive form of cannibalism was practised.   Lust for flesh, coupled with the only just less bestial motive of the ultimate revenge, was paramount among these particular Nigerian tribes.   The Tangales even had a ritual prayer—or rather, an incantation—which was both an expression of hatred and lust and an incitement to greater displays of these primitive emotions:

> Here is my enemy.   He hates me, and I hate him.   He kills me when he meets me.   My god has now brought him under my feet.   Let my enemy's people have their strength taken from them. Let their eyes become blind.   When the warriors of my tribe go to enemies' territory, let all the enemies quickly die at their hands. If any of this enemy's spirit survives, may he come back to possess his own father and his own mother and all the members of his family!

The sheer viciousness of the incantation is somehow reminiscent of that terrible cry of Baxbakualanuxsiwae: "Hap!   Hap! Hap!   Hap!"   Lust for human flesh as food may have been uppermost in the hearts of the Tangales, but the veins of revenge and scorn were threaded through it like the lines of gristle in the red flesh they so much enjoyed.

Another anthropologist, P. A. Talbot, writing at almost exactly the same time as C. K. Meek, adds fragmentary information about other tribes not referred to by his colleague. He makes the uncompromising statement that the practice of cannibalism, with its almost invariable accompaniment of head-hunting, seems to have been almost universal throughout the Nigerian tribes with whom he had had contact, save for the Edo, among whom, curiously enough, the eating of human flesh was tabu, and the Yoruba, among whom the practice was mainly restricted to the custom of the chiefs: that of eating a part only of either the head or the heart of their predecessors in office.   The reason (if not the excuse) for this practice is easy enough to appreciate.

Talbot goes on to state that, so far as he could ascertain, the practice of cannibalism bore no relation to the state of development, or 'morality', of the tribes.   It was common, he had found, even among those tribes which in other respects had the most enlightened standards.   Tribesmen, when interrogated, he says, stated categorically that they ate human flesh because of their great longing for meat.

All animal and bird flesh (he says) is much liked in those parts, but in very many of them it can only be regarded as a luxury, since—at any rate with the poorer peoples—it is not very often that a man can afford to kill even a fowl.   Human flesh is preferred above all other flesh *for its succulence*, and that of the monkey is generally considered to come next.   The parts in greatest favour are the palms of the hands, the fingers, and toes; and, of a woman, the breast.   The younger the person, the tenderer will be the flesh. . . .

It is interesting to contrast this attitude with that of the other Nigerian tribes, such as the Hill Angas mentioned by C. K. Meek, who were unwilling to partake of the flesh of young people.   It tends to confirm the distinction: that these other tribes were concerned with the eating of human flesh for its own sake, and without any secondary motive, such as the transference of virtue from the dead to the living.

Directly an enemy was slain (Talbot continues), his head—and sometimes his body, if the people were strongly cannibalistic—was taken to the village and a great dance given, either at once, or after the skull had been cleaned of its flesh by boiling, or by being buried for a time in the ground.   At the feast, every man-slayer of the village danced round, generally with a skull in one hand and his machete in the other.   Sometimes the body of the enemy was brought in whole; sometimes it was cut in pieces in advance to facilitate transport.   It was then boiled in native pots and shared out, occasionally among the man-slayer's family and friends, but sometimes among all the people of the village, until it was wholly consumed.   In some tribes it was forbidden for women and children to partake of human flesh; in others, for example among the Kalabari, the eldest sister of the hut was forced to taste it, however strongly she might protest.

Among the Abadja, the whole body of anyone slain was ordinarily taken back to the village and there consumed, though it was tabu to eat women or children.   A man only divided his 'kill' among his own family.   The body was cut up and cooked in pots; the fingers, palms of the hands, and toes were considered the best eating.   Sometimes, if a family had been satisfied, part of the body would be dried and put away for later.

When an Nkanu warrior brought a head back, everyone who heard of the deed gave him a present, and much palm-wine was drunk.   The trophy was boiled, and the flesh cut away.   The skull was then taken out, accompanied with all the others in the village, and the flesh was then boiled and eaten.

Much cruelty was practised among certain of these tribes.   For example, the Bafum-Bansaw, who frequently tortured their prisoners before putting them to death.   Palm-oil was boiled in a big pot, and then by means of a gourd enema it was pumped into the bowels and stomachs of the prisoners.   This practice was said to make the bodies much more succulent than they would otherwise have been.   The bodies were left until the palm-oil had permeated them, and then cut up and devoured. . . .

This anthropologist concludes his observations by remarking succinctly: "There was no idea of inheriting the courage of the dead foe by imbibing bravery with his flesh; this was the simplest form of cannibalism: Man's flesh is best of all, and afterwards follows monkey's flesh."

George Basden wrote in the dual capacity of amateur anthropologist and missionary. As one would expect, therefore, his report, which was written at about the same time as Meek and Talbot were doing research in Nigeria, is marked with a more personal note than the others. One has the very clear impression from what he wrote that this was something he had both seen and personally reacted to strongly. He, too, contrives to maintain a skilful balance between cold reportage and the emotional comment, and his report is the more valuable for that reason. He is particularly concerned with the Ibo tribe, whose territory was bounded by one bank of the great River Niger.

The Ibo country lies within the recognised Negro belt, and the people bear the main characteristics of that stock. Cannibalism, human sacrifices and other savage customs were real facts, and flourished within five miles of Onitsha, and no one would dare swear that the inhabitants of even that town were all entirely innocent. It is well within living memory (Basden was writing only thirty-odd years ago) that human sacrifices were offered— the death and burial of a king or notable chief being the most usual occasions.

At one period I was living in a tiny hut set up in the bush some five miles east of Onitsha, surrounded by a number of settlements. Between two of these there was a feud of long standing. At intervals war broke out in earnest. During the last campaign one party captured, and afterwards ate, seven of their opponents, whilst the other party secured only four victims.

One morning I was walking alone, when I came upon a bundle of sticks lying in the path; to this bundle was attached a clean and fresh human skull, which I judged from the teeth and size to be that of a young man. It had been utilised as a fetich. It would act as a solemn warning to would-be thieves, and such a powerful 'ju-ju' would ensure the owner's finding his property intact however long it was left on the road. It was in close proximity to this place that, as was well known, a cannibal feast had lately been held. . . .

Amongst our lads there was a small boy whose father had been a servant to the Niger Company. Whilst carrying a message to Obushi, the father had been murdered, and his body disposed of according to time-honoured custom. On one occasion I was resting outside my hut when a man of unprepossessing appearance came along and entered into conversation. His eldest son, then a small lad, had been placed by his father in the care of a missionary, in order that he might receive instruction. In the course of his remarks, he solemnly asserted that it would be of great benefit to his son if he were provided with human flesh sometimes as part of his diet. He maintained that if this were done a proper man's spirit would develop in the lad.

Basden goes on to say that the further south one went, the more pronounced were the cannibalistic tendencies among the tribes. Though it was generally known that the custom of feasting upon captives taken in battle was prevalent throughout most of Nigeria, in the southern parts there existed a regular traffic in human flesh. Strangers trespassing over frontiers

were captured with the deliberate intention of killing and
devouring them; bodies were even purchased, or bartered
with other tribes whose larders were better stocked.   Human
flesh was, in fact, a marketable commodity, with a recognised
market price; it was looked upon, in the southern parts of
Nigeria particularly, as a staple form of diet.

It is not long (Basden writes) since a certain Chief managed to get
possession of one of his opponents against whom he had a grudge
of long standing.   He derived satisfaction from first lopping off
his ears and nose, and afterwards flaying him alive.   The carcass
was eaten, and the skin converted into a drum head.

There is not a shadow of doubt that, could the history of the
Ibos be clearly traced, a host of such-like stories would have to be
recorded.   I have become acquainted with many erstwhile
cannibals, and quite good-natured folk many of them are.   One
week-end I was staying at a place a few miles south-east of
Onitsha.   My quarters were very circumscribed, the only accommodation available being a tiny thatched lean-to shed against the
compound wall, usually occupied by the goats and fowls.   My
boys and carriers shared the limited accommodation, lying at
night alongside the camp-bed.   After the evening meal, we settled
down for the night, long before our customary bedtime;   con-
sequently the men chatted freely.   Presently I became interested
in their conversation, and amongst other items of news, I gathered
that they had all had a share in cannibal feasts.

At first they were reticent, but gradually they opened out, and
announced what they considered to be the choicest titbits.   Those
they affirmed, were the knuckles.   They were strapping young
fellows, whom I had got to know sufficiently well to induce them
to travel round with me.   Since then, they have all become
Christians;   one, a much-respected evangelist!

Another missionary, Father Bubendorf of Freiburg, who was
stationed near Onitsha at about the same time, had occasion to
make a journey from his mission into adjoining territory.   He
reported that he had been a horrified eye-witness of the
slaughter of a group of captives outside the hut of a tribal
chief:

Every moment, men, women and even children passed me.   One
would be carrying a human leg on his shoulder, another would be
carrying the lungs or the heart of some unfortunate Kroo-boy in
his or her hands.   Several times I myself was offered my choice of
one of these morsels, dripping with gore.

The Rev. E. Deas, of the United Presbyterian Mission, confirmed the many reports of the existence of cannibal markets in many parts of Nigeria, and Bishop Crowther wrote:

> Cannibalism is widespread from the delta of the Niger for a long way up its course. Among the Okrika Tribe, a hundred and fifty prisoners were taken from a tribe on the opposite side of the river and divided amongst the chiefs. With the exception of eleven, who fell to the lot of converted chiefs, and were therefore spared, the remaining 139 prisoners were divided up among the chiefs and the men who had captured them, and killed and devoured by them.

A correspondent of *The Saturday Review* wrote of the unmistakable lust for human flesh among the tribesmen of West Africa, and Nigeria in particular, and added: "Young boys are brought from the dark interior, kept in pens, fattened upon bananas, and finally killed and baked."

CHAPTER SIX

THE LEOPARD SOCIETIES OF SIERRA LEONE

So SMALL, in comparison with the vast area of Nigeria, that it is almost lost between French Guinea and the Ivory Coast, nearly at the westernmost curve of West Africa, is the Protectorate of Sierra Leone. Here the tribes are naturally less scattered; there is greater homogeneity; communications are less difficult. Today, like Nigeria, it is rapidly taking a more and more important place in the list of exporting countries, with its resources of iron ore, palm kernels and cocoa; and—more valuable if on a smaller scale—diamonds and gold. But only yesterday, or the day before, it was the home of the dreadful Leopard Societies: one of the very few examples where cannibalism has come to be so highly organised, so close-knit in its ceremonials and tabus, that it has acquired a name; and a name which those who understand its connotations can hardly hear without a shudder.

The Leopard Societies of Sierra Leone existed within the memory of living man; indeed, there are those who suspect that even now the tradition is not entirely dead. For by very long tradition, members of the exclusive Leopard Societies were privileged people: like the Hamatsa of the Kwakiutl Indians, they had rights over their fellow-men that could not be called in question. They were, so to speak, a trade union; and a powerful one at that. Furthermore, they had agents, or branches, of their trade union tucked unobtrusively into communities and settlements large and small among the mountains, on the plains, on the river banks, in the forests and scrub throughout the land. There was a sort of freemasonry about their organisation that was a very terrible thing.

Since the members of the Leopard Societies were privileged men (no women were included), there was keen competition for membership; and since competition was keen, conditions of membership, and above all the initiation-rites, were harsh and forbidding. A man had to pay dearly for membership. We shall see—far away on the other side of this great continent, among the closed ranks of the Mau Mau—initiation rites that have something in common with those of the Leopard Societies.

Any native of Sierra Leone who desired to become a member of the Leopard Society—to become, that is, a 'Leopard Man' —had first to ascertain who the nearest king, or priest, of the cult might be. Having found and identified him—not necessarily an easy matter—he had to approach him, and humbly ask him for *borfimor*, a word best translated by the word 'medicine', but in the sense of the corresponding word 'medicine-man'. He would be told that the king, or priest, had not the absolute power of decision in this matter, but that there were others to be consulted.

If the candidate for membership were approved, then a message would come to him that he was to take a certain road, or track through the forest, where he would 'meet' the *borfimor*. Having set out along the track, he would in due course encounter a group of men who would ask him if he was looking for the *borfimor*. He would naturally answer that he was, whereupon he would be asked what he wanted the 'medicine' for. There was a traditional answer to this formal question— an odd reply which has no obvious explanation. "To play *jagay*," he had to reply, mentioning a traditional West African game that is played with cowrie-shells and roughly resembles 'knuckle-bones'.

If his reply was acceptable he was then called upon to swear, and after that there was no turning back. The whole party would proceed along the track through the forest or the bush, coming (as if by chance) upon a red box, in which the *borfimor* had already been placed. The candidate for membership was then given a 'leopard-knife'.

The 'leopard-knife' varied slightly in detail, but was in essence a very terrible weapon. It might be a sort of pronged knife, with a double point, or a double knife with two prongs each. The prongs, or blades, were double-edged, and in some cases were set at an angle to the part that was gripped by the user. Whatever their form, they were murderous weapons.

Having received the 'leopard-knife', the candidate for

membership held it firmly and tapped on the side of the box containing the *borfimor*. As he did this, he repeated an oath: "I come now to get this medicine from these people. After this, if I reveal any secret, or betray any fellow-member, then as I walk along a track a snake shall bite me; as I go on the sea my canoe shall overturn and drown me; in the open places when I walk, the lightning shall strike me dead."

When the oath had been administered, the party broke up and separated for a space of three days. Then they met once more, to seek a victim. But before setting forth on their quest they took a meal together, prepared and served by the men who had met the candidate and admitted him to membership. After the meal was ended, the new member was told that he had eaten the flesh of a human being, and that act had set the final seal on his membership of the Leopard Society.

Originally, the victim had to be a girl, freeborn (as opposed to being the daughter of a slave or captive) and over fourteen years old. If possible, she should be the eldest child of the family providing her. Each initiate of the Leopard Society had to produce as a sacrifice one person of his own blood, or, failing that, of the blood of his wife's family. In more recent years, the victim could be a woman or a girl, a man or a boy, though still the eldest girl was preferred.

Before the killing of a victim, the 'medicine' could be 'started' by putting into the box pieces of the flesh of a new-born child who had died at birth, together with certain other ingredients; but it was held by the members of the society that a medicine made in this way was useful only as a temporary measure: it had no real power as a *borfimor*.

Two established members of the society accompany the initiate on his quest for a victim. Their object is to 'beg' for a victim; but the form which the begging takes admits of no argument. The group, consisting usually of five men, meet the mother, or guardian, of the intended victim in a lonely place, and speak to her of the necessity of the sacrifice for "the well-being of the tribe". Or it may be that it is a father or brother who is approached, and asked for a son or brother. Traditionally, the man or the woman refuses; but half-heartedly only: they know that the Leopard Society has singled them out as a 'tool', and that to refuse to co-operate would mean more sacrifices, including themselves. By co-operating, they become agents of the society.

When the victim has been agreed upon, and 'offered', the Leopard Men disperse into the forest or bushland. There, they wander about all through the succeeding night, imitating the roar of the true leopard, and only ceasing to roar when the first light of day begins to penetrate the trees. This roaring has to be maintained throughout the whole period leading to the actual capture of the victim, and during the ceremony of killing, or sacrificing, the victim as well.

The next stage is the selection of a member of the society whose strength and animal agility have long been recognised: it is he who is to capture the intended victim. He bears a title, Yongolado—Man-with-teeth-and-claws. He is equipped with a leopard-skin and a pair of leopard-knives. The leopard-skin is kept by the chief man of the society, and is never handled by anyone except himself, and the Yongolado, except on this special occasion. Secrecy surrounds every detail of the procedure. The skin, rolled round and containing the knives, is handed, under cover of darkness, from the chief man of the society to a trusted lieutenant; from him it passes to another, and another, and another, so that no member can say either from whom he received it or to whom he handed it on; until at last it comes into the hands of the Yongolado.

The Yongolado puts on the leopard-skin, and looks about him. He may find that other members of the society have joined him, also wearing some part of the insignia of the leopard. Their faces, like his, will now be covered with the leopard's mask, and they will all be holding leopard-knives in their hands, protruding through the end of the skins like great claws.

In many parts of the hinterland of Sierra Leone, the forest, or at any rate the bush, came, and sometimes still comes, to within a matter of yards of the outer huts of any settlement. The Leopard Men approach to the fringe of the undergrowth, and make their sinister whistling cry—an echo, here, of the whistle of Baxbakualanuxsiwae that preceded his devouring of human flesh among the Kwakiutl Indians. The Headman of the village recognises the whistle, and he and any Leopard Men in the village leave their huts and go out to meet the others in the darkness.

Before leaving their village, they have arranged that the victim shall be set on a track that leads into the undergrowth, for traditionally the capture and sacrifice must take place in secret and in darkness.

The Leopard Men lie concealed on each side of the track until a favourable moment arrives. The victim—a man, a woman, or, more probably, a girl or a boy—approaches. The track lies among thick undergrowth, beneath heavy trees. Creepers hang down from the trees and intertwine at head-height. The scrub to left and right of the track is as impene-trable as a wall. The night is thick, the air heavy with the menace of jungle life.

The victim is allowed to pass the first of the Leopard Men, those who have joined in the expedition, perhaps from other villages. She—for it is usually a girl—perhaps slows down her walk a little, for the track she is following is crooked and tortuous, difficult even for her accustomed feet to follow. But in the darkness, even her slightest, hesitant movements can be seen by the men lying in wait till the moment arrives which they judge to be the right one.

At last it is the moment. The silence of the sleeping jungle is broken by a deep-throated growl. The intended victim pauses in her tracks. And at that moment the Yongolado springs from his hiding-place close alongside. He leaps on to the back of his victim and in one swift movement tears open her throat. This is the signal for the other Leopard Men to close in, and between them they carry their victim further into the bush or forest. As they do so, one of their number, especially appointed for the purpose, and shod with pieces of wood carved to repre-sent the paw-and-claw-marks of a real leopard, sets to work to make as many leopard tracks as possible, and all forming a trail running into the trees in a different direction from that taken by the main party.

When the Yongolado has reached an agreed spot, in a clear-ing among the trees and bush, he throws the body to the ground. The lower part of the belly is cut across with a sharp-bladed knife, and the cut is continued up each side of the body as far as the collar-bone. The flesh is lifted and the entrails carefully examined. The liver, heart and intestines are then removed, and the head is hacked off. The body is then divided horizontally at the waist, and lengthwise from the neck to the crutch. The four quarters thus produced are further sub-divided, and the smaller portions systematically distributed. Each portion is quickly wrapped in banana leaves. The face is cut away from the head so that the victim cannot be identified by anyone who has not already become privy to the secret.

The liver is the most important part of the victim to be removed from her body. It is this which enables the Leopard Men to know whether their next *borfimor*, or medicine, will be a powerful one. If the liver is as it should be, then the whole of the victim is suitable for their purposes. But the gall-bladder, too, must be very carefully scrutinised; for they believe that if the victim has, before her death, been involved in any form of witchcraft, this will be revealed by the condition of her gall-bladder.

The ritual of slaughter, and subsequent examination of the victim's corpse, varies among the different sects of Leopard Men. In the case of one society, the victim was immediately killed, but was forced to sit down on the ground beneath a tree. The chief for whom the particular sacrifice had been planned, as representative of his people whose welfare needed this additional stimulus, then came forward and sat astride the victim's shoulders. The others then came forward, and as many as could do so laid a hand either on the chief or on the victim, and those who could not do so laid a hand on each other, so that all were making a chain of contact. The Yongolado then prayed that good medicine should come of the sacrifice, and then came forward and, in the customary manner, tore out the victim's throat.

Next, the belly was opened, in the usual manner, a bowl being placed beneath it to catch the spilled blood. An assistant thrust his hand deep into the belly and quickly tore out the liver and intestines. Another then thrust in his hand and tore away some fat. When the blood had ceased to flow, and the bowl was full, the intestines, liver, fat and blood were taken away to a hut. The victim herself, who might still be partly alive in spite of the loss of blood and the agony she had gone through, was then carried to a platform outside the chief's hut, and left there tethered to a post.

The following morning the body was taken back into a secret

part of the forest, and cut to pieces. The breast was carefully cut away, and some of the ribs removed. This was the chief's portion, and one of his wives would be in attendance to collect the portion and take it away, to be cooked for him. The legs were then cut off, opened, and the bones extracted. The head was cut off, skinned and all its flesh removed. The leg and thigh bones and the skull were then buried under a palm-tree. The remainder of the body was then cut into small portions, and in due course, at the bidding of the chief, the people came out to partake of the feast. At his arrival, having had his own meal, he would be presented with the hands and the feet of the victim, which were his also if he chose to exercise his right. By tradition, however, he would hand these special delicacies to minor chieftains in his tribe, or others to whom he wished to show some particular mark of favour.

There followed a curious piece of ritual which seems to have been peculiar to some parts of Sierra Leone. When the feast was over, and everyone had eaten his portion, banana leaves and stalks were cut and an effigy of the late victim was constructed of them. The effigy was fastened to a pole and ceremonially despatched to the village by which the victim had been provided. A small portion of the victim's body was, by a piece of cruel irony, given to the father or mother of the victim, who was traditionally present at the ceremony and had of course connived at the sacrifice. A piece of the skin of the victim's forehead was always preserved to be laid over the *borfimor*, and a piece of the fat of the kidney was set aside to be rubbed on it.

Amid such a welter of ritual it is not easy to decide which in fact is the true motive for the killing and eating of a victim. Those who condemn cannibalism outright as a disgusting and inexcusable practice insist that among the tribesmen of Sierra Leone such slaughter served one purpose only: that of glutting a savage appetite for human flesh. But surely, with a ritual so elaborate, even if so fierce and merciless in its detail, there must be more behind it than a mere lust for flesh?

Questioned, tribesmen have declared emphatically that their reason for killing and devouring human beings is to create a powerful medicine, the *borfimor* which is so jealously guarded, so secretly used. Possession of a powerful *borfimor*, they claimed, gave them supremacy over other men—particularly over the unwanted white man, who had so many powers that they themselves did not possess. "White men," one member of a Leopard Society said when questioned, "have more power than black men. But by this eating of human flesh we obtain some power which the white man does not possess. Also, it is a power that prevents the white man from knowing everything that we do." In that statement there is probably more truth than the speaker himself appreciated.

CHAPTER SEVEN

CANNIBALISM IN THE CONGO BASIN

J UST AS the Amazon Basin drains an enormous area of Central South America, on the Equator, so in Africa the River Congo, 3,000 miles in length, drains a similar enormous area in the heart of Equatorial Africa—an area of something like a million square miles. It sweeps in a great half-circle from its source among the mountains south of the Equator, north-westwards across it, and then south-westwards to the Atlantic. The area through which it, and its innumerable tributaries, flow is known as the Congo Basin—the Belgian Congo; a fertile, tropical region producing not only palm-oil, cotton and cocoa, but copper, tin, gold and—what is worth vastly more than gold today—radium. This is the dark region first explored by David Livingstone, and by the man who went out in search of him and greeted him in the world-famous phrase, H. M. Stanley.

Today, of course, it is a country largely opened up and made accessible. Railways and good roads give access to its innermost recesses; it has its own airport; the Belgian Congo has become, in a few short decades, part of the international industrial scene. It is not necessary, however, to turn many pages back to find a very different scene.

James Dennis, in a survey of what in his day was known about the incidence of cannibalism, refers particularly to the Belgian Congo: "In the central part of Africa, from the east coast to the west, especially up and down the many tributaries of the Congo, cannibalism is still practised with every accompaniment of atrocious cruelty," he wrote at the turn of the century, basing his observations on reports from travellers, missionaries, and the experiences of Sidney Langford Hinde, a former captain in the Congo Free State Force, whose book was published in 1897.

Hinde was involved in the war between the Zanzibar Arabs, who were seeking to exploit the natives and the native resources of the Congo Basin for their own purposes, and the Belgians who were determined to make the region one of value to Western Europe.   For his services he was made a Chevalier de l'Ordre Royal du Lion.

Nearly all the tribes in the Congo Basin (he wrote) either are, or have been, cannibals; and among some of them the practice is on the increase.   Races who until lately do not seem to have been cannibals, though situated in a country surrounded by cannibal races, have, from increased intercourse with their neighbours, learned to eat human flesh.

Soon after the Station of Equator was established, the residents discovered that a wholesale human traffic was being carried on by the natives of the district between this station and Lake M'Zumba. The captains of the steamers have often assured me that whenever they try to buy goats from the natives, slaves are demanded in exchange; the natives often come aboard with tusks of ivory with the intention of buying a slave, complaining that *meat is now scarce in their neighbourhood.*

There is not the slightest doubt in my mind that they prefer human flesh to any other.   During all the time I lived among cannibal races I never came across a single case of their eating any kind of flesh raw; they invariably either boil, roast or smoke it. This custom of smoking flesh to make it keep would have been very useful to us, as we were often without meat for long periods. We could, however, never buy smoked meat in the markets, it being impossible to be sure that it was not human flesh.

The preference of different tribes for various parts of the human body is interesting.   Some cut long steaks from the flesh of the thighs, legs or arms; others prefer the hands and feet; and though the great majority do not eat the head, I have come across more than one tribe which prefers this to any other part.   Almost all use some part of the intestines on account of the fat they contain.

A young Basongo chief came to our Commandant while at dinner in his tent and asked for the loan of his knife, which, without thinking, the Commandant gave him.   He immediately disappeared behind the tent and cut the throat of a little slave-girl belonging to him, and was in the act of cooking her when one of our soldiers saw him.   This cannibal was immediately put in irons, but almost immediately after his liberation he was brought in by some of our soldiers who said he was eating children in and about our cantonment.   He had a bag slung round his neck which, on examining it, we found contained an arm and a leg of a young child.

A man with his eyes open has no difficulty in knowing, from the horrible remains he is obliged to pass on his way, what people have preceded him, on the road or battlefield; —with this difference: that on a battlefield he will find those parts left to the jackals which the human wolves have not found to their taste; whereas on the road, by the smouldering camp fires, are the whitening bones, cracked and broken, which form the relics of these disgusting banquets.   What struck me most, during my expeditions through the country, was the number of partially cut-up bodies I found. Some of them were minus the hands and feet, and some with steaks cut from the thighs or elsewhere; others had the entrails or head removed.   Neither old nor young, women or children, are exempt from serving as food for their conquerors or neighbours.

Hinde's report is laconic: the writing of a man accustomed to the brutalities of war.   He accepted what he saw, and makes few comments that bear any signs of deep feeling.   In general his observations seem to be borne out by those of others who have written about these tribes, but he appears to be alone in his belief that the Congo cannibals never eat their human flesh uncooked.

Very different is the writing of missionaries like Grenfell, Bentley, Forfeitt, Lewis, Phillips and their colleagues of the Baptist Missionary Society who were working in the Congo Basin in the latter years of the nineteenth century and early years of the present century.   The Rev. W. Holman Bentley— who incidentally received the same award as Hinde from the Belgian authorities—spent twenty years in the region, and the two volumes of his *Pioneering on the Congo* paint a detailed and often deeply moving picture of their experiences.

The whole wide country (he wrote) seemed to be given up to cannibalism, from the Mobangi (a major tributary of the Congo) to Stanley Falls, for six hundred miles on both sides of the main river, and the Mobangi as well.   Often did the natives beg Grenfell to sell some of his steamer hands, especially his coast people; coming from the shore of the great salt sea, they must be very 'sweet'—salt is spoken of as sweet, in the same way as sugar. They offered two or three of their women for one of those coast men.   They could not understand the objections raised to the practice.   "You eat fowls and goats, and we eat men; why not? What is the difference?"   The son of Matabwiki, chief of Liboko, when asked whether he ever ate human flesh, said: "Ah!   I wish that I could eat everybody on earth!"   Happily his stomach and arm were not equal to the carrying out of his fiendish will.

Fiendish?   Yet there is something free and lovable in many of these wild men; splendid possibilities when the grace of God gets a hold of them.   Bapulula, the brother of that 'fiend', worked with us for two years—a fine, bright, intelligent fellow; we liked him very much.

Bentley says that, bad as cannibalism was on the Congo, it was even worse on the Mobangi.   Tribes there kept and fattened slaves for butchery as we do cattle and poultry.   There were organised raids along the river and forays into the jungle to unsuspecting settlements where the people were overpowered and brought away. . . .

They divided up their human booty and kept them, tied up and starving, until they were fortunate enough to· catch some more and so make up a cargo worth taking to the Mobangi.   When times were bad, these poor starving wretches might often be seen tied up, just kept alive with the minimum of food.   A party would be made up and two or three canoes would be filled with these human cattle.   They would paddle down the Lulongo, cross the main river when the wind was not blowing, make up the Mobangi and sell their freight in some of the towns for ivory. The purchasers would then feed up their starvelings until they were fat enough for the market, then butcher them and sell the meat in small joints.   What was left over, if there was much on the market, would be dried on a rack over the fire, or spitted, and the end of the spit stuck in the ground by a slow fire, until it could be kept for weeks and sold at leisure.

Sometimes a section of the people would club together to buy a large piece of the body wholesale, to be retailed out again; or a family man would buy a whole leg to divide up between his wives, children and slaves.   Dear little bright-eyed boys and girls grew up accustomed to these scenes from day to day.   They ate their own morsels from time to time, in the haphazard way that they have, and carried the rest of their portion in their hands, on a skewer or in a leaf, lest anyone should steal and eat it.   To this awful depth have these children of the Heavenly Father fallen! This is no worked-up picture, it is the daily life of thousands of people at the present time in Darkest Africa.

Bentley says that he discussed the question of eating human flesh with a fellow missionary who had had experience in other parts of the world.   This missionary had asked a converted savage just why he had always preferred human flesh to that of animals.   The answer—as so often in such cases—was simple, and difficult to challenge: "You white men consider pork to be the tastiest of meat, but pork is not to be compared with human flesh."   In other words, human flesh was preferable; and why should one not eat what one preferred?   "Why," asked another tribesman, when accused of eating human flesh, "do you interfere with us?   We do not trouble you when you kill your

goats. We buy our meat, and kill it; it is not your affair."
One old man with whom Bentley talked told him that he had
recently killed and eaten one of his seven wives. She had been
guilty of some breach of tribal and family law, and he and his
other wives had made a feast of her—as an example and a
warning!

Bentley quotes a letter from a colleague of his named
Stapleton, who, with another missionary, had established a
mission station at Mosembe, in the heart of the territory of the
dreaded Bangala tribes, whose reputation even among other
tribes in the Congo Basin was such that they were spoken of
with bated breath. There had been an inter-tribal fight,
ending in victory:

> At about twelve o'clock a long procession of men marched through
> the station laden with spoil. Fifty men carried as many goats,
> most of which had been speared; others, less fortunate, brought
> away fish-nets, stools and plantain.
> Whilst this was proceeding, as a kind of introduction to what
> would follow, two men passed, one carrying a human neck poised
> aloft upon a spear, the other an arm; both had been lopped off an
> unfortunate man who had been killed and left on the field. Later
> on, we were horrified by a more ghastly sight. A party of warriors
> returned who had joined somewhat late in the chase. They
> marched in single file past our house. In the middle of the line
> three men bore the remaining parts of the mutilated body. One
> carried the still bleeding trunk; he had slung the other arm
> through a large wound in the abdomen and, suspended on this,
> the ghastly burden swung at his side. Two others shouldered the
> legs.
> It was a sickening sight; the more so as we were assured that
> these would be cooked and eaten in the evening. Needless to say,
> we did not visit the scene of the feast. A few of the young men
> went down for a share, but were too late: the flesh had been eaten.
> However, they were invited to partake of the vegetables still
> remaining in the water in which the corpse had been boiled.
> Both Weeks and myself found it difficult to eat our evening meal,
> and you will hardly wonder that in our dreams for a few nights,
> men carrying mutilated limbs were the chief figures, and that
> these limbs were sometimes *our own*.
> Two days later, a lad walked into the station carrying in a plan-
> tain-leaf some of the flesh that had been roasted, and one of our
> workmen eagerly joined him in disposing of the dainty morsels.
> This cooked flesh we saw. The day following the attack our
> people visited the creek towns which had been left at their mercy.
> A sick woman had been left in one of the huts. She was dis-

covered, and some of the doughty warriors recounted with much glee and mock imitation of her agonies how they had burned her to death in her hut.   To burn alive a poor, sick, deserted woman is regarded as a huge joke.   Yet usually these Bangalas are merry, manly fellows, very friendly in conversation and quite demonstrative in their affection; but when the lust of blood is upon them, deeds which fill us with horror are the merest incidents of the fight, to them.

Of these Bangalas, the missionary Grenfell reported that the women of the tribe "cram dogs with food as we do chickens, in order that they may be plump for killing and eating.   Some Bangala at Lukungu market bought a bit of meat.   A dog ate it.   They wanted their *own* bit of meat, so seized and opened the dog to get it—thus succeeding in getting what they also prized: the carcass of the dog."

The Bambala, these missionaries found, regarded as special delicacies human flesh that had been buried for some days; also a large, thick, white beetle grub found in palm-trees (probably the grub referred to in the Introduction), and human blood boiled with manioc flour.   The women of the tribe were forbidden to touch human flesh, but had found many ways of circumventing the tabu, and were particularly addicted to human flesh, extracted from graves and in an advanced state of decomposition.

A later traveller in the Congo, an artist and sculptor named Herbert Ward, knew the region in the early years of this century.   He admits: "No high motive took me to Africa.   I went there simply and solely to gratify my love of adventure."   It is obvious from his book that he had not only courage but a remarkable gift for getting on to human terms with natives who were still cannibals.   He found, in addition to the cruelty and degradation, abundant good-humour—a quality that subsequent travellers and settlers have frequently mentioned.

The impression I received from personal intercourse (he writes) was that the cannibals of the forest were infinitely more sympathetic than the people of the open country, where the trading instinct is inborn.   The cannibals are not schemers, and they are not mean.   In direct opposition to all natural conjectures, they are among the best types of men.

"Do you people eat human bodies?" said I one day, upon entering a native village, and pointed to a quantity of meat, spitted upon long skewers, being smoke-dried over numerous smouldering fires. "Io; yo te?" was the instant reply—"Yes; don't you?" And a few minutes later the chieftain of the village came forward with an offering which consisted of large and generous portions of flesh, only too obviously of human origin. He seemed genuinely disappointed when I refused.

Once in the great forest, when camping for the night with a party of Arab raiders and their native followers, we were compelled to change the position of our tent owing to the offensive smell of human flesh, which was being cooked on all sides of us. A native chief stated to me that the time occupied in devouring a human body varied according to whether the latter happened to be one of his enemies, when he would eat the body himself, or merely a slave, who would be divided between his followers.

Ward describes the slave-markets he has seen on the banks of various of the Congo tributaries, where there was an organised traffic in human beings destined for slavery and eventual butchery for human consumption; they were normally bartered in exchange for ivory. . . .

A visit to one of these slave-depots revealed a condition of savagery and suffering beyond all ordinary powers of description. It was no uncommon experience to witness upwards of a hundred captives, of both sexes and all ages, including infants in their mothers' arms, lying in groups; masses of utterly forlorn humanity, with eyes downcast in a stony stare, with bodies attenuated by starvation, and with skin of that dull grey hue which among coloured races is always indicative of physical disorder. The captives were exposed for sale with the sinister fate in view of being killed and eaten.

Proportionately, a greater number of men than women fall victims to cannibalism, the reason being that women who are still young are esteemed as being of greater value by reason of their utility in growing and cooking food.

Probably the most inhuman practice of all is to be met with among the tribes who deliberately hawk the victim piecemeal whilst still alive. Incredible as it may appear, captives are led from place to place in order that individuals may have the opportunity of indicating, by external marks on the body, the portion they desire to acquire. The distinguishing marks are generally made by means of coloured clay or strips of grass tied in a peculiar fashion. The astounding stoicism of the victims, who thus witness the bargaining for their limbs piecemeal, is only equalled by the callousness with which they walk forward to meet their fate.

There is a pronounced absence of ceremonial in association with the cannibalistic practices reported by such eye-witnesses as these.   Indeed, apart from some grisly burial-rites described by some of the missionaries such as Grenfell, Bentley and others who were serving in the Baptist Mission fields of the Congo Basin about the turn of the century, when wives, relatives and slaves of chiefs who had died were slaughtered on his grave and then cooked and eaten by the remainder of the tribesmen, there is hardly any evidence whatsoever that cannibalism was anything other than a lust for the taste of human flesh.

Writing many years later than anyone who has been referred to in this chapter, the traveller Lewis Cotlow, F.R.G.S., has something to say of the Congo as he knew it in recent years. In his very readable book, *Zanzabuku*, he describes how he has just left Fort Portal, in Uganda, and is heading for the eastern border of the Belgian Congo, skirting as he does so the southern slopes of Mount Ruwenzori:

> In half an hour I thought I had my reward, for we encountered along the road a group of Bantu Negroes, much smaller than average height. "Pygmies?" I asked Cezaire, hopefully. "Bamba," he answered. "Part Pygmy, part Bantu. Their teeth are filed to sharp points, supposedly from the time not so very long ago when they were cannibals."
>
> Cezaire told me that there were still cases of cannibalism in Central Africa, most of it on bodies that had just been buried. The authorities in some localities still had trouble over it occasionally, and there were tales of isolated tribes who practised it regularly, as they always had. . . .

Cotlow had noticed the filed teeth—the universal sign of cannibalistic tradition—but he did not, himself, witness any actual cannibalism.   He mentions however the distinguished German ethnologist, Schweinfurth, who had lived with the Mangbetu before that tribe came under the influence of the Europeans generally.   The German had wanted to take home skulls and human bones for research, and therefore offered gifts to the tribesmen if they would let him have some.   "In a very short time," says Cotlow, "he had accumulated a great pile, although he was disappointed to find that most of the skulls had been shattered—so that the Mangbetu gourmands could get at the brains, a great delicacy.   Still, he came home with forty excellent skulls, out of the two hundred he collected.   Another German reported of the Mangbetu that they delighted in meals of human flesh. He had been unable, he said, to find a grave anywhere—a fact which held considerable significance."

Cotlow remarks that the authorities, in an attempt to explain why it should be that some tribes are cannibals while others are not, suggested that the Mangbetu "ate human flesh because they raised no cattle." The Zulu and the Masai were believed never to have indulged in cannibalism—and they were cattle-breeders. On the other hand, the Mangbetu did raise poultry, so any possible craving for meat could be satisfied that way, if their cannibalistic tendencies were to be attributed solely to a desire for meat as food.

There is a tail-piece to Cotlow's observations:

No doubt all eating of human flesh among the Mangbetu had ceased by this time, but on my first trip I received some vague and confusing answers to my questions about it. One honest ex-plorer told me that, tired of roundabout investigation, he asked an old Mangbetu, "Do you eat human meat?" The ancient one was silently thoughtful for a moment, and then said, looking down his nose: "It is very hard to stop old habits."

Cotlow's book was published in 1957. The three trips he made among the tribes of the Congo Basin and elsewhere in Equatorial Africa took place in the years 1937, 1946, and 1954. Even though the record he is quoting dates back to the earliest of his expeditions, that is a period of only twenty years: a flicker of a page or two in the long, and still largely untold, story of this part of a Dark Continent.

Fort Portal, the point from which Cotlow began the expedi-tion referred to, is just within the confines of the British Pro-tectorate of Uganda, a province bounded on the north by the Sudan, on the east by Kenya, and on the south by Tanganyika. The Belgian Congo is its big neighbour on the west, and about half of Lake Victoria lies within its boundaries.

Certainly the Bagesu, and probably other tribes in the region that have been less exhaustively studied, practised the custom of disposing of their dead by devouring them; a custom which the German mentioned by Cotlow will have recognised as explaining why he never found any graves among the tribes he had met with.

John Roscoe, writing between the two World Wars, states clearly that the custom of eating the bodies of the dead was common to all the clans of the numerous Bagesu tribe, and that the practice took place during the period allocated to mourning:

> For various reasons, the custom was kept secret, and even members of the tribe were not permitted to look on during the ceremony, which was performed by night. Yet the custom was known to all, and each family was aware of what was going on, though they never sought to watch their neighbours' doings.
>
> When a man died, the body was kept in the house until the evening, when the relatives who had been summoned gathered for the mourning. In some exceptional instances it took one or two days to bring the relatives together, but as a rule all was ready by the evening of the day of death, and at sunset the body was carried to the nearest waste ground and deposited there. At the same time, men of the clan hid themselves in different places round about and, as darkness deepened, they blew upon gourd horns, making a noise like the cry of jackals.
>
> The villagers said that the jackals were coming to eat the dead, and the young people were warned not to go outside. When darkness set in, and it was felt to be safe to work without intrusion from inquisitive onlookers, a number of elderly women relatives of the dead man went to the place where the body lay, and cut it up, carrying back the pieces they wanted to the house of mourning, and leaving the remains to be devoured by wild animals.
>
> For the next three, or sometimes four, days the relatives mourned in the house in which the death had taken place, and there they cooked and ate the flesh of the dead, destroying the bones by fire and leaving nothing. There was no 'purification', or 'shaving' when this mourning was ended; sometimes an ox was killed for a feast when the heir was announced, but as a rule the people simply returned to their ordinary life without any ceremony. The widows, however, burned their grass girdles, and either went about naked or wore the small aprons used by unmarried girls.

Tribesmen offered by way of explanation of their custom of devouring their dead this odd belief: If, they said, they were to allow a body to be buried in the ground and, in the natural course of things, to decay, the ghost of the dead person would haunt the district near his grave and, by way of revenge for being allowed to decay, cause illness to the children.

Roscoe writes about one or two other tribes of Uganda. Of the Bakongo, a small tribe whose stamping-ground was on the eastern slopes of Mt Ruwenzori, he says that though there is evidence that they were once cannibals, they were now hunters of four-legged meat-on-the-hoof: they would kill and eat any-thing from rats to leopards.   They maintained that they buried their dead in the proper way, but it was suspected that in fact the ancient custom of devouring them still persisted among the more remote clans.

On the opposite slopes of Mt Ruwenzori lived the Bambwas. These tribesmen, Roscoe says, as recently as the first years of this century were eating human flesh.   He declares that he actually saw this going on, and the practice of filing the teeth to a sharp point was universal amongst them.

Among the tribes which were no longer cannibal, he says, he noticed some curious customs connected with death and burial:

> When a man died, his legs were bent up and his hands were crossed in front of him with the arms straight.   This was some-times done before death, and the limbs tied lest they should be stretched out and become rigid in that position.   All the orna-ments were removed from the dead man.   The grave was dug *in the hut*, the body placed in it on an old sleeping mat, in a sitting posture, and the grave was then filled in with earth.   A woman, on the other hand, was buried *outside* the hut, lying on her back, with her legs bent up and her hands on either side of her head.
>
> The brother of a dead man took possession of his widows at once, but one widow was left in the hut for a month to guard the grave, and the mourners also remained there for a month, during which they carried out a daily programme of mourning and wail-ing.   At the end of the month, a goat was killed and its head placed on the grave.   The mourners ate the meat, then washed, shaved their heads and cut their nails.   The hair and nail-parings of each person were tied in a bundle and fastened to the roof of the hut.   They then left the hut; the posts were cut and the hut fell down on the grave.   This ended the mourning, and no further notice was taken of the place; though the ghost was supposed to continue to hover near it.

This alternative method of burial, by digging the grave inside the hut and then causing the hut to collapse over the grave, may of course be the explanation why that other traveller failed during his travels in the region to find any graves at all, and therefore made the logical deduction that the custom of the tribes in the locality was to devour the bodies of their dead.

Another writer, this time in *The Saturday Review*, comments on the fact that, though cannibalism no doubt existed even till comparatively recent times in East Africa, it was accompanied by less brutality than the cannibalism noted in Equatorial Africa and particularly in the West. "An element of *domestic economy* seems to pervade cannibal customs in the east," he wrote. "The flesh of the old, the infirm, and the useless is dried and preserved, with a sort of reverence, in the family larder. It is offered to guests as a special compliment, to refuse which would be a deadly insult, while its acceptance secures friendship. Many travellers in East Africa have eaten thus sacramentally of the ancestors of some dark-skinned potentate."

At the time of the taking over of the Sudan Zandeland by the Anglo-Egyptian Administration in the early part of this century there was certainly a good deal of cannibalism in the region. Indeed, Basil Spence makes the point that the word 'Zande' and the word 'cannibal' are interchangeable. "The very origin of the Azande," he says, "makes them suspect; for they came from the western part of Africa, though at present the majority of them live in the Belgian Congo and French Equatorial Africa." He goes on to say:

> Innumerable acts of cannibalism have been reported from time to time by both Belgians and French, the most recent of which I have actual knowledge being the waylaying by a party of Azande of a Belgian officer proceeding on leave from the Lado Enclave (now Western Mongolla); they tore him limb from limb and ate him *raw*. This occurred twelve years ago. . . .

Spence is writing in 1920, so that this episode occurred well into the present century. He goes on to say that the Azande of the Bahr el Ghazal are an offshoot of the other Azande—the cream, he says, of the fighters. They had been seen to drive a lion off its somewhat decayed 'kill' in order to devour it themselves, and to tear up and eat a putrid, semi-liquefied elephant; certainly they devoured the dead on a field of battle, rather than leave the corpses to rot or be eaten by animals. The Azande, he says, invariably admit their cannibalistic practices—even those who allege that they have recently been converted from them.

An interesting piece of corroborative evidence of this is quoted by another authority, E. E. Evans-Pritchard, writing in a very recent issue of the magazine *Africa*. He quotes the statement of a Zande in whose integrity he has absolute

confidence: a statement which he took down verbatim from
the man, and says he has every reason to believe in its every
detail. . . .

> In the past, the Azande were just like animals of the bush (says
> this man, Kuagbiaru by name).   They killed people and ate their
> fellows just like lions, leopards and wild dogs.   In the past, when
> a man died a Zande sharpened his knife, moved over to the corpse
> and cut off the flesh, about two basketfuls of it, and went with the
> flesh to his home.   He took a very big pot and placed the human
> flesh in it till it was filled, and then put it on the fire.   It stewed
> for a long time, then he took it off the fire to put it on a drying
> platform over a fire to dry.   He took it from there and cooked it
> in his own pot, by himself.   That pot he used for eating human
> flesh another man would not touch in any circumstances; it was
> kept apart by itself always; only he himself touched it.
> His fire place was by itself on one side.   When he was of a mind
> to eat his man, he lit his fire by himself at the base of some tree
> and he took his dried human flesh, some three or four pieces of it,
> and put them on the fire in a pot.   He closed the mouth of the pot
> with another little pot.   It went on stewing till it was cooked.
> Meanwhile his wife ground sesame to go with it.   He did all the
> cooking of the meat himself.   His wife cooked porridge and gave
> it to him by the side of his flesh.   He ate his porridge and flesh till
> he was satisfied, and then covered over the mouth of the pot and
> put it at the side of the granary till he was hungry again.
> A Zande ate flesh because it made good meat.   A Zande used
> to say thus: "What is a stranger to me?"   Since it was a stranger,
> he ate him up entirely because he was meat.   The man whose
> forbears ate men, also ate men himself, when he grew up.   Some
> Azande feared other Azande who ate human flesh, and thought of
> them as lions, leopards, hyenas and wild dogs. . . .

We have here almost the sole evidence that there existed,
among these people of the Congo Basin and its outlying districts, a hint of ritual, ritual of course associated with deep-
hidden and hardly-realised fear.   But it is one small piece of
such evidence amid a welter of more blatant examples of sheer
lust for the taste of human flesh.

A much more recent traveller in Central Africa than any of
those quoted hitherto, H. C. Engert, is convinced from his
own experiences that cannibalism still exists as a regular practice.   In a book written as recently as 1956, and describing a
journey that he has made in East, Central and West Africa
since the Second World War, he mentions meeting a Danish
vet. who told him that when he and his porters were in the

northern part of the Congo they ran short of food. The villagers whom they encountered were short of food too, and had none to offer. But they came at length to a village where a tasty stew was offered to his party. "The flesh," the Dane told him, "was soft and tender." Having enjoyed their meal, they asked where the meat had come from. "A woman belong village," was the answer.

Engert, who is evidently an intelligent and highly observant traveller, and incidentally a brilliant photographer, adds:

Cannibalism is far from being dead in Africa, for it is almost impossible to control the natives in the bush. I remember one District Officer standing at his door one night, listening to the drums, saying to me: "They are chopping someone." "Why don't you do anything about it?" I asked. "How can I? If I try to send my native policeman, he will only pretend that he has been; he would be much too frightened to go. We take action if we have proof, or if we find bones."

I myself (Engert continues) once lived in a cannibal village for a time, and found some bones. The natives were worried about this, but I am no policeman. They were pleasant enough people. It was just an old custom which dies hard. Thousands of natives —and I think this is no exaggeration—are still eaten in Africa every year, for it is difficult to break old habits.

Equatorial Africa: stretching along the Equator from the French Gaboon by way of the Belgian Congo, Uganda, to Kenya—two thousand miles and more; and all the territory on the hottest latitude. Is there perhaps a reason here for the prevalence of this custom of devouring human flesh? The custom was rife also, in the Amazon Basin—which also, it will be remembered, lies athwart the Equator; as does the 'cannibal' island of Borneo.

Charles Kingsley's niece, who was intrepid enough to explore the territory of the Fangs of Gaboon in the last years of the nineteenth century, travelling more than two hundred miles up one of its most difficult rivers, encountered cannibalism almost universally throughout this westernmost region of Equatorial Africa. She found the natives determined to kill and devour some of her attendants, who had been collected from a neighbouring tribe with whom there was a feud. She noticed the filed teeth, but as a niece of the Rev. Charles Kingsley, was perhaps too serious-minded to comment on the appropriateness of the name borne by the tribe with these filed teeth: the Fangs. She reported that nowhere did she come across any burial-places, and stated emphatically that the Fangs were a tribe that devoured their dead. She actually saw in some of their huts fragments of human bodies being stored in just the same way as civilised peoples keep foodstuffs in their larders. Her statements, on which sceptics might be inclined to cast doubt, suggesting that this was a panic observation by an impressionable woman, are borne out by the Rev. W. S. Bannerman, an American Presbyterian missionary of the Gaboon Mission.

At the eastern end of Equatorial Africa lies Kenya, associated all too much in our minds, these days, with the horrors of Mau Mau. This aspect of cannibalism and sacrifice will, however, be dealt with later, in a different context.

Most anthropologists and travellers generally are agreed that the practice of eating human flesh is entirely absent in the north and the south of the continent of Africa. E. O. James, however, quoting from some reference in *The Golden Bough*, says that "among the Bechuans (a tribe inhabiting territory south of Northern Rhodesia) a short, stout man was slain in the midst of the wheat to serve as 'seed'. After his blood had coagulated in the sun, it was burned along with the frontal bone and the brain; the ashes were then scattered over the ground to fertilise it." This, of course, is human sacrifice: the sort of ritual that has been noted among the Aztecs and elsewhere. James says that it took place also in West Africa, where "in March, a man and a woman were killed with spades and hoes in order that their bodies might be buried in the newly-tilled field." But of the Bechuans' ceremony he has one more, terse, remark to make: "The rest of the body was eaten."

CHAPTER EIGHT

HEAD-HUNTERS AND HUMAN SACRIFICE
IN INDONESIA

Borneo, the third largest island in the world, lies between the Malay Peninsula and New Guinea. To the north are the scattered Philippines, and immediately to the south stretches the long curving island of Java, with its smaller attendant islands running eastwards to Timor, just short of North Australia itself. Borneo lies almost exactly astride the Equator. Its best-known inhabitants are the tribes known as the Dyaks; and the Dyaks have had a reputation as merciless head-hunters since first men began trading among the innumerable islands of the Indian Archipelago. Head-hunting and cannibalism, more often than not, are dual practices.

The custom of head-hunting is probably as ancient as the Dyaks' existence as a nation (wrote Sir Hugh Low, in a memoir on Sarawak, the northern part of Borneo). Possibly their original motive was akin to that of a non-Dyak Borneo tribe, who held that human sacrifice was the most acceptable form of sacrifice to the tribal gods. Some tribes believe that the persons whose heads they take will become their slaves in the next world.

Feasts are held with specific objects in view: to make the rice crop flourish, to cause the forests to abound with wild animals, to enable their dogs and snares to be successful in securing game, to have the streams and rivers swarm with fish, to give health and activity to the people themselves, and to ensure fertility among their women. All these blessings are, it is believed, most efficiently and certainly secured for the tribe by the capture of a victim and the feasting upon his head.

Another observer, this time an official of the Sarawak Government Service, supplies details connected with the manner in which these men actually severed their victims' heads. Such detail is interesting in that it shows that, even among the members of a large tribe like that of the Dyaks, there may be subtle and even significant variations of practice:

The way of cutting off their heads varies with the different tribes. The Sea Dyaks, for instance, sever the head at the neck, and so preserve *both* jaws.   Among the Hill Dyaks, on the other hand, heads are very carelessly taken, being split open or slashed across with *parangs*.   Often it may be seen that quite large portions have been hacked out of the heads.   Others again cut off the head so close to the trunk that great skill and a practised hand must have been used.

Many tribesmen habitually carry about their person a little basket destined to receive a head.   It is always very neatly plaited, ornamented with a variety of shells, and hung about with human hair.   But only those Dyaks who have lawfully obtained such a head, as opposed to those who steal, or 'find' them, may include this human hair ornamentation to their macabre baskets.

The Sea Dyaks scoop out the brains by way of the nostrils, and then hang up the head to dry in the smoke of a wood fire—usually the fire which is maintained anyway for the cooking of all the food for the members of the tribe.   Every now and then they will leave their pre-occupations, saunter across to the fire, and tear or slash off a piece of the skin and burnt flesh of the cheek or chin, and eat it.   They believe that by so doing they will add immediately to their store of courage and fearlessness.

The brains are not always extracted by way of the nostrils, however.   Sometimes a piece of bamboo, carved into the semblance of a spoon, is thrust into the lowest part of the skull, and the brains gradually extracted by the occipital orifice. . . .

It is not usual, in these official reports, particularly when they emanate from official, or even semi-official, sources, for the writer to insert the sort of comment that is found as a tailpiece to this description by a Sarawak Government employee:

> The brains are thus extracted from the skull much as one extracts stuffing from the Xmas turkey from an orifice that seems to have been designed to make the procedure as difficult as possible!

The writer has already referred to the matter of the use of human hair as ornamentation for these baskets which the Dyaks carried with them to contain their skull trophies.   He adds a curious detail or two about these skulls, to which it is not easy to find exact parallels anywhere else among headhunting and cannibalistic tribes.

> They cut off the hair from the skulls to use for ornamentation also to their sword-hilts and sheaths.   But in the meantime someone must always keep an alert eye on the progress of the cooking of the skulls.   For instance, the lower jaw of a skull must never be permitted to sag or drop.   If it shows signs of this, it must be carefully bound up.   If teeth fall out, or have perhaps already been knocked out in battle or afterwards, the cavities must at once be

filled with imitation teeth, made of wood. The eye-sockets, too, must be plugged; and the nostrils through which the brains have been extracted. The tongue must always have been cut off at the root.

Another Government official, this time an Assistant Resident in Upper Sarawak, sent in a report in the form of random jottings resulting from an extended tour that he made through the territory:

> Among Dyak and Milano tribes, in many parts of this country, it is the practice still to cut up and consume the *raw heart* of a warrior killed in battle, under the idea that those who partake of the dish will in due course increase their courage. Though I personally have never met with cannibals in Borneo (he was writing at the tail-end of the nineteenth century), I am sure from the careful inquiries I have made that the practice of eating human beings has not long died out; indeed, I feel fairly confident that the practice still exists in obscure and little-known places in the remote interior.
>
> I was assured by a traveller with whom I spoke at some length that when, for instance, he visited the Meribun and Jincang Dyaks, he found them to be practising cannibalism. These particular tribes live not far from the head-waters of the Sadong River. At Sungei Meribun, the cannibals had been seen by this traveller feasting on the flesh of a human body. Traditionally, only the heads of the victims are eaten, but when an individual member of their own tribe happens to die, the body is sold, and anyone who wishes to do so, not excluding women and even children, may take part in the feast.
>
> In this particular instance the body was that of a comparatively young man, and it was noticeable that the most favoured portions were the soles of his feet and the palms of his hands. Another tribe, this traveller told me, the Jincangs, will devour the whole of the body with the exception of the entrails, which are carefully avoided by all who take part in the feasting.

The traveller appears to have been a particularly observant individual—and it is reasonable to suppose that to take a keen interest in such activities may at times lay the observer open to the charge of prying, for which sensitive tribesmen may have their own scale of penalties. He observed in particular a tribe of Dyaks known as the Janakang, who, he reported,

> Practise certain refinements—if the word can be fairly used in such a grisly context—in the matter of eating human flesh. They do not, like some other Dyak tribes, eat indiscriminately all parts of the body. Rather, they practise a form of epicureanism. First

in favour among the delicacies comes the human tongue; then comes the brain; and then the muscles of the thigh and calf. These particular tribesmen, though by no means alone in the habit, file their teeth to exceedingly sharp points, to enable them to tear at this tough, sinewy flesh.

This traveller seems to have managed to get on speaking terms with these Dyaks—a somewhat hazardous procedure in the circumstances. He asked them why they practised cannibalism, and the reply came in the form of another question: "If we do not eat of warriors' flesh," they asked, "how can we ourselves hope to become as fearless as they?"

Sir James Brooke, the first Rajah of Sarawak, went very carefully into the available evidence of cannibalism in the country for which he was largely responsible. It is very clear that he was not easily persuaded, that he made a practice of checking and re-checking evidence, checking the credentials of those who sent in reports to him, and personally interviewing anyone from whom he thought it might be possible to obtain authoritative information.

Among those from whom he collected information were three men whom he refers to as "intelligent Dyaks from the interior". They were persuaded to spend some time at the Residence, where they were interrogated carefully, after being assured that they would be well treated. "They spoke," Rajah Brooke says, "in the most frank manner to be conceived—as direct and unimpeachable evidence as I have ever heard offered, sometimes when they were together, sometimes by individual apart, in conversation with numerous persons. I examined them myself," he adds, "and entertain no doubt of the correctness of their statements, as far as their personal knowledge is concerned. The witnesses themselves stated over and over again, with the utmost clearness, how much they had *seen*, and how much they had only *heard*. There was such perfect good faith, and simplicity, in their stories as to carry conviction of their truth."

The three "intelligent Dyaks from the interior" were named Kusu, Gajah and Rinong, and their stories, recounted at different times and over a period of time, with repetitions omitted, add up to the following:

We are of the tribe of Sibaru, which is likewise the name of a branch of the Kapuas River. We are two thousand fighting men.

We have none of us been up to the interior of the Kapuas, where the Kayans live, but they often come down to Santang, where we meet them. They are very numerous and very powerful and independent. Many of them are reported to be cannibals, and we know these reports are true, for we have seen things with our own eyes.

There was a war a few years ago between Malays and Dyaks, and the Dyak forces included many Kayans. I, Kusu, saw these Kayans run small spits of iron, from eight inches to a foot long, into the fleshy parts of dead men's arms, from the elbow to the shoulder, and into the fleshy parts of their legs from above their ankles, beneath the calf, to the knee-joint. Then they sliced off the flesh through which they had thrust their spits, and put the flesh into baskets which they had prepared in readiness.

The spits which they use are also prepared especially for such occasions and are carried in a case beneath the sheaths which hold their knives. The Kayans prize heads in exactly the same way as other Dyaks prize them. They take also the flesh from all parts of the bodies of their victims, leaving only the largest bones. Not wishing to share their booty with other warriors after the battle, they carried off the portions of flesh, broiled them on hot stones and then entered their canoes and had their feast without fear of interruption from the others. It was not I, Kusu, and Gajah and Rinong alone who witnessed these things, but others also who had been in the battle. The flesh, when it was being cooked, smelled like hog's flesh.

The second Dyak took up the tale from his friend Kusu, stressing the fact that that was by no means the only time they had witnessed cannibalism. He referred especially to the Dyaks of Jangkang, who lived, he said, on the banks of a tributary of the Sangow River. These Dyaks had made a foray against another tribe, the Ungias, and having taken many prisoners and killed many others, they approached the speaker's own settlement:

They carried with them several baskets of human flesh. They cooked and ate this flesh outside the hut where I live, but it had been broiled before they arrived. I knew that it was human flesh for I saw one of the party turn the hand of a dead man at the fire. I could see that he turned it by the fingers. Kusu and Rinong and I saw them eat this hand on the bank of the river, close beside my hut. We talked to them about what they had done, and they laughed and were proud.

The Jangkang eat anyone who is killed in fighting. They even kill their own sick and infirm, if they are near death, and eat them. At Santang a party of this tribe was staying, and one of them

climbed into a mango tree and fell from it and broke his arm.
Otherwise he was not much hurt.   But his companions at once
slit his throat and ate his whole body.   We did not see this, but
some of our friends at Santang told us about it, and they are
friends whose word we trust.   We have also been told that at
their feast which they call Makantaun, a man will borrow a fat
child from his neighbour to make up part of the feast; later he
will repay his neighbour perhaps with a fat child of his own.
We have heard this thing, and we believe it, though we have not
seen it with our own eyes.

A successor of Sir James Brooke was inclined to question this
information on the strength of investigations which he himself
made some years afterwards.   But he does say that some travellers in the Kapuas district came across a number of lengths
of bamboo which appeared to have been hidden away as though
their owners had taken fright at the rumoured approach of
white men.   When these pieces of bamboo were carefully
inspected they were found to be hollow canes packed tightly
with human flesh—"'iron rations'," as he remarked of them,
"of the most hideous type."

Another traveller, in the eastern part of Borneo, reported
that he had noticed that a number of the Dyak tribes were very
careful to avoid all contact with a tribe known as the Trings.
He made discreet inquiries as to the reason for this unusual
form of boycotting, and learned that the Trings were despised
by the more advanced Dyak tribes for continuing the practice
of cannibalism which they themselves had now abandoned.
The traveller, a man named Carl Bock, was told that the Trings
considered the most succulent portions of a human being to be,
first the palms of his hands, then the knees, and then the brain.
"Bai, bai, bai!" the man said to him, meaning "Good, good,
good!"   And as he spoke the words he pointed meaningly to
Carl Bock's hands, knees and forehead.   This Tring informant
stated proudly that he had tasted the flesh and blood of over
seventy victims—men, women and children.   "The blood of
their hands and knees and brain," he ended, "now runs in my
own blood-stream!"

Unlike many of the tribes whose activities have already been
considered, the Dyaks made a habit of organising large-scale
expeditions for the express purpose of collecting victims;
whether primarily for the securing of fresh heads, or primarily

for the purpose of securing further supplies of human flesh to eat, is unimportant, for the two motives seem to have been virtually indistinguishable. They seem to have taken pleasure in the sheer detail of organisation of these expeditions; much as a commander in charge of the planning of some piece of strategy in modern warfare must be obsessed by the detail of logistics and other vital elements. An elaborate account of a typical expedition has been pieced together by one John Dalton:

The perseverance of the Dyaks during an expedition is wonderful. They get their information in advance from the women of some distant campong who have been taken prisoner in a foray. In proceeding towards a campong, their canoes are never seen on the river in day-time; they invariably commence their journeys about half an hour after dark falls. They pull rapidly and silently up the river, close to the bank. One boat keeps immediately behind another, and the handles of the paddles are covered with the soft bark of a tree so that no noise whatsoever is made.

After paddling without intermission, about half an hour before daylight they pull their canoes up on the river bank amongst the trees of the thick jungle, so that from the river it is quite impossible to see them or discover their tracks. Should their chieftain, or the leader of the expedition, feel the desire for human flesh, then one of the followers is killed. This not only provides him with a good meal, but provides also a head.

Some of the tribesmen then ascend the tallest trees in order to examine the surrounding territory and see whether a campong, or even an isolated hut or two, lies near at hand. They discover this from the smoke of the fires. Should it be a solitary hut, then they swiftly surround it and take very good care that not one of its occupants escapes. Should it prove to be a campong of any considerable size, they go much more warily to work.

Dalton then goes on to describe the precautions taken by the leader of the expedition. One third of his party is sent on in advance, through the thickest part of the intervening jungle; they station themselves around the perimeter of the campong, well out of sight, and with extra sentinels wherever a track leads through the jungle to or from the settlement. The remainder of the expedition go ahead by canoe, timing their arrival at their destination for about one hour before daybreak. Once arrived, the warriors put on their fighting equipment, which has in the meanwhile been stored in the bottom of their canoes. They moor their canoes, and then set out across land through the shelter of the trees and scrub.

Just before daybreak, they start to throw on to the thatched roofs of the huts 'fire-balls' made of the dry and highly inflammable bark of certain trees, and, Dalton continues:

> The hut roofs immediately and simultaneously burst into flames. Then the war-cry of the warriors is heard amid the crackle of blazing thatch and of the collapsing hut-poles and walls. The work of the massacre begins at once, in the pandemonium that ensues. The male inhabitants of each hut are speared or hacked to pieces as they stumble down the ladders from their huts, many of which stand high on stilts, in a desperate attempt to escape the leaping flames. The flames give sufficient light for the warriors to distinguish between men and women.
>
> The women and the children—those who are not burned alive —escape into the jungle by the well-known tracks; but only to find these already guarded by sentries, from whom there is no escaping. They have no choice but to surrender, and are thus rounded up and placed under guards.

Dalton then describes the elaborate precautions taken by the expedition to ensure that no one shall escape capture, even though he may have miraculously escaped death by the burning of his hut or at the hands of the warriors closing in about the campong and hacking their way through the spaces between hut and hut. The tracks are guarded; the bank of the river is guarded; sentinel canoes lie in midstream on the look-out for anyone foolish enough to try to swim across to the further side. The campaign is successful down to the smallest detail.

The timing of these expeditions, too, is skilful and intelligent. The tribesmen believe that men and women sleep most soundly in the hour that immediately precedes daylight; that is why they choose this moment for their surprise attacks. They welcome a little light rainfall, believing that people sleep more soundly when rain is falling from the skies; but this rain must only be very light—otherwise it will soak the thatch and extinguish the fire-balls, so that the element of surprise and the resultant panic will be lost.

The old women who are captured are immediately killed off. The heads of male prisoners are cut off, the brains being extracted as soon as possible and held over fire to pickle them and thus preserve them. Dalton speaks of a chief whom he

knew, named Selgie, whose warriors brought back with them
from one such expedition, which had lasted some six weeks in
all, over *seven hundred* human heads, of which number the
chief's own share amounted to more than one third. "There
is," he adds, "no degree of suffering a Dyak will not cheerfully
endure if the recompense is to be even a single additional head."
And he adds a personal reminiscence:

> I have been present when Selgie has taken two campongs. The
> inhabitants were surprised and the fighting as a consequence was
> all on one side, though in a few instances some resistance was
> offered. I did not observe them attempt to parry blows with any
> weapons; rather, they took them on their shields or on their
> bamboo caps. The noise was terrific during such a massacre—
> for it can be called no less than that, and is joined in heartily by
> such of the tribe's women as have prevailed upon the warriors to
> allow them places in the canoes. An old Dyak loves to dwell on
> his success in expeditions such as these; and the terror of the
> women and children he has seen captured, *mutilated*, and then
> mercilessly killed affords a fruitful source of gratification and even
> amusement when they are gathered together to talk over past
> exploits.

In the neighbouring large island of Sumatra, according to
Dr Maynard, whose comments on the Fiji Islanders have
already been referred to, there were cannibalistic practices in
every way comparable with those of the Dyaks, and even of the
more ferocious Fijians themselves.

> The code of the Battas of Sumatra (he wrote) condemns to be
> eaten alive those guilty of adultery, those who commit theft at
> night, prisoners of war, those who treacherously attack the in-
> habitants of a house, or a lonely man. The execution takes place
> without delay, in the presence of the whole population. In cases
> of adultery, one last formality is necessary: the relatives of the
> criminals must be present at the carrying out of the sentence.
> The husband, the wife, or the persons most directly offended,
> have the right to retain the ears of the condemned for themselves.
> Then, each according to his rank chooses his fragment, and the
> chief judge cuts off the head and hangs it like a trophy at the door
> of his hut.
> The brain, to which they attribute magical properties, is pre-
> served in a gourd. The intestines are not devoured, but the
> soles of the feet, and the heart, cooked with rice and salt, are re-
> garded as a delicious dish. The flesh is always eaten raw, or
> grilled at the place of punishment, and the use of palm wine and
> other strong liquors is strongly interdicted at these judicial feasts,

where the men alone have the right to be present. Sometimes also they collect the blood in bamboo stems. In defiance of the law, the women use a thousand subterfuges, and employ all their seductions, in order to share in this secret and horrible feast.

Some travellers affirm that the Battas prefer human flesh to all other, but only indulge in it during warfare and following the death sentence. Others accuse them of immolating, in times of peace, from sixty to a hundred slaves annually. But today the Battas no longer put their parents to death when age has rendered them useless as workers or fighters. Formerly, every year at the time of the ripening of the citrons, old men were to be seen voluntarily submitting to death. The family assembled; the victim, weighed down by age, collected all his energy and sprang towards the branch of a tree, there to remain suspended by both arms until his strength failed and he fell to the ground. Then the neighbours and children, who had been dancing round him in a circle, sang this refrain: "When the fruit is ripe it needs must fall!" They thereupon precipitated themselves upon him, beat him to death, dismembered him and devoured his flesh, soaking it in *samboul* or sprinkling it with *kari*. When an Englishman offers tea and milk, the Battas often reject them with scorn, retorting: "Only children drink milk; Battas drink blood!"

E. O. James, whose researches into cannibal and other rites among the Aztecs and other communities have already been referred to, has a general comment to make on Borneo and tribes in adjoining islands and parts of the mainland such as Burma and Siam. Concerned, as he tends to be generally, with the ceremonial aspect of human sacrifice, he finds a deeper motive underlying the practices which have been described as characteristic of the Dyaks and neighbouring tribes.

In Indonesia (he writes) head-hunting occupied a position equivalent to that of human sacrifice in relation to agriculture and the cult of the dead, the underlying motive in both rites being apparently identical. The head was considered to be especially rich in 'soul-substance'. The Karens of Burma, for instance, suppose that the *tso*, or 'life-principle', resides in the upper part of the head (as the Nootka of British Columbia regard the soul as a tiny man who lives in the crown, and the vibrations of the membrane in the fontanel of infants is explained among the Ao Naga tribes as due to the movements of the soul); and in Siam the greatest care has to be exercised in cutting the hair, lest the indwelling *khuan* be disturbed. The numerous tabus surrounding the cutting of the hair, and the elaborate protection of the head by various coverings and devices, take their rise in the belief that the soul is therein located. There can be little doubt that the practice of head-hunting is based on this same notion.

It is a welcome relief, sometimes, to pass from factual reports of head-hunting expeditions and the various grisly practices that follow such expeditions if they have been successful, to the deliberate and measured commentary of a man of James's calibre. He remarks, pursuing his highly specialised thesis by way of the tribes in the Naga Hills, where, he maintains, head-hunting was closely associated with the well-being of the tribal crops and cattle-breeding, that even among the Kayans of Borneo—against whom such adverse criticism was levelled by the three 'intelligent Dyaks from the interior'—the custom of head-hunting was associated with the growing of rice crops.

In Borneo (he says) the head is believed to contain the ghost, or *toh*, which, so long as it is not neglected, produces fertility in the soil, promotes the growth of the crops, and brings prosperity to the community in general and to the person who captures the head in particular. The soul is conceived of as a sort of egg, or bladder, filled with a vaporous substance which is spread over the fields as a magical manure when the bladder bursts. The grain is fertilised, since the vapour holds the vitalising principle. And when the grain is eaten as food, its life-giving power is communicated to the blood, and thence imparted to the seminal fluid, by means of which men and animals are enabled to propagate life.

There is, then, an intimate connection between the soul and fertilisation, and head-hunting is largely prompted by the idea of securing additional soul-substance to increase the productivity of the soil and, indirectly, the fertility of the tribesmen and tribeswomen. It adds to the *vital essence* in the village: hence it is essential that as many heads as possible shall be acquired. Just as the Aztecs carried on wars to secure sacrificial victims, so the head-hunting expeditions became a normal feature of native life.

James's theory—admittedly not a novel one, for other anthropologists before and since his day have elaborated it—may be taken as a sort of 'justification' of these practices. But it does not altogether fit in with the verifiable facts, as quoted. If, for example, the 'soul-substance' does live within the skull, behind the forehead, whether as a 'tiny man' or in any other image, then the Dyak practice of immediately smoking the skull over flames, of scooping out the contents, of snatching mouthfuls before the smoking process is even completed, is difficult to explain. Had they *no* superstitious fear in this regard?

CHAPTER NINE

NEW GUINEA: 'REVENGE' CANNIBALISM AND TABU

TRAVELLING EAST from Borneo, which lies surrounded by the South China, the Java and the Celebes Seas, we come to New Guinea, the second largest island on the world's surface, and find ourselves back in the Pacific Ocean once again.

New Guinea lies just to the south of the Equator, its northernmost tip almost on it. The island is almost equally divided, from north to south, by an arbitrary straight line. To the west of it is that half of New Guinea which belongs to the Dutch; to the east is the half that is administered by Great Britain and Australia—which is, by the vast scale of the Pacific, a mere stone's-throw to the south. The south-eastern portion of New Guinea, with its huge curve of bay fronting the romantically named Coral Sea, is more generally known as Papua. We are back, now, in that region of the Pacific Islands known as Melanesia—the 'Black Islands' where people with dark skins and crinkly hair are found.

And—metaphorically speaking at any rate—certainly New Guinea may be considered 'black': here, until only the day before yesterday, cannibalism in its most brutal and horrific forms was universally practised. Indeed, this is one of the very few regions left of which no one dare say for certain that, even in the mid-twentieth century, the eating of human flesh is no more than a memory. There remain great tracts of New Guinea virtually unexplored, and certainly unmapped.

Most, if not all, of the motives for cannibalism that have so far been encountered seem to prevail here—or to have prevailed until all too recently. Revenge is a dominating motive; the transfer of desirable qualities from the dead to the living; the prevention of any form of after-life for the victim, including the possibility of his haunting his killers; and, sometimes to the exclusion, or at any rate subordination, of all other motives: the sheer lust for human flesh, coupled with an accompanying passion for sheer cruelty that is unsurpassed in any other part of the world. Yet the complicated pattern of tabu is as pronounced here as it is anywhere in the world, with the most extraordinary variations from tribe to tribe—almost, one would say, from parish to parish.

The Rev. James Chalmers, one of a long line of amazingly courageous missionaries who have worked there, and all too often fallen victims to the very practices they had devoted their lives to attempting to eradicate, was successful in discovering the legend underlying cannibalism in New Guinea. There is a curious parallel, here, to the Garden of Eden story, and one is inclined to suspect that the native who told him the legend was already a convert, and had learned at any rate the basic Old Testament story!

I asked him (Chalmers records) *why* they ate human flesh. He told me that it was the women of the tribes who first urged the men to kill their fellow human beings for the purpose of eating them. The husbands were, the man told me, returning from a successful hunt far inland. As was their custom, they were blowing their conch-shells and singing and dancing.

As they approached the village, coming down the river in their canoes piled high with wallabies, boars and cassowaries, the women called out to them: "What success, husbands, that you sing and dance so?" "Great success," the men shouted back. "Plenty to eat. Here, come and see for yourselves."

The women approached the canoes, and when they saw what was in them, they called out: "What, just that dirty stuff?" And then, in voices of scorn: "Who is going to eat that? Is that what you call successful hunting?"

Then the men began reasoning among themselves: "What do our wives mean, mocking us like this?" And one of them, wiser than the others, said after much thought: "I know. They want the flesh of *man*!"

Then, throwing the wallabies and boars and cassowaries over the sides of their canoes, they went quickly along the river to a neighbouring village and brought back with them ten bodies. But, the man said to me, the men returned in their canoes without their usual singing and rejoicing.

When the women who were waiting for them on the river bank saw them approaching the village, they called out: "What have our husbands brought for us to eat, this time?" And then they looked, but their husbands did not look at them, only cast their eyes downwards at what lay in their canoes. "Yes, that is right!" shouted the women. "Dance and sing again, now, for you have brought back with you something worth dancing and singing about!"

Then the ten bodies were taken out of the canoes and put on the river bank. And the women cooked them, and pronounced them good. And after a while, the men also said that the flesh was good. And from that day till now, the men and women of these tribes have always said that the flesh of human beings is better than the flesh of any other animal.

And certainly all the evidence points to the fact that, whatever the origin of cannibalism may have been, here in New Guinea—and the legend is of course quite worthless except for the odd light it sheds on a relationship between a missionary and a native in the latter end of the nineteenth century—the practice was long established by the time the first white men landed on its inhospitable shores, and was an unconscionable time a-dying. Writing only forty years ago, J. H. P. Murray, Lieutenant-Governor and Chief Judicial Officer in Papua, added unwittingly a footnote: "Certain tribes here like human flesh and do not see why they should not eat it. Indeed, I have never been able to give a convincing answer to a native who says to me, 'Why should I not eat human flesh?'"

Writing very much more recently on this same subject, a Government anthropologist researching into the Papuan Orokaiva Society had this to say: "The reason for cannibalism itself has been given by these natives as the simple desire for *good food*. Anthropologically speaking, the fact that we ourselves should persist in a superstitious, or at least sentimental, prejudice against human flesh is more puzzling than the fact that the Orokaiva, a born hunter, should see fit to enjoy perfectly good meat when he gets it."

Such an observation as this is of course a far cry from the comment of the traveller Alfred St Johnston, who made it very clear that he himself would be glad to break with such 'superstitious nonsense' and indulge in cannibalism with the natives of Fiji. This anthropologist, F. E. Williams, reported back to his government in detail, his report characteristic, both in its detail and in its attitude, of many such reports:

The corpses of grown men were tied by hands and feet to a pole and carried face downward. In the case of a child, one hand was tied to one foot, and a warrior would sling the body over his shoulder as a hunter might a wallaby's. Usually the victim was dead before being bound in this manner. An ingenious, if grue-some, method of carrying human flesh was observed by a former Resident Magistrate in the Division. The limbs had been peculiarly treated. The ankle-joints had been severed, leaving the Achilles tendon intact. The bones of the leg had been excised and the pelvical bone removed. The ham had been neatly cut off. The boneless leg was wrapped carefully round a three-foot stick and the foot secured to the stick by a piece of vine. In this manner the flesh could be carried comfortably on one's back.

Brought home by the raiders, the corpse of the victim was set upright in the village, still attached to its pole. During the night there was dancing to the accompaniment of the drum and the *hui*, a trumpet of wood or shell. In the morning the body was taken down to the stream and cut up in the running water, in order to wash away the blood. Various portions were then distributed, as they are in the case of a pig, and little odds and ends were given to the children, who played at roasting them in the fires.

Williams turns next, as all true anthropologists do, to the various tabus that attended the consumption of human flesh, which, as has been stated already, covered a wide range. Here, as among certain other tribes, the actual slayer of the victim was debarred from partaking of the victim's flesh.

This rule was rigidly observed. However, though the slayer might not eat of the slain, he was permitted to bite into small por-tions of the liver, after it had been ceremonially treated with sym-bolic herbs. Possibly the slayer believed that he thus assimilated some of the courage and fierceness of his victim; but it must be remembered that the liver is regarded as the seat of fear as well as of the more warlike emotions.

This tabu on the flesh of the slain among the Orokaiva applies not only to the slayer but to his father, mother and nearest rela-tives. If they were rash enough to partake, their genitalia would swell, their joints grow crooked and their heads turn bald. In view of such alarming risks, it seems likely that there was thought to be in the person of the slain something like infection to that of the slayer. The slayer would always be prompt to remove his perineal band and wear a leaf, or nothing at all, until he reached home and could effect a change of clothing. If he had despatched his victim with a club, he would straightway change this for another man's; on no account must he shoulder the club that struck the mortal blow, for he would then run the risk of a swollen or distorted shoulder-joint.

Again, the slayer must perform certain rites, and observe cer-tain tabus. He must not drink pure water out of the river but only that which has been stirred up and made muddy by the feet of a *non-slayer*. He must not eat *taro* cooked in the pot, but only that which has been roasted on the open fire. He must abstain from sexual intercourse. These restrictions last for several days, and then the slayer eats the same purificatory stew—*suna*—which is given to initiates at the end of their seclusion.

Among the Binandele tribe there is a peculiar rite which immediately precedes the ceremonial eating of the *suna*. The slayer climbs into a certain tree which contains a nest of those large and aggressive insects commonly known as 'green ants'. The tree is always swarming with them. While he crouches in a fork of the tree, branches are broken off and laid over him so that he is almost completely covered and thoroughly bitten. Having endured this for some time, he climbs down from the tree and eats the *suna*, steaming himself over the dish and sponging his joints with handfuls of the stewed leaves.

Williams adds that these rites and tabus are not merely purificatory; they are also, as are others like them, defensive. They serve the vital purpose of driving away the *asisi*, as these natives call the spirit or ghost of the man who has been slain. Not only is the slayer held to be unclean for a given period of time till he is purified; he is at the mercy of the ghost of the victim, and must be protected from it. There seems to be a close parallel here, even in matters of small detail, between the Orokaiva and the Kwakiutl Indians.

The practice of secrecy—the passing from hand to hand, as it were, of the responsibility for the actual killing—which has been noted for example among the members of the Sierra Leone Leopard Societies attains a curiously high level among these New Guinea tribes; notably among those of the Purari Delta. J. H. P. Murray, the Lieutenant-Governor and Chief Judicial Officer in Papua already referred to, has this to say about them:

> The people of the Purari Delta are naturally secretive as to their religious beliefs and practices, and not inclined to discuss them with strangers, but information emerges in the course of trials and official investigations. For instance, in the year 1909 I tried a man called Avai, a native of Baimuru, who was charged with the murder of a woman of Baroi. His statement contained some curious details. He said: "Bai-i told us to kill three Baroi people. We caught Aimari and his two wives, in Era Bay. Kairi killed Aimari. I killed one wife, and Iomu the other. I killed the woman with a dagger of cassowary bone. We put the bodies in the canoe and took them back with us. I did not bite

off the woman's nose. It is not our custom to bite off the nose of a person you have killed. If I kill a man or a woman, someone else bites off his nose. We bite off the noses of people that *others* have killed. We *bite* them off; we do not *cut* them off.

"We left the three bodies in our canoe till morning. Then we took them into our village and put them on the platform. Then we singed them, cut them up into small pieces, mixed the pieces with sago, cooked them, wrapped them up in leaves of nipa-palm, and distributed them. I ate a hand of one woman, but it was not the hand of the woman I myself killed. It is not our custom to eat a person we have ourselves killed. But if, after killing a man, you go and sit on a coconut, with also a coconut under each heel, and get your daughter to boil the man's heart, then you may drink the water in which the heart has been boiled. And you may eat a little of the heart also, but you must be sitting on the coconuts all the time."

The simplicity of the statement is convincing. It was Murray who observed that he had never, in all the course of his career as a judicial officer in Papua, been able to think of a really convincing answer to the man under trial for cannibalism who asks him, simply: "Why should I not eat human flesh?" He records elsewhere that many of the tribesmen of whom he has knowledge regard human flesh as civilised men regard beef and mutton. He quotes a witness in a trial who said in evidence: "We boil the bodies. We cut them up and boil them in a pot. We boil babies too. We cut them up like a pig. We eat them cold or hot. We eat the legs first. We eat them because they are like fish. We have fish in the creeks, and kangaroos in the grass. But men are our real food."

This small detail of biting off the nose of a victim interested the anthropologist, Williams, when he was inquiring into the customs of the tribes of the Purari Delta. He found that among them there was a frequent need of human victims in connection with a curious, and unique, ceremony known as *Gopi*—a ceremonial attending the initiation of young tribesmen. As with the Leopard Men in Sierra Leone, the raids were carefully organised, stealthy and usually carried out under cover of darkness. But not always. He cites a specific instance which was brought to his attention:

A gang of Kairu men in canoes spotted a solitary member of another tribe alone in his canoe. They pursued him into the bush, where he was overtaken and struck down with a cassowary dagger. He was then dragged back to the water's edge, where *another member* of the raiding party was called on to deliver the finishing blow. This is a characteristic feature of all such raids.

The man who captures, or fetches down, the victim is called *Kenia Vake*, and to him belongs the honour and glory of the occasion. But he himself does not actually despatch the victim; anyone close at hand may be called upon. This second person, besides slaying the captive, enjoys the singular privilege of biting off his nose. He is known as the *Poke Vake*, or 'Nose-man'.

Among these people, the human victim was not always ceremonially dissected, but was sometimes left lying on the floor so that anyone who wished to do so could come and hack off a morsel to his liking.

This occasional casualness in the matter of the distribution and consumption of human meat seems to have been a characteristic of these Purari Delta and other New Guinea tribesmen. Sir William MacGregor, who wrote the Foreword to Murray's book, had this to say:

There suddenly began to appear in sight, with the first dim grey of dawn, the leading war-canoes of a powerful native armada. They came on up the river out of the semi-darkness with swift and steady strokes of the paddle, with a silence and regularity that was almost spectral.

When I examined their canoes I found that the marauders had captured some ten or twelve people. There were, in four separate canoes, four adult, undivided dead bodies. In another there was the body of a little girl of seven or eight, still tied by the hands and feet to the pole on which her tender little body had been carried.

A village had been raided, and the canoes were full of plunder. A host of miscellaneous articles had been collected, all of which were lying about in the canoes, with here and there a human hand protruding.

A nearer examination showed that the member had been detached, clumsily and unskilfully hacked from the body by an inexperienced hand, and that it was already half-cooked, probably to keep it longer sweet. On the platforms of the canoes were also little made-up parcels and packets of human flesh, deftly enveloped in leaves and tied with bark. On some of the platforms were large and small uncovered pieces, some cooked and ready for the table, others apparently the remains left over from an interrupted meal. One of these was a large portion of the back of a child, half cooked, and corresponding exactly to what is known to the cook as a 'saddle'. In the holds of the canoes were coils of human intestines, sorted as one folds a fishing-line, with a stick through the coil supporting it by resting on the edges of the canoe so as to let the coil fall into the hold but without the lower end reaching down to the bilge-water.

Murray himself reports the case of a young man near Port Moresby who was unfortunate enough to fall into the river and be snatched at by a crocodile. Only a portion of his body, however, was eaten by the crocodile. The young man's wife and children, accompanied by his father and mother and some close friends, thereupon sat down by the river side and ate the remains of the body. When questioned about their apparently callous act, they answered that they had done what they did "out of affection".

Probably the greatest authority on the tribes of New Guinea was C. G. Seligmann, who has written at great length, and with an immense amount of documentation, about their habits and customs, their religious and magical ceremonials, their tabus and traditions. He states categorically: "In the vast majority of cases of cannibalism in the south-eastern districts, the eating of human flesh was part of the solemn act of revenge, which it was the duty of each community to take on behalf of its own members killed and eaten by other communities with whom it was at enmity."

He does, however, add that in a certain number of cases, which he considers to have been small, human flesh was devoured not specifically as an act of revenge but because it was enjoyed. Complete strangers trespassing over the territory of these tribes were commonly killed and devoured, he says; and adds: "There was, of course, no large or constant supply of food of this kind." This is hardly surprising in view of the notorious customs of the New Guinea tribes!

The two main factors concerned in the cannibalism of south-eastern New Guinea (Seligmann writes) were the duty of taking vengeance for a member of the hamlet-group killed, and the desire for human flesh, for which undoubtedly there was a very strong liking. The individual or individuals eaten in revenge for a comrade who had been eaten by a hostile community had the title *Maia*, or *Maiha*. The usage connected with such warfare undertaken to obtain *Maiha*, and the ceremonial observed at the ensuing cannibal feast, can best be illustrated by taking an actual instance.

It became known at Maivara that a Wagawaga canoe was about to visit Basiliki, so three canoes put off quietly at night and

an ambush was formed behind an island which the Wagawaga
canoe would pass.   The ambush was successful and two prisoners,
a man of the Garuboi clan and a girl of about ten belonging to
another clan, came into the Maivara men's hands.   The prisoners
were bound and flung into one of the Maivara canoes, which then
leisurely started for home.   They took care, however, to pass close
to Wagawaga on their way.

When opposite Wagawaga, the canoes approached to within
two hundred yards of the shore, the men gesticulating and waving
and blowing conch-shells.   Then they halted, and gave the dance
called *Besa*, or *Boriri*, which is used on such occasions.   The captives were made to stand up and were then stripped naked.   The
man's perineal band was waved in the air by the captors, who
yelled the names of the prisoners and detailed how they would be
cooked and eaten.   Then the canoes continued on their way, and
on arrival the man was duly eaten after the usual preliminaries,
though the girl, as was the custom sometimes, was adopted by a
woman of the Maivara tribe.

Seligmann goes on to describe how the Wagawaga menfolk,
wild with anger and frustration, began to prepare a retaliatory
move.   When the time came, they set out, entered the Maivara
River, and about midnight surrounded an isolated hut, and
captured a prisoner.   Once clear of the river and the shore, the
Wagawaga men danced their *Boriri* dance and hurled insults at
the Maivara men who had run out to see what was happening.

Then (he goes on) the canoes returned triumphantly to Wagawaga, where the captive was pitched into shallow water, speared
by as many warriors as could reach him there, and then dragged
ashore.   The greatest care was taken not to kill the captive at this
stage, for it was necessary that he should be more or less severely
wounded by the next-of-kin of the man for whom the revenge was
being taken.   In this instance, the brother of the dead man, who
was not a member of the war party, slashed him across the
shoulder with a tomahawk.   Even now, the victim was not killed;
and if, as rarely happened, he was mortally injured, it was looked
upon as a regrettable mishap.

The next stage was for the widow of the man for whom revenge
was being exacted to blind the *Maiha*.   This she would do by
thrusting pointed sticks into the victim's eyes, taunting him the
while in some such terms as these: "With your eyes you saw my
husband killed; now will your eyes be no more use to you!"
Then the dead man's sister's children spear the victim until he
dies, and his body is then carved up by the men.

Alternatively, he would be dragged to the stone circle of the
clan that was especially reserved for cannibal feasts.   There he

would be enveloped in dry coconut leaves and lashed to a tree, usually a coconut tree, which always stands in the middle of these stone circles. The leaves would then be ignited, and as a rule the victim in due course expired.

Seligmann adds that cases have been known where a prisoner, mutilated and terribly burned by this practice, managed to escape from the tree because the flames happened to burn through the lashings before actually bringing about his death; but this chance was a rare one indeed, for the victim would normally be under close observation by the relatives of the dead man for whom the revenge was being taken, and by those waiting in expectation of the feast to come.

In New Guinea, human flesh was usually boiled, though it was also the practice, if rather less general, to cook it in the native ovens. The penis, which was especially esteemed as food, was usually split and then roasted on hot ashes. The best pieces were the tongue, the hands, feet and *mammae*; the brain, extracted from the *foramen magnum* of the boiled skull, was broken up and considered a very special delicacy. The intestines and solid viscera, as well as the testes and vulva, were also eaten, and there were a few members of the tribes who preferred to eat human flesh raw, though this was much more difficult than eating it when it had been properly cooked.

Human flesh (says Seligmann, as a result of his inquiries among the tribesmen, mainly in south-eastern New Guinea) is stated to resemble pig in flavour, but to make better food, since—although they both taste much alike—the former has the more delicate flavour, as well as the further advantage, claimed for it by everyone who can be persuaded to talk freely on the subject, that it never produces any painful feeling of satiety, or induces vomiting. It has been emphasised by these people that if too much pig flesh were eaten, a man's stomach would swell up and he would be sick; but that human flesh might be eaten until a man found it impossible to swallow any more, without producing these unpleasant symptoms.

Seligmann adds that, throughout his inquiries into this aspect of the subject, he never found anyone to admit that there had been more than the rarest cases of an individual's having reached satiety in this respect.

In cases where two prisoners had been brought back to the village at the same time, it was the practice of these tribes to kill and then roast one of them before the eyes of the other, "so that the second victim could fully appreciate the agony he would suffer when his turn came. A further refinement of barbarism was to thrust splinters of wood into the victim's flesh, then light them and allow them to burn down to the skin. The pith contained in the mid-rib of a coconut-leaf was held," Seligmann reports, "to be particularly suitable food to eat with roasted human flesh. The burned corpse was laid on a pandanus-leaf mat, cut up, and then eaten partly inside and partly beyond the limit of the tribe's stone circle."

There was a much rarer, but still widely prevalent, form of cannibalism in New Guinea. This consisted of the eating of bodies exhumed for the purpose some time after they had been buried. Seligmann admits that he found difficulty in ascertaining these details, but is convinced that the practice was in existence at the turn of the century, at any rate in the region of Milne Bay, which is at the extreme south-easternmost tip of the island.

> The court at Samarai tried a case of desecration of sepulchre, two adult women and a girl—mother and two daughters—being the offenders. The little child of the elder of the two daughters had died, and had been buried in the usual manner. About one day after the burial, the three accused had dug up the body, and eaten it. The woman belonged to a village near the head of Milne Bay. They protested that what they had done had always been, and still remained, a custom of their country. In the light of their statement, the penalty they incurred was only a short term of imprisonment.

It was harder still, Seligmann found, to obtain reliable information on yet another aspect of this, for sorcerers and sorcery were involved here, and it was virtually impossible to get tribesmen to open their mouths on the subject. A certain amount of information, however, was collected:

> That sorcerers made a practice of exhuming and eating corpses seems to indicate that their object was to perform an act of magic. The natives themselves constantly assert that graves of their dead are opened secretly by their local sorcerers.
> Few, if any, of the sorcerers will admit that they carry out this practice with the sole object of obtaining food. In many cases the sorcerers are women. Some women of the tribe, anxious themselves to acquire the status and power of a sorcerer, or a *Parauma*, as the sorcerer is called along the whole coast, indulge

in this practice as the surest means to this desirable end. A girl who was asked, during an official inquiry, about a certain woman regarded by her tribe as a *Parauma*, answered, after a good deal of hesitation and prevarication: "Perhaps—who knows?—she eats a buried body."

The existence of sorcerers, or witches, is confirmed by a missionary, the Rev. W. E. Bromilow, who reported from Dobu, in the south-eastern part of New Guinea. But in his report it is evident that the activities of witches were not so much secretly feared as openly condemned—even by tribes among whom normal cannibalism was practised.

Witches (Bromilow writes) are said to eat the bodies of the dead. We have often heard reports of evil spirits and witches eating dead bodies, but thought them exaggerated. However, there is apparently a clear case on the spot. An old woman died in one of the villages near us, and a week or two afterwards a most horrible report was circulated. The grave of the old woman had been disturbed, and on inquiry it was found that the deceased woman's own sister had taken out the body, and with some of her fellow-witches had partaken of a cannibal feast.

Some of her male relations wished to strangle her right off, and throw her into the sea, but our presence prevented them and she was allowed to go away. She herself denied the story, but when a Government Officer took evidence on the case, he opened the grave and found that the body had in fact been removed. There is certainly real horror at the affair in the minds of many, and as soon as the report began to get about, no one would eat from any pot she had been boiling, and many would not even touch any fruit or other edible she had handled.

A. P. Rice, the American anthropologist who has already been quoted in connection with the cannibalistic practices of the Fijian Islanders, reports one curious custom among the Papuans of which no mention is made by Seligmann:

One of the New Guinea Papuan tribes has the custom of taking out its grandparents, when they have become too old to be of any use to the tribe, and tying each of them loosely in the branches of a tree. The populace will then form a ring round the tree and indulge in an elaborate dance, which has some affinity with the traditional Maypole dance. As they dance, they cry out in chorus a refrain which has a somewhat sinister double-barrelled meaning: "The Fruit is Ripe! The Fruit is Ripe!" Then, having repeated this cry, they close in upon the tree and violently shake its branches, so that the old men and women come hurtling to the ground below, there to be seized and devoured by the younger members of the tribe.

It would seem that, throughout New Guinea, no one would ever eat the flesh of a man he had himself killed, or even of a prisoner he had himself captured. Writing about this very emphatic tabu, and its consequences, Seligmann states:

The actual killer or captor of the man who was to be eaten would go straight to his own hut, and stay there for about a month, living on roast *taro* and hot coconut milk; his wife would continue to share his hut, but must for that period sleep apart from him. He remains thus isolated in his hut because he is afraid of the 'blood' of the dead man, and it is for this reason that he does not join his fellow-warriors in partaking of the flesh. For if he were to do this, he believes, his belly would become 'full of blood', and he would promptly die.

There is, however, something more subtle in all this than the actual blood, though it is in fact connected with blood. He goes in terror not only of the blood, but of the smell, or 'vapour', of the blood. It is as though certain imperceptible qualities emanating from the blood lingered about the scene of the cannibal feast and adhered to a greater or lesser degree to all those who had taken part in it; adhered, what is more, long after all physical traces had been removed. These emanations, or influences, were held to be specially injurious to the provider of the feast. It was to avoid them so far as was possible that the seclusion within the hut lasted a whole month. The provider of the feast—for this same reason—would not take lime from the lime gourd of any member of his tribe or clan who had taken part in the feast.

The homicide's brother would prepare the skull and take it to the platform of the hut. He had the right to wear on the upper arm an armlet which was made of the lower jaw of the *Maiha*. His cervical vertebrae might also be worn, but it had to be attached to the man's back hair, which is usually allowed to grow very long at Wagawaga.

A man or woman killed and eaten otherwise than as payment for the death of a clansman was called *Idaidaga*. A stranger, for example, might be killed and eaten for no other cause than a desire for a favourite food. Whoever actually killed the stranger had to abstain from his flesh, and indeed follow all the rules that applied to the killer of a *Maiha*.

The victim, if he was taken alive, was dragged to his captor's tribe's stone circle, speared—but not mortally wounded—and then roasted and cut up in the usual way. His flesh was distributed by his captor's brother, who called the name of each recipient. All members of the tribe who had attained the age of puberty, whether male or female, were permitted to eat of this flesh, though it appears that the women did not invariably avail themselves of the privilege. There were naturally fewer abstainers among the menfolk, but the old and toothless were forced by circumstances to abstain from the eating of flesh which they had regarded as a delicacy since their earliest manhood. Indeed, at Wagawaga this fact was so clearly recognised that when human flesh—usually in supply inadequate to the demand—was being distributed among the tribe, the names of the aged and the toothless were not even called.

Before leaving New Guinea, among whose numerous tribes the variations of practice and tabu are so many that it seems at times as though there can be no end to them, it is worth seeing what two later travellers, one writing shortly before the First World War, the other writing within the last year or two, have had to say.

H. Wilfred Walker, F.R.G.S., had travelled widely in the South Pacific and was interested in the smaller islands as well as the larger ones. In the early years of this century he joined a punitive expedition led by the Resident Magistrate against the Dobodura Tribe.

We decided (he writes) to rush the village of Kanau, but when we got there we found it deserted. In the centre of the village was a kind of small, raised platform, on which were rows of human skulls and quantities of bones, the remnants of many a gruesome cannibal feast. Many of the skulls were quite fresh, with small bits of meat still sticking to them, but for all that, they had been picked very clean. Every skull had a large hole punched in the side, varying in size but uniform as regards position. The explanation for this we soon learnt from the Notus, and later it was confirmed by our prisoners.

When the Doboduras capture an enemy, they slowly torture him to death, practically eating him alive. When he is almost dead, they made a hole in the side of the head and scoop out his brains with a kind of wooden spoon. These brains, which are eaten warm and fresh, were regarded as a great delicacy. No doubt the Notus recognised some of their relatives amid the ghastly relics. . . .

Walker describes some further aspects of the expedition, in the same laconic style, and then picks up his story with rather more emotion, though his reactions are kept well under control, his effects being gained as often as not by understatement:

We sat talking in subdued tones for some time, expecting every minute to hear the thrilling war-cry of the Doboduras. We

could hear the dismal falsetto howls of the native dogs in the distance, and they were not particularly exhilarating at such a time,
and I more than once mistook them for distant war-cries.

The Papuans do not as a rule torture their prisoners for the
mere idea of torture, though they have often been known to roast
a man alive—for the reason that his meat is supposed to taste
better thus.   I have heard of cases of white men having been
roasted alive, one case being that of the two miners, Campion and
King.   But we had learned that this Dobodura tribe had a system
of torture that was brutal beyond words.

In the first place they always try to wound slightly, and capture
a man alive, so that they can have fresh meat for many days.
They keep their prisoners tied up alive in the huts, and cut out
pieces of their flesh just when they want them; we were told that,
incredible as it may seem, they sometimes manage to keep them
alive for a week or more, and have some preparation which prevents them from bleeding to death.

Monkton advised both Acland and myself to shoot ourselves
with our revolvers if we saw that we were overwhelmed, so as to
escape these terrible tortures, and he assured us that he should
keep the last bullet in his revolver for himself.

The other traveller is a Dane named Jens Bjerre, who wrote
about a New Guinea cannibal tribe in a book published as
recently as 1956.   The tribe, known as the Kukukuku, seem
to have been every bit as savage as the Doboduras of whom
Walker was writing in his report at the end of the punitive
expedition:

When a party of warriors takes an enemy prisoner (Bjerre writes),
either in combat or by abduction, they tie the captive to a thin
tree-trunk and bring him horizontally back to their village.   So
that their prisoner shall not escape, they then break his legs with
a blow of the club, bind him to a tree and adorn him with shells
and feathers in preparation for the forthcoming orgy.   Fresh
vegetables are brought in from the fields and a big hole is dug in
the ground for an oven.   As a rule, the children are allowed to
'play' with the prisoner; that is to say, to use him as a target, and
finally stone him to death.   This process is designed to harden the
children and teach them to kill with rapture.

When the prisoner has been killed, his arms and legs are cut off
with a bamboo knife.   The flesh is then cut up into small pieces,
wrapped in bark and cooked, together with the vegetables, in the
oven in the ground.   Men, women and children all take part in
the ensuing orgy, usually to the accompaniment of dances and
jubilant songs.

Only enemies are eaten.   If the victim is a young, strong

warrior, the muscular parts of his body are given to the village boys, so that they can absorb the dead man's power and valour.

It will be noticed that Jens Bjerre writes in the present tense: as if he had witnessed these things himself. This is unlikely, to say the least; for in New Guinea it seems that these cannibal practices were well on the way out by the turn of the century. Pockets of resistance, so to speak, will certainly have survived until very much more recently; and possibly survive still in the remote and unmapped hinterland of New Guinea. The island lies close enough to the Equator (the line of latitude on which so many cannibal-infested territories seem to have survived longer than elsewhere) to be suspect still; but with the rapid increase in ease of communication, particularly through aerial survey, it seems unlikely that even these hypothetical pockets of resistance can survive much longer.

CHAPTER TEN

CANNIBAL PRACTICES AMONG THE MELANESIANS

LYING SOME five hundred miles off the north-east coast of New Guinea, and stretching south-eastwards for some two thousand miles, in the direction of the North Island of New Zealand, there is a chain of large and small islands, separated from one another often by only narrow channels, and occupied by Melanesians of whom, in the case of the New Hebrideans at any rate, an encyclopaedia published in 1951 is able to state categorically: "They are still cannibals."

The islands consist of a number of large groups, such as those constituting New Britain, New Ireland, the Solomons, the New Hebrides and New Caledonia. They are tropical in their vegetation, producing in many cases coffee and cocoa, cotton and copra; many of them are volcanic. Though they are, geographically, South Sea Islands, with the inevitable associations of such islands, they are in many ways exceptionally forbidding territory. Not least because of their tradition of cannibalism and brutality to travellers and traders, their sheer intractability in the face of western influence, their rigid adherence to their old ways of life, however heavy the pressure may be that is brought to bear on them. Sandwiched between New Guinea, with its formidable record of man-eating, and the Fiji Islands with a record hardly less formidable, it is perhaps hardly surprising that they should stick so tenaciously to tradition.

The well-known traveller, Martin Johnson, was in the New Hebrides immediately before, and perhaps actually during, the First World War. He writes, as so many travellers in these parts have done, rather as if their senses have been dulled by what they saw. Nor can they be entirely blamed for this, since familiarity with conditions, however startling and dangerous they may have seemed at first impact, must breed, if not contempt at least comfortable acceptance!

We walked (he writes) for about three hours without seeing any signs of a village. Then we heard, faint in the distance, the sound of a tom-tom. Soon we were within hearing of a chanted song. We advanced with caution, until we reached the edge of a village clearing. From behind a clump of bushes we could watch the natives who danced there. The dance was just the ordinary native hay-foot, straw-foot, around the devil-devils in the centre of the clearing; now slow, now gradually increasing in tempo till it was a run.

What interested me was the feast that was in preparation. On a long stick, over the fire, were a dozen pieces of meat. More meat was grilling on the embers of another fire. On leaves near by were the entrails of the animal that was cooking. I do not know what it was that made us suspect the nature of this meat. It certainly was not much different in appearance from pork. But some sixth sense whispered to me that it was *not* pork.

For an hour we watched, and took long-range photographs. The dance continued monotonously. The meat sizzled slowly over the fire—and nothing happened. Then I gave one of the Tongoa boys a radium flare and told him to go into the clearing, drop the flare into the fire, and run to one side, out of the picture. He did as I asked him. The natives stopped dancing, and watched him as he approached. He threw the flare into the fire, and jumped aside.

As they stooped down close to the flames to see what he had thrown there, the flare took fire, and sent its blinding white light into their faces. With a yell, they sprang back, and ran in terror directly towards us. Then they turned and ran in the opposite direction. The half-minute flare burned out; so they grabbed the meat from the fire and carried it away with them into the bush.

My boys sprang into the clearing. I, with my camera on my shoulder, was just behind them. When I came up to them, they were standing by the fire, looking at the only remnant of the feast that was left on the embers. It was a charred human head, with rolled leaves plugging the eye-sockets! I had proved what I had set out to prove: that cannibalism is still practised in the South Seas. I was so happy that I yelled!

After photographing the evidence, I wrapped the head carefully in leaves, to take away with me. We picked the fire over, but could find no other remainder of the gruesome feast. In one of the huts, however, we discovered a quantity of human hair, laid out on a green leaf, to be made into ornaments. Some of the cannibals returned and, from a distance, watched as we searched their huts. I then took their pictures. They grinned into the camera, as innocent as children. Later, we invited them to take a meal with us. They ate our trade salmon and biscuits with gusto and smacked their lips over the coffee; but their favourite dish of 'long pig' was not on the bill of fare!

More thoughtful by far than Martin Johnson's is a report by a missionary in the New Hebrides, the Rev. Oscar Michelsen. He is less concerned to get photographs, and prove to his own satisfaction the existence of a deplorable custom among the New Hebrideans, than to express his despair at the infinitesimally slow progress his mission seems to be making. Martin Johnson was writing of the Malekula region; Michelsen is writing of experiences on the cluster of tiny islands that cling to the edge of the larger ones.

One day when I was on Nguna (he writes) news arrived of a fearful massacre having been committed on the island of Efate, the other side of Nguna Bay. Another missionary, Mr Milne, and I repaired to the spot and ascertained the facts.

A number of natives from the island of Makura had arrived in Efate, just opposite Nguna, to dig some *taumako*, a vegetable similar in appearance to the potato. The chief who instigated and led in the massacre had been among Europeans, in Queensland and elsewhere, for thirteen years, and could speak English well. He denied having killed anyone; but while the words were in his mouth, evidences of his guilt were forthcoming. In the surf on the beach lay the trunk of a human body; in a canoe alongside was the head; and the arms and legs were roasting on a fire in a neighbouring village.

Confronted with proofs of his crime, the brutal fellow readily excused himself. The things said by missionaries, he agreed willingly enough, were quite right and good for the white man; but they *do not suit the black man*.

Seeing that we could accomplish nothing, we left for the mission station in the boat which had conveyed us across the bay. When we were a short distance out from land, we saw a procession going along the beach. The body of a man, lashed to a pole, was being carried by two persons. A conch-shell was blown, and some young men went in front, swinging spears over their heads. This was in bravado of the act of murder. Others followed, filled with the same evil spirit. When the true facts came to light, our worst fears were realised: for several persons had been killed, and their bodies had been distributed as presents to friends among the tribe.

Michelsen has already made the point that, according to his observations and such research as he had been able to make in the district with which he was primarily concerned, though "the depraved appetite of fallen man, in his lowest estate (as he puts it) is gratified by the taste of human flesh", there is another, and more positive motive. This is "a wish to show how entirely they can vanquish their enemies: they make food of them! Malakaleo, a chief at first bitterly opposed to the Gospel, answered a message from his enemies with the threat: 'We will eat you!'" He ends his note on the massacre on Efate with a paragraph illustrating the connection between the massacre and his reference to the motive of revenge coupled with absolute destruction:

> The crime was excused by the statement that, some time previously, a number of natives of Epi, working for a planter on Efate, had stolen his boat in order to make their way home. While passing Makura, they were induced by the natives to go ashore—and forthwith were murdered and eaten. The Chief of Makura, on whose order this horrid deed was committed, was the very man whose mutilated body we had found in the surf at Efate. Thus the act was an act of revenge.

A. P. Rice, referring specifically to the natives of the New Hebrides, states that the body of killed or captured enemies were dressed for the ovens with the least possible delay after they were brought in to the villages, and served with yams by way of embellishment. The blacker the flesh, he was informed, the more palatable it is held to be by the cannibals, and certainly black flesh was infinitely preferred by them to that of white men. Among these natives, as among others already considered, the term 'fish' is habitually used to describe a human body brought in for consumption.

Opinion seems to vary in regard to the Solomon Islands. R. H. Codrington, writing at the turn of the century, actually states that the practice of cannibalism has "recently extended itself" there. The older natives, he says, told him that human flesh never used to be eaten except in the form of a sacrifice, and that even as a sacrificial ceremony this was merely something introduced "from islands to the west"—presumably New Guinea. Native tribes occupying the coast were still relatively free from the practice, but most of them stated that, far inland, cannibalism would be found.

It was, Codrington declared, a regrettable fact that it was the *young* Solomon Islanders, rather than the old, who had become addicted to cannibalism in recent years. They habitually feasted on the bodies of men slain in battle, which, they said, was a practice of the natives of the island of San

Cristoval. There, they assured Codrington, the tribesmen habitually killed for the sole purpose of obtaining human flesh for consumption; and they killed in sufficient quantities to be able to sell the flesh among other tribes.

On Leper's Island, it appeared, human flesh is still devoured. But there the brave enemy is not devoured; rather it is the murderer, or someone who has brought hatred down upon him among his fellow tribesmen or neighbouring tribesmen. He is eaten in anger and scorn, after being cooked like a pig, and the men, women and older boys eat of his flesh—as a gesture, rather than to satisfy mere appetite.

A. I. Hopkins, however, writing some thirty years later than Codrington, after spending a quarter of a century in the region, says: "The practice of cannibalism is virtually extinct. But there are plenty of old men still alive who have occasionally eaten human flesh, though very few—if any—youths. It is not a thing the average native cares to talk much about, or is now proud of, or attempts ever to justify." The 'old men' Hopkins refers to may of course be the 'young men' of Codrington's report some years earlier.

But Hopkins challenges Codrington's statement by observing that it was the Spaniards who first viewed cannibalism in the Solomons with horror. If this is indeed the fact, then the practice must have been established for a very long time indeed. "One of the Spaniards' first experiences," he says, "was the offer of a man's leg in sign of friendship, and their rejection of it with gestures of loathing was to the natives a declaration of hostility and a spurning of their proffered peace-offering."

The bush folk in the larger islands, such as Mala, Guadalcanal and San Cristoval, Hopkins continues, were cannibals, though in Bugotu and Gela they were not. Victims were sometimes kept alive in the villages, ready to be killed and cooked when a festive occasion occurred. He adds:

Men have told me how, as children, they were given bits from the feast; sometimes, if they were reluctant and likely to refuse, they were told that it was pig's flesh that they were being offered. Children were given such morsels that they might get some portion of the personal qualities of the victim—courage, strength, swiftness, or whatever it might be. Also, they thus shared in the *mana* of the victim's tribe, and in the tribal sacrifice were thus pleasing to their spirits.

In Mala, the coast people were never cannibals, so they say, and probably truly; though there may have been rare exceptions. But in the bush it was a not uncommon practice up to recent years. In 1905 or 1906 I came into close contact with a village where they had very recently eaten two men killed in a fight. A few years later, two women were captured and eaten near the Government Station. It was merely, I was told, as an act of defiance and a gesture of contempt on the part of some bush-rangers 'wanted' by the Government.

Hopkins states that the tribe from which a member had been captured, or killed, and then devoured, lost all prestige. If the man was devoured, so also was his *mana*, which was inseparable in thought from the *mana* of the whole tribe. Thus their virtue was gone. "The best thing they could do, then," Hopkins ends, "was to break up and disperse and lose themselves among friendly and allied tribes."

A woman missionary, Florence Coombe, writing of the same regions as Hopkins, and not many years earlier, mentions a priest who was working in San Cristoval and came upon a party of natives in the act of cooking an enemy. He wrote to her:

My sense of disgust and indignation was great; one felt inclined to upset the oven and its contents, but the thought occurred that he who did so would in all probability be the oven's next occupant. They seemed to have no idea then of the white man's horror, continuing to laugh and joke about their victim's last struggles, and sticking his finger-joints in their hair among their combs.

Florence Coombe goes on to remind us of "still another idea struggling thus repulsively—yet surely to our sight with a wonderful pathos—to realise itself":

A powerful chief who has long been dreaded and admired is slain in battle, and the yearning of all the men who were his enemies to obtain a portion of his spirit—that *mana* which is the secret of his valour and success—develops into an almost religious ceremony. A mouthful of the brave man's flesh and blood is thought to convey his coveted power.

It is typical of Florence Coombe's thoughtful and sometimes inspired writing on this sordid subject that she can end her observations thus: "In this act of cannibalism we seem to detect the germ of a Divine Truth."

Desire for the *mana*, and fear of the *mana*, are both found among these islands.   The Rev. George Brown, a missionary among the Melanesians, observed a curious custom which he reported back to his headquarters:

> A man who is cutting up a body will sometimes tie something over his mouth and nose during the operation in order to keep the spirit of the dead man from entering into him.   For the same reason, when a body is being eaten, the doors of the huts are shut, and afterwards the people all shout, blow horns, shake spears, etc., to frighten away the ghost of the man they have eaten.
>
> In the Shortlands group of the Solomon Islands there is a small, rocky islet in the port to which the natives take any person they may capture, to kill him there.   They do not like to kill anyone in the village, for fear of the spirit of the dead man making trouble afterwards.

Brown speculated much about the various motives underlying the cannibalism to be observed among these Melanesian islands. He came to the conclusion that, in the main, cannibalism there was "generally a semi-sacred rite, and in most cases practised to discharge an obligation to the spirits of the dead".   Very often, of course, this was inextricably associated with the motive of revenge.   The family of a murdered man will obtain a portion of flesh from a member of the tribe to which the murder belonged.   They return with the flesh, cut it into portions and distribute them among the family and close relatives of the murdered man.   At a given signal they devour these portions of flesh while gathered in the man's hut, and a special portion of the flesh is offered ceremonially on a kind of altar built on a dead tree, called the *ragau*, which has been brought to the hut —this being an offer to the spirit of the murdered man.

> Thus (says Brown) they have now discharged all obligations to the spirit of the murdered man.   They have provided him with food, finishing up by giving him a portion of flesh from a man of the village from which the slayer came.   Now they want to get rid of him.   They therefore pull up the *ragau* and ceremonially throw it away in the direction of the village from which the murderer came; after this, they let the murdered man's hut collapse in ruins.

Brown states that there is always a clear distinction made, among these people, between a man murdered or killed in battle, and a man who has died from any other cause.   But there is no doubt in his mind that the principal reason for cannibalism among the tribes with whom he had contact was that of obligation towards a dead relative. His opinion was confirmed for him in a conversation he reports between himself and a tribesman, who spoke as follows: "Suppose my brother is killed by Outam (a neighbouring tribe): by and by I hear of some Outam man killed by another tribe. I go and buy a piece of the body, and place it in my dead brother's house as an offering to him." He adds that in some parts of the islands a man will not bathe or wash until his revenge is completely satisfied. The Kababaia, for instance, ate the hair, the intestines, and even the excrement, of a man from a village who had killed some of their relatives.

In general, he adds, where cannibalism is fully recognised, all parts of the victim's body would be eaten. . . .

> But the hands and breasts of women were esteemed the choice parts. Some of the bones were kept to be used as weights on the ends of spears. Skulls were put on a dead branch of a tree and placed either on the beach or near the hut of the person who had killed the former owners. On the piece of land on which I lived in Port Hunter there were seven of these ghastly objects at a short distance from my house. I wanted to get rid of them, but judged it expedient to leave them alone, for fear the people might be angry if I took them down, and so replace them by putting my own skull in their place.

It is perhaps a testimony (if not a tribute) to the implacability of these islanders, and their reluctance to forgo their traditional practices, that the Rev. George Brown, D.D., Melanesian missionary, like the unnamed priest in San Cristoval whose comment was quoted by Florence Coombe, is less willing to take risks than, say, some of the courageous missionaries quoted in connection with the Fijian Islanders!

A. P. Rice gives some grim details about cannibalistic practices in the most south-easterly of this whole long necklace of islands constituting Melanesia, the one that approaches most nearly to the North Island of New Zealand. This is New Caledonia.

> Here (he writes) the women of the tribes used to pick out the best-covered corpses on the field of battle and dress them for the ovens while the warriors were still engaged in killing others. Heated stones were thrown into makeshift ovens on the very fringe of the

battlefield so that there need be no delay in feasting once the victory was won. . . .

Incidentally, he does not explain what happened when, as must often have been the case, the tide of battle turned. Did the ultimate victors utilise the ovens which the women of the defeated side had so optimistically prepared, and roast in them the bodies of the men who had expected to triumph over them? If so, it was a nice example of 'the biter bit'.

In New Caledonia (Rice continues) it was the hands that were considered the choicest portions, and these by prescriptive right became the portion of the tribal priests. These would follow the warriors, and the women of the warring tribe, and take up positions in the rear of the battle. So important was it to them that they, and they alone, should be given the hands of the enemies slain in battle that they would actually fast rather than accept anything inferior.

On this island, too, there was no prohibition against women partaking of human flesh. Nor was there any tabu against the eating of the corpse of a chief. On the other hand, if the corpse of a chief was on offer, it was obligatory that every man, woman and even small child must receive at least a mouthful. Another important tabu on this island concerned the corpses of women. If by any chance the body of a woman happened to be included in the feast, then however far demand exceeded supply, the torso must be cast away and only the arms and legs divided into portions.

Possibly because the cluster of islands known as New Ireland happens to be so near to New Guinea, where cannibalism lingered so long, and took so many horrible forms, the few authenticated records which we possess of the practice there make grisly reading.

Hugh Hastings Romilly, Deputy Commissioner for the Western Pacific and Acting Special Commissioner for New Guinea itself, made an official report to his Government which makes scarifying reading, and the only consolation to be set against it is the fact that the report was published as long ago as 1866. However, in view of what has been written about adjacent and neighbouring islands to the east and south-east of New Guinea, it is perhaps too much to hope that the practice died out there any sooner than it did elsewhere; if as soon.

On my arrival in New Ireland (he writes) there was a great sound of merry-making and laughter. On the branches of a big tree in the centre of the clear space were six corpses, hanging by their necks, their toes just touching the ground. After a long pull at my flask, I sat down, with my back to the tree, and watched the women.

They had made fires and were now boiling large pots of water. As soon as the water boiled, it was ladled out in coconut-shells and poured over the bodies one by one, after which they were carefully scraped with bamboo knives. This was simply the process of scalding and scraping that every dead pig goes through after it has been killed. The hair of the head was carefully cut off and preserved, to adorn some future head-dress.

The women all this time were laughing and joking, discussing the points of each man. The whole thing was done in the most matter-of-fact way possible. When the bodies had been thoroughly scraped, nothing more was done until the return of the men of the village.

Then the business of the evening commenced. A mat of plaited palm-leaves was laid down, and one of the bodies was cut down from the tree. A very old man, apparently the 'father' of the tribe, advanced into the centre of the crowd, where an open space had been left to give him room to conduct his operations. He had five or six bamboo knives in his hand, and with his thumbnail he was stripping the fibres off their edges, leaving them as sharp as razors.

The body was then placed on the mat, and 'cleaned'—some of the more perishable parts being thrown to the women as one throws scraps to the dogs. These were barely warmed at the fire before they were devoured. The head was then cut off and carefully placed on one side, on a leaf.

In due course all six bodies were similarly prepared, and cut up into very small pieces. Each piece was carefully wrapped in a stout leaf and bound up tightly with sinnet. The thigh and shin-bones, however, were preserved intact. They are used for making handles for spears.

When all six bodies had been cut up, the pile of little parcels wrapped in green leaves had assumed considerable dimensions. Then, the ovens were opened. The flesh was divided into as many parts as there were ovens, a little pile was put into each oven and covered over with hot stones. The bones and other parts which were not wanted were wrapped in mats and carried into the bush to be buried.

The flesh in the ovens had to be cooked for three days, or till the tough leaves in which it was wrapped were nearly consumed. When taken out of the ovens, the method of eating it is as follows: the head of the eater is thrown back, somewhat after the fashion of an Italian eating macaroni; the leaf is opened at one end and the contents are then pressed into the mouth till the last are finished.

As my interpreter remarked to me: "They cookum that fellow

three day. By-um-by cookum he finish, that fellow all same grease!"

Romilly adds that for some days afterwards, when the very last scraps of human flesh have been finished, members of the tribe refrain from washing so as to preserve as long as possible the memory of their feast.

It is perhaps not surprising, in view of the general attitude towards the killing and eating of their fellows that prevails almost throughout Melanesia, that myth and legend are rare. It is when the devouring of a human being is closely identified with sacrifice either to a tribal god or to a god of sun and rain that the legends are begotten and elaborated with the passing of time. This has been seen among the Aztecs and among the Kwakiutl Indians, to mention only two peoples out of many.

But legend is not entirely absent in Melanesia, even though the general motive for killing and feasting on human flesh is either the lust for succulent meat or a desire to obtain revenge on some other party. The island of San Cristoval—to which so many other islanders point as the *fons et origo* of their own cannibalistic practices—has a typical example of such a myth: a myth which has the 'fairy-tale' quality found throughout Grimm, Perrault and Hans Andersen, in which the youngest of a family of brothers always comes out best in the end. And, characteristically, the myth involves the cooking of flesh.

In olden times (runs the legend) there was a family of brothers who lived together on San Cristoval. The name of the eldest of these brothers was Warohunugaraiia. A day came when the brothers decided to build a canoe-house, and while they were at work, a new brother was born in the family, and named Warohunugamwanehaora. Immediately he was born he grew up, and, with his umbilical cord still unsevered, but coiled round and round his neck, went off to see what his elder brothers were doing.

His elder brothers were not at all pleased at the advent of their new brother, and bade him pack off and leave them alone. They were all the more resentful of him when they found that, even though he was younger by far than either of them, he could do all that they could do, and do it with much greater ease and much better altogether.

They began therefore to hate him, and started thinking of

ways in which they might rid themselves of him. First they dug a deep post-hole and told him to jump down into it and see what was there. When he did so, they dropped a huge hut-post down on top of him, and packed it well with earth and stones—only to find when they relaxed from their labours that their young brother was sitting perched on the very top of the pole, grinning down at them.

They tried to force him to enter the open jaws of a giant clam, but their young brother easily tricked them, and actually made use of the giant clam as a canoe that got him back to his brothers' canoe-house before they arrived themselves. They forced him to jump on to the back of a man-eating fish, telling him that it was a reef; the dreaded *ulahu* swallowed him whole, but their clever brother carved his way out and escaped. They made him climb a great tree, and by some magic of their own made the tree grow ever taller and taller as their young brother clambered down it. But he triumphed over them by forcing the tree to bend its topmost branch over until it almost touched the ground, when he could jump off with ease.

Finally (the legend runs) the brothers got together and decided on a plan which they knew would put an end to him once and for all. "We will make a big oven, and throw him into it, and then cook him—and *eat him*," they said.

They made him help to dig the oven, made him collect masses of firewood and pile it on until the fire was very very hot. They watched to see that the stones in the bottom of the oven were red-hot. Then they told their brother to place leaves at the bottom. And as soon as he began to do this, they picked him up and threw him on to the leaves, which already were flaming high from the heat of the red-hot stones. Hastily they threw more stones down on top of their brother, every one of them hotter than the last, until he was quite covered by them. Then they sat back, laughing and watching the steam rise between the cracks in the great heap of red-hot stones, and talked gaily about the feast that was preparing for them down in the bottom of the oven.

Presently they heard something go 'Crack!' "That's his eye," said one brother, and rubbed his hands in anticipation. Then there was another 'Crack!' "That's his other eye!" said the brother. "He must be very nearly cooked by now."

"But let us make quite sure," said the other. "Not till we touch the stones and find that they are quite cold to our hands shall we know that our brother is cooked and ready for us to eat him."

At last they felt that the time had come for them to open up the oven. When they did so, they found that the heat had been so fierce that even the stones themselves had changed their shape and were quite soft. But even as they removed the last of the stones from the very bottom of the oven, a voice close behind them said: "Am I quite cooked, dear brothers?"—and there was their youngest brother sitting on the stump of a tree watching them, and his umbilical cord was still coiled three times round his neck.

Then their youngest brother got up from the tree-stump and came over to where Warohunugaraiia and his brother were standing on the edge of the oven, for by now he had begun to be annoyed at their continued efforts to get rid of him, especially the last one. "You do nothing but try to harm me, Brother," he said, "whereas I have done nothing to harm you. But now it is my turn at last."

Then he heated a very small oven, and took only a very small bundle of firewood, and heated it no more than to a gentle heat. He then said to his eldest brother: "Lie down in the oven, Brother," and his brother, mocking him, did so.

Then Warohunugamwanehaora swiftly piled the heated stones upon his eldest brother, and tied them together with his umbilical cord in a knot that no one could possibly unloose. After that, he sat with his second brother, and waited and watched for a little while, for just three days, before taking away the stones. And there lay Warohunugaraiia, cooked exactly as meat should be cooked, neither too much nor too little. And Warohunugamwanehaora and his second brother together feasted upon him, leaving not one morsel of flesh however small upon his bones.

So runs the legend of the three brothers of San Cristoval, cited by the islanders to explain—if not to justify—their addiction to the practice of cannibalism: what was instilled into them by their ancestors, they maintain, is a custom that they do right to follow.

CHAPTER ELEVEN

CANNIBAL PRACTICES AMONG THE POLYNESIANS

POLYNESIA—THE 'Many Islands'—in general seems to have been less riddled by cannibalism than the islands large and small lying to the west of the International Date Line. Samoa, Tonga (or the Friendly Islands), the Marquesas, the Society Islands, to mention only the main groups that lie south of the Equator in this vast expanse of the Pacific Ocean that separates Chile and Peru in the east from Australia in the west, all show signs and symptoms of the past existence of the practice, but in the main it certainly began to die out among those islands long before the process began in Melanesia.

The Samoans, in defence of the existence of the practice in the past, tell the legend which, like similar legends 'justifying' the practice among other tribes, involves a mythical being whose influence was maintained down the generations.

In their case it was a mythical cannibal deity somewhat reminiscent of the Kwakiutl Indians' Baxbakualanuxsiwae. This cannibal's name was Maniloa, and he dwelt in a deep ravine through which travellers had to pass between settlement and settlement. He had built a spidery bridge of plaited lianas across the ravine at the very threshold of his lair. Every time a traveller reached the centre of the bridge, Maniloa would emerge from hiding, give a mighty wrench to the lianas that composed the bridge, and the luckless traveller would be cata-pulted through the air, to drop on the cannibal's doorstep. So great was the power of Maniloa's roaring voice which accom-panied his seizing of the bridge, say the Samoans, that waterfalls leapt from the mountainsides and trees were uprooted.

The cannibal devoured his victims whole, without waiting to chop them up, and after a time the Samoans gathered together and tracked him to his lair, by-passing the spidery bridge and descending upon him from the mountainside. By setting upon him while he slept, they succeeded in killing him. But—they add in explanation of the practice of eating human flesh which they admit survived until comparatively recently—in doing so, the giant cannibal's spirit entered into them, and for ever afterwards they, like him, killed human beings and made banquets of their flesh.

The Rev. George Brown came across a variant of the myth. The Samoans told him that there had been an old devil named Tupuivao who lived at Apolima. His custom was to string a piece of sinnet across a track that passed near his cave, and to tie one end of the sinnet to his big toe. As soon as he was awakened from sleep or rest by a jerk at his toe, he knew that a traveller had passed that way. He immediately rushed out and clubbed the traveller to death and ate him whole. Brown adds that this legend, in addition to 'justifying' the tradition of cannibalism in Samoa, is the origin of a popular Samoan saying applied to anyone who has just escaped danger by a narrow margin: '*Faafetai ua to i tua apolima*'.

Brown refers to the Samoans as a 'superior' race, and indeed there is much evidence that this was true. He found no evidence that the Samoans ate human flesh, as the Fijians did, for the sheer gratification of appetite. On the other hand, he found little or no evidence that cannibalism among the Samoans was part of a sacrificial ceremony. Human flesh was eaten during periods of famine, and Brown mentions one such period in the second half of the nineteenth century, when strangers were killed and eaten to stave off hunger.

But there is a relic of the practice still to be seen, Brown says:

When a group of Samoans went to beg pardon for any offence, they bowed down in front of the offended chief's house, and each man held in his hand a small bundle of firewood, some leaves, stones, and earth. These were symbolic of the deepest humiliation, and meant: "Here we are, the people who have so deeply sinned. And here are the stones, the firewood and leaves and earth to make the oven in which you can cook us, and eat us, if it be your will." In most cases the offended chief would come out of his house with a fine mat in his hand, which he would give to the suppliants, 'to cover their disgrace'.

Brown adds that if proof is needed that cannibalism was regularly practised in Samoa, it lies in the fact that the Samoan language has a word for it: *faiaso*. They say that this was the name of a famous chieftain among them who claimed to have devoured the most desirable portions of a human being every day of his adult life. Parallel evidence, he says, lies in the fact that there is the widespread custom of using terms of abuse mentioning some parts of the human body—with the stated wish that someone might come along and devour them. "Sometimes, too," he adds, "to show their satisfaction at a victory over a deceased foe, his eye or tongue was taken out and placed in readiness on a bread-fruit leaf used as a plate."

A. P. Rice states emphatically that cannibalism in Samoa never reached the depths of depravity which it held in the Fiji Islands. Human flesh was eaten by way of revenge. He quotes a statement by someone who was acquainted with Samoa a hundred years before, to the effect that cannibalism there was restricted to the bodies of men slain in battle, and the only exceptions were in times of severe famine. He admitted, however, that when such times came along, Samoan chiefs deliberately went to war, tribe against tribe, to procure what they considered to be 'legitimate' food. It was considered a deep disgrace when a human being was captured and killed for consumption, and tribes were careful to bury the bones of their own dead in pits beneath the floors of their huts—for even to have the bones stolen by another tribe would bring disgrace that could hardly be lived down.

The Tonga Islands, though they are still nearer to Fiji than Samoa, and might therefore be expected to have come under Fijian influence, are generally reported to have been almost entirely clear of cannibalism. Captain Cook, during his second and greatest voyage, which began in 1772 and ended three years later after his discovery of the Melanesian islands of New Caledonia, declared that cannibalism was unknown there, except in cases of acute famine. It was he who gave them the name, the Friendly Isles. The story is told that when, after a skirmish, a party of Tongan warriors returned with some prisoners, and cooked and ate portions of their bodies, as they had heard that other tribes were accustomed to do, the remainder of their tribe boycotted them.

Some later voyagers stated that a cult of cannibalism had recently begun to show itself—among the younger warriors only, however.   They admitted, when pressed, that they had been incited to do this by what the Fijians did.   They declared that by eating human flesh they were asserting their manliness and giving strength to their fighting qualities.

When the Tongans did eat human flesh, they were careful to cleanse and purify it by washing it in the sea; the bodies were disembowelled before being spitted and roasted over fires. Alternatively, the bodies were cut up into small portions, wrapped in plantain-leaves and baked or roasted on hot stones.

There is an interesting eye-witness account of cannibalism in the Tonga Islands which was reported by one William Mariner to a doctor named John Martin.   It is interesting not only because of its vivid detail, but because it bears out what has been said about the instinctive reluctance of the Tongans to indulge in the eating of human flesh until the Fiji Islanders brought their powerful influence to bear on them.   Martin was a chance-met acquaintance of Mariner, a man who himself had lived on the various Tonga Isles for many years.

The doctor states emphatically that the Tongans ought not to be considered essentially as cannibals—in spite of Mariner's account of a skirmish and its grisly results.   "Far from its being a general practice," he says, "when some tribesmen have returned from a foray, and it is known to others in their village that they have indulged in such inhuman practices, most persons who know of it, particularly the women, avoid them. They call out to them: '*Ia-whe moe ky-tangata!*'   This means: 'Keep off!   You are eaters of human flesh!'"

William Mariner, whose story Martin quotes, became involved in inter-tribal skirmishing some time in the early nineteenth century, perhaps fifty years after Captain Cook's visit.   It is very clear from what he has to say that whether or not cannibalism existed in Cook's day, it did exist in Mariner's.

He was with one of the Tongan tribes, and reports that the warriors kept on falling into cleverly concealed pits, called *lovosas*, at the bottom of which sharpened bamboo stakes were set.   Mariner himself fell into one of these pits, and was rescued in the nick of time by the warriors nearest to hand. . . .

While this was going forward, a Hapai chief, at some distance from his friends, met another Tongan chief under the same circumstances. They immediately engaged with their clubs. One, however, being soon disarmed, and the other having broken his club, they fought with their fists; till at last, so weak that they could not strike, they grappled with each other and fell to the ground. The Tonga chief, incapable of injuring his antagonist in any other way, got his fingers into his mouth, but the other gnawed them terribly.

The Hapai men returned with about fifteen prisoners. Some of the younger chiefs, *who had contracted the Fiji habits,* proposed to kill the prisoners and then roast and eat them. The proposal was readily agreed to: by some because they like this sort of diet, by others because they wanted to try it, thinking it manly and warlike to do so.

Some of the prisoners were soon dispatched. Their flesh was cut up into small portions, washed with sea-water, wrapped up in plantain-leaves, and roasted under hot stones. Two or three of them were also baked whole, the same as a pig.

The carcass was rubbed over with the juicy substance of the banana-tree, after which it was thrown for a few minutes on the fire. Then, when it was warm, it was scraped with mussel-shells or knives, and then washed. It was next laid on its back, when the cook cut open the throat and drew forth the windpipe and gullet, passed a skewer behind them, and tied a string tight round the latter, afterwards to be divided.

He then cut a circular portion from the belly, from four to six inches in diameter, and drew forth the entrails, separating the attachments either by force or by the use of bamboo. The diaphragm was then divided, and the gullet, windpipe, contents of the chest, stomach and liver, were all drawn away together, along with his bowels. From these, the liver was separated, to be baked with the carcass; the remainder was washed and cooked over hot embers, to be shared out and eaten in the meantime.

The whole inside of the carcass was next filled with hot stones, each wrapped in bread-fruit leaves, and all the apertures were closed up quickly, with plugs of leaves. The carcass was then laid, with the belly downwards, in a hole in the ground lined with hot stones, a fire having previously been made there for that purpose, but prevented from touching them by small branches of the bread-fruit tree. A few other branches were then laid across the back of the carcass, and plenty of banana-leaves strewn, or rather heaped, over the whole; upon which, again, a mound of earth was raised so that no steam could escape. The liver, as aforementioned, was first placed beside the carcass, and sometimes yams also. By these means, the carcass could very well be cooked in about half an hour.

Martin, it must be remembered, was a doctor; this may perhaps account for the loving detail he includes about the cutting-up and organising of the carcass; the process of cooking which he describes is obviously based on the same principle as our modern pressure-cookers, and it will be noticed that the carcass is ready for distribution within half an hour. This contrasts strongly with the practice in New Ireland described by Romilly, where the period of cooking lasted for three days.

Martin's story comes shortly to an end:

> A few days now elapsed without any signs of the canoes from Hapai (Mariner had told him), and the distress of those who did not choose to eat human flesh was very great. Mr Mariner had been two days and a half without eating anything, when, passing by a hut where they were cooking something, he walked in, with the pleasing thought of getting something that his stomach would bear, even if it were only a piece of rat.
>
> On inquiry, he was told that they had got some *pork*, and a man offered him a piece of liver, which he eagerly accepted. He was raising it to his mouth when he saw by the smile on the countenance of the man that it was *human* liver. Overcome by disgust, he threw it into the man's face, who only laughed and asked him if it was not better to eat good meat than die of hunger. . . .

The Marquesas, a group of South Pacific islands belonging to the French, and a long way to the north-east of the main Polynesian groups, had a bad reputation for cannibalism. Hermann Melville, author of *Moby Dick*, was a captive on the islands for several months in the middle of the last century. He states that it was quite evident that the Marquesan tribesmen knew that cannibalism was severely frowned upon by white men, and would go to some lengths to conceal their practices, rather than come into open conflict with them. But they had no intention of giving up those practices for all that.

During his enforced sojourn there, Melville one day saw the return of a war party, who brought home with them a considerable number of prisoners. Celebration of the victory, he says, began almost immediately; but he himself, though he says that otherwise he was being leniently treated, was kept rigorously away from the place where the ceremony was being prepared. He knew, however, from the sound and rhythm of the tribal drum-beating, what was afoot. It was, he reports, a very special feast, at which only tribal chiefs and priests were present.

On the day following the feast he found himself once more

free to wander about as he chose. He went in the direction from which the drum-beating had seemed to come to him. And there, on the unmistakable scene of the orgy, he saw a large wooden vessel that looked as much as anything like an upturned canoe. Peering beneath it, stealthily, he saw heaped together what he describes as a tangle of fresh human bones.

It was (says the anthropologist, A. P. Rice) considered a great triumph among the Marquesans to eat the body of a dead man. They treated their captives with very great cruelty. They broke their legs to prevent them from attempting to escape before being eaten, but kept them alive so that they could brood over their impending fate.

Their arms were broken so that they could not retaliate in any way against their maltreatment. The Marquesans threw them on the ground and leaped on their chests so that their ribs were broken and pierced their lungs, so that they could not even voice their protests against the cruelty to which they were submitted. Rough poles were thrust up through the natural orifices of their bodies and slowly turned in their intestines. Finally, when the hour had come for them to be prepared for the feast, they were spitted on long poles that entered between their legs and emerged from their mouths, and dragged thus at the stern of the war canoes to the place where the feast was to be held.

With this tribe, as with many others, the bodies of women were in great demand. Very often a man who was condemned to be killed and eaten could be visited by his relatives, always naked and painted black. There are records of cases where the relatives have volunteered to be killed and eaten in their stead, but it is probable that the bodies of these self-sacrificing individuals merely constituted an additional course when the time came.

Rice remarks on the curious fact that the tribesmen in the Society Islands, who are the Marquesans' nearest neighbours, have given no sign of having been addicted to cannibalism; indeed, he says, "they look upon cannibalism with horror". He offers no explanation of this, and it is not easy to find one. The islands are near enough to the Marquesans to be in contact with those fierce tribes; and the Fijians had the reputation for wide travel among the archipelagos, and must surely have reached their shores. Even if this was not the case, tribesmen from other groups of islands between Fiji and the Society Islands, will surely have spread stories of these practices; and primitive peoples are notoriously imitative.

He makes no reference whatsoever to a far-flung outpost of

Polynesia, the tiny, almost legendary, island known as Easter Island. This lies more than two thousand miles to the west of Chile—to which it belongs; but even though it is so far out in the Pacific Ocean, it is still remote from the main groups of islands constituting Polynesia: a lump of volcanic rock perhaps fifty square miles in extent, famous for the enormous figures carved out of the lava that covers so much of the island.

Alfred Métraux, the distinguished French anthropologist and scientist, in a book published as recently as 1957, explodes a good many of the myths which have surrounded Easter Island, particularly in regard to its 'statues'. He also has something to say on the subject of cannibalism as practised there:

> Victoria Rapahango told us that in her youth she had known the last cannibals on the island. They were the terror of little children. Every Easter Islander knows that his ancestors were *kai-tangata*—'man-eaters'. Some make jokes about it; others take offence at any allusion to this custom, which has become in their eyes barbarous and shameful. According to Father Roussel, cannibalism did not disappear from Easter Island until after the introduction of Christianity. Shortly before this, the natives are said to have eaten a number of men, including two Peruvian traders. Cannibal feasts were held in secluded spots, and women and children were rarely admitted. The natives told Father Zumbohm that the fingers and toes were the choicest morsels. The captives destined to be eaten were shut up in huts in front of the sanctuaries. There they were kept until the moment when they were sacrificed to the gods.
>
> But the Easter Islanders' cannibalism was not exclusively a religious rite, or the expression of an urge to revenge; it was also induced by a simple liking for human flesh that could impel a man to kill for no other reason than his desire for fresh meat. Women and children were the principal victims of these inveterate cannibals. The reprisals that followed such crimes were all the more violent because an act of cannibalism committed against a member of a family was a terrible insult to the whole family. As among the ancient Maori, those who had taken part in the meal were entitled to show their teeth to the relatives of the victim, and say: "Your flesh has stuck between my teeth." Such remarks were capable of rousing those to whom they were addressed to a murderous rage not very different from the Malay *amok*.

Métraux, who was reporting on the scientific expedition of which he had been a member in the 1930's, describes the Easter Islanders' mode of fighting. Hostile tribes, he says, provoked one another with violent insults, and commenced battle by throwing stones. . . .

In the hands of the Easter Islanders these were a redoubtable weapon, of which they made frequent use. The hail of stones was followed by a volley of javelins, whose obsidian points tore the skin and opened gaping wounds. After this exchange of missiles, the warriors attacked with the little, short flat club identical with the New Zealand *patu*. Some, however, preferred the long club with sharp edges.

Blows fell thick and fast until one group, having lost some of its warriors, fled from the field. The victors rushed in pursuit of the vanquished, slaying or taking prisoner those who fell into their hands. After this, they entered the enemy's territory, where they burnt down the huts and laid waste the crops. Women and children were led into captivity.

If earlier battles had exacerbated passions and created a spirit of revenge, the prisoners were tortured. Their skulls were broken with blows from an axe, they were buried alive, or trampled upon until their bellies burst and their entrails spilled out. To escape these reprisals, the vanquished fled across the island and hid in caves. Traditional legends of the island relate the outcome of these battles in almost stereotyped sentences: "They were cut in pieces. The vanquished, seized with panic, took refuge in caverns, where the victors sought them out. The men, women and children who were captured were eaten." If a high-ranking chief figured among the prisoners, he was not only eaten, but his skull was burnt, to inflict the supreme outrage on his memory and his family.

Métraux ends his account of this mode of warfare with the comment: "The attraction of these military expeditions was rendered even greater by the prospect of banquets consisting of the corpses of the enemy. After all," he adds, perhaps by way of extenuation, "Man was the only large mammal whose flesh was available."

Before leaving Polynesia, brief mention must be made of the Hawaiian Islands, a group of some twenty or more volcanic islands lying far to the north of the Equator, that is in the North, not the South Pacific. Their capital is, of course, Honolulu. Few, if any, Pacific islands are better known, or have had more written about them, than these. The American Naval Base of Pearl Harbour lies in their midst; the main Pacific air routes meet at Honolulu, and the great Pacific shipping routes. Captain Cook discovered these islands in 1778; and it was in

Hawaii that Captain Cook, only a year later, met his tragic end.

Judge Fornander of Honolulu stated categorically that the Hawaiians felt deep abhorrence for the practice of cannibalism, which they knew to exist elsewhere in the Pacific. Yet it was in Hawaii that Cook died, and the manner of his death bore striking resemblances to the very practices the Hawaiians claimed to abhor. There have been a number of versions of this, of which the circumstantial account by Captain King is probably the most reliable:

> About 8 o'clock, it being very dark, a canoe was heard paddling towards the ship. There were two persons in the canoe, and when they came on board they threw themselves at our feet, and appeared exceedingly frightened. After lamenting with abundance of tears the loss of 'Orono'—as the natives called Captain Cook—one of them told us that he had brought us a part of the body.
>
> He then presented to us a small bundle wrapped up in cloth, which he had brought under his arm. It is impossible to describe the horror which seized us on finding it a piece of human flesh about 9 or 10 pounds' weight. This, he said, was all that remained of the body of 'Orono'; the rest was cut to pieces, and burnt; but the head and all the bones, except what belonged to the trunk, were in the possession of Terreeoboo. What we were looking at had been allotted to Kaoo, the chief of the priests, to be made use of in some religious ceremony. He said he had brought it as a proof of his innocence, and his attachment to us.

Captain Cook, as far as can be ascertained from conflicting reports, had attempted to persuade a Hawaiian chief to accompany him back to his boat; the gesture had been tragically misinterpreted.

CHAPTER TWELVE

CANNIBALISM AMONG THE AUSTRALIAN BLACKFELLOWS

THE DENSITY-OF-POPULATION map of Australia shows at a glance that, with the exception of a fringe along the eastern seaboard, very narrow at the northern end but bulging slightly around Sydney, Canberra and Melbourne, and a small bulge around Perth in the south-westernmost corner of the continent, practically the whole of its three million square miles of territory is occupied by fewer than five persons to the square mile. The total population is less than that of London; and of the eight million-odd, only 50,000 or so are aborigines surviving into the twentieth century.

The aborigines, living much as Stone Age man lived, without permanent dwellings, without any but the most rudimentary knowledge of agriculture, are commonly called 'Blackfellows'; they were in occupation of the habitable portions of Australia long before Captain Cook discovered Botany Bay and, as it were, 'put on the map' a continent that had been tentatively touched upon by a Portuguese at the beginning of the seventeenth century, and landed upon by William Dampier at the end of that century.

They are at once a dangerous and a pitiful community, as any community must be that survives only against great odds; their habits and customs seem to have been less thoroughly investigated than those of many other primitive peoples in other parts of the world. But there is no doubt that cannibalism existed among them until recent times, and possibly in such dangerous areas as Arnhem Land, in the far north of Northern Territory, may exist to this day. Motives for the eating of human flesh, as elsewhere, are varied, and often closely intertwined. The need of sacrifice; the demands of magic; the desire for revenge: all these are present, as elsewhere; but in the case of the Blackfellows they are perhaps less clearly evolved and crystallised.

Colin Simpson, writing of the Australian aborigine only five or six years ago, had this to say:

The eating of human flesh was not practised by the Australian native to the extent that it was by the South Sea Islander. The term 'cannibalism' is usually taken to mean gorging on human flesh, and with relish; and that seems a valid description of the cannibalism of the Melanesian *indigènes* of New Caledonia, who appear to have regarded man-meat much as we regard the Sunday joint. Not all cannibalism is the same in purpose.

In hard summers, the new-born children were all eaten by the Kaura tribe in the neighbourhood of Adelaide, according to Dr McKinley. In 1933 I was able to talk to old men who had eaten human flesh. The chief of Yam Island described to me how he had eaten finely-chopped man-meat mixed with crocodile-meat, at his initiation. He added that it had made him sick. The purpose, as he put it, was "to make heart come strong inside".

In the Wotjobaluk tribe, a couple who already had a child might kill their new-born and feed its muscle-flesh to the other one to make it strong. The baby was killed ritually, by striking its head against the shoulder of its elder brother or sister.

Human flesh-eating among many tribes was a sign of respect for the dead. At a Dieri burial, relatives received, in strict order of precedence, small portions of the body-fat to eat. "We eat him," a tribesman said, "because we knew him and were fond of him." But revenge cannibalism is typified in the custom of the Ngarigo tribe, who ate the flesh of the hands and feet of slain enemies, and accompanied the eating with loud expressions of contempt for the people killed.

Simpson made reference to 'initiation'. A Professor of Anthropology in the University of Sydney, A. P. Elkin, develops this aspect of cannibalism among the Australian aborigines. In Central and Western Australia, he says, the young men spend a good deal of their period of seclusion in pairs, so assisting one another to obtain food. . . .

In nearly all tribes from the west to the east (he writes) and from the north to the south, at some part of the initiation series a blood rite is performed. It consists of anointing the newly initiated with arm-blood from the older men, or else giving them some of this to drink. The older men also anoint themselves, or each other, and drink blood. This blood is sacred; there is a secret name for it, and it is usually associated with some mythical hero's act.

It gives life, strength and courage, and so fits the candidates for the revelations that are to be made. At the same time it unites them to the elders of whose blood they have partaken; indeed, it does more: it unites them to the initiation-heroes, for the blood taken under such conditions is the hero's, or ancestor's, life, and so to drink it brings the initiated into the mythical world. A special song must be chanted while this blood is being drawn, and this changes it—consecrates it, as we would say—and gives it sacramental efficacy.

Elkin goes on to remark that he has heard a missionary speak with loathing of this rite of blood-drinking. But he adds that such an attitude is surely unreasonable for a Christian, especially one with strongly developed sacramental views. If, he says, we ourselves cannot tolerate blood drinking, then we might at least appreciate the symbolism, and recommend the substitution of some such liquid as wine—which, after all, is our own practice.

He goes on to speak of cannibalism among the aborigines in connection with burial rites noted among many of the Queensland tribes, and others too:

> The body (he says) was dried over a fire or in the sun, after the internal organs had been removed through an incision and it had been packed, bound up and, usually, painted. It is then made up into a bundle, and is carried around by the mourners until their grief has been assuaged. It is finally disposed of by interment, cremation, or by being put inside a hollow tree. In some districts, the preparation is complicated by cannibalism, so that the bundle consists only of the bones, or the bones and the dried skin.
>
> Cannibalism (Elkin concludes) forms a ceremony, not only in connection with mummification in parts of Queensland, but also precedes the exposure of the body on the tree-stage among other tribes. Parts of the body have to be eaten by prescribed relations. Practised in Queensland, as part of burial, cannibalism was considered a most honourable rite, to be used only for persons of worth. It was, incidentally, a quick method of preparing the 'mummy', the flesh being eaten instead of merely being dried in the sun or over a fire.

A good deal of highly intelligent research into the customs and traditions of the Australian Blackfellow has been carried through, largely in the course of their duties, by members of the Australian Mounted Police and Patrol Officers in the Native Affairs Branch. Two of the former group, G. Horne and G. Aiston, paid especial attention to the customs of the Wonkonguru tribe, in whose case, they say, cannibalism, though it existed, was not so much a general practice as a precaution against magic—and in one case to ensure a supply of food. The two motives are by no means necessarily unconnected.

The first case (they report) was at Apawandinna, half way from Cowarie. A very fat Blackfellow chased an emu and became overheated in the chase, and died. The other Blackfellows were very worried over the death. They examined the man, but could not find anything to show as a cause of his death. He was a good-natured man, very popular with the tribe, so that it was unlikely that he had been 'boned'—a form of magic widely practised among the Wonkonguru tribe.

Finally, the old men of the tribe decided to cook the body. They cut it up and distributed it right round the camps of the tribe, which at that time extended from Killalpaninna to Birdsville in Queensland. The idea of the old men was that if the dead man had been 'boned', his flesh would poison the man who had 'boned' him, and anyone who was innocent would be protected from such a death by eating a piece of him. I talked it over with one old man who had eaten it in order that the rest would not think him guilty of 'boning' the dead man. He put it to me this way: "'Spose 'em me no eat 'em. 'Nother fella say, Him kill 'em. Me eat 'em, then all right."

This is clearly 'magic': the magic of sudden death, and precaution against sudden death, as understood by the Blackfellows. The reference to 'boning', however, perhaps needs explanation. Horne and Aiston put the matter thus:

The pointing-bone is called by the Wonkonguru *wirra garoo*. It consists of a bone, or stick, having bands marked round it and a hair string stuck to one end. Each man makes the bones to his own liking, but of course he follows the general patterns that have been used possibly for centuries. The bands determine the life of the person aimed at, for as each is burnt, the man is supposed to get more sick; and when the burning reaches the last band, the man dies.

The method of using a bone varies slightly. If a man has sufficient confidence in himself, he will seize the bone in his left hand with two fingers extended along it. He then takes up the hair string with his right hand and pulls it tight against his right hip. Then, kneeling down, he points the bone towards his enemy. After he has sung a song, he covers the point of his bone with pitch to keep in the poison that has been 'sung' into it, and the man then waits until he hears that his enemy is ill. The bone in the meantime is buried in a hole in the sand and covered up with feathers.

When the enemy becomes ill, the bone-pointer digs up his bone and burns about half an inch off its point. He then covers up the burn with more pitch, and again hides the bone. The sick man in the meantime, suspecting that he has been 'boned', steadily gets worse. His friends travel in all directions, searching for the man who is 'boning' him. Usually some man who is a general nuisance to the camps is finally settled upon as the one who is doing the 'boning', and then—unless he can get into sanctuary—he is killed, or at least very badly knocked about.

The Blackfellows are very frightened of the bone magic, and it is impossible to persuade them that there is nothing in it. They distrust white men's medicine because, they maintain, it is not powerful enough to cope with the poison of the bone.

Horne and Aiston were reporting on the Australian aborigines as they knew them thirty and more years ago. It would seem, from the few reliable reports that have come from the country in more recent years, that the mills of change grind very slowly indeed; and perhaps this is inevitable. Australia is an enormously large territory; desert and wilderness and their inevitable concomitant of thirst—thirst that means death —make the prospect of travelling into the interior enough to daunt most men. Those who go there, go as a matter of duty; it is hard to think of anything in the nature of a mission, as ordinarily understood, among these roving tribes.

Nevertheless, there have been officers who have looked upon their duties as something more than the fulfilling of the bare letter-of-the-law. Syd Kyle-Little must be one of these—as the pages of his recently published *Whispering Wind* reveal. He writes with understanding, even with affection, of the Blackfellow whom it was his duty to control when necessary, guide where possible. He clearly had an extraordinary flair for coming to terms with the natives, though he is under no illusion as to the danger involved in exercising any sort of authority over them: they are primitives of the primitives. . . .

It appeared that a white man by himself on such a mission as mine might easily find himself wrapped in pandanus-leaves and roasting quietly on the ashes of an Arnhem Land fire. "From well corroborated evidence, a form of cannibalism is still practised by three groups between the Blyth and Liverpool Rivers," Gordon Sweeney, a Patrol Officer in the Native Affairs Branch, one of my predecessors, wrote. "The bodies of all except the children, old people, and the diseased are cut up after death, the bones taken out and the flesh cooked and eaten. There appears to be no special ceremony at the time, or ceremonial significance attached to this practice, at least among two groups, the Manbuloi and the

Gumauwurrk.   A third group, the Rauwarang, do not allow the children to eat.   The bones are shortly afterwards handed to the relative who is to carry them at the usual Buguburrt corroboree, which under this name is practised throughout the social area. The reason given for the cannibal practice in all three groups is that the people think that eating human flesh will make them clever at hunting, at spearing kangaroos, finding wild honey, getting yams, etc.''

Kyle-Little describes in his book a mission which he under-took in 1946, and the quotation which had made him think so hard came from a comment from one of his immediate predecessors.   He continues thus:

I wondered about Sweeney's warnings of cannibalism.   I had known the Australian aborigine for too long to believe that he was a blood-thirsty, man-eating savage.   Provoked, he *was* savage. But I did not mean to be provocative.   As for man-eating, I discovered later that this was only partly true.   The Liverpool River natives did not kill men for food.   They ate human flesh largely from superstitious beliefs.   If they killed a worthy man in battle, they ate his heart, believing that they would inherit his valour and power.   They ate his brain because they knew it represented the seat of his knowledge.   If they killed a fast runner, they ate part of his legs, hoping thereby to acquire his speed.

Kyle-Little—who uses as title for his book the name which the Blackfellows ultimately gave him, as a sign of their respect—completed his mission, and returned to write his very revealing book.   If he encountered any cannibalism, it was not 'Whispering Wind' who was personally involved.   And E. O. James, who has written so much on different aspects of cannibalism in so many different parts of the world, and with such acute perception of the distinctions, confirms what the Patrol Officer had had to say: "Among the native tribes of Australia, the bodies of those who fall in battle, honoured chiefs, and new-born infants, are frequently consumed to obtain their qualities, just as in the Torres Straits (which separate the northernmost territory of Australia from the southernmost part of New Guinea) the tongue and sweat of a slain enemy are imbibed to get his bravery."

CHAPTER THIRTEEN

CANNIBAL PRACTICES AMONG THE MAORI OF NEW ZEALAND

THE POPULATION of New Zealand is barely a quarter that of Australia, so the New Zealand Maori form a very much higher proportion of the total than the Australian Blackfellows do in their country, for there are some 50,000 of them still.

The Maori are thought to have migrated to the North Island of New Zealand some hundreds of years ago—perhaps from Hawaii, perhaps from elsewhere. They may have drifted across the South Pacific, from island group to island group, in the course of centuries, absorbing some of the characteristics of the various tribes with whom they fought, and perhaps later temporarily settled down, as they did so. To judge from their fierceness, and the late survival of cannibalism among them, it would not be unfair to suggest that they absorbed more than a little of the Fiji Islanders' traditions. It has been suggested that they may have originated in India or Central Asia, and have reached New Zealand by way of Malaya; but basically they are Polynesian, though generally speaking the savagery of their ways in the not-so-distant past would suggest Melanesian rather than Polynesian traditions.

Elsdon Best, an authority on the Maori, is clearly puzzled by the deeply-ingrained habit of cannibalism of which he found so much evidence in the course of his researches. "How is it," he asks, "that our Maori has become such a pronounced cannibal in these islands?" Rightly or wrongly, he attributes the origin of the Maori to the Society Islands, which, as we have already seen, were not a hotbed of cannibalism. "Was cannibalism, as a common custom, *acquired* by the Maori?" he asks. And adds: "The dreadful Maori custom—or at least occasional habit—of exhuming and eating buried human bodies was also a *Fijian* custom."

Captain Cook was horrified by the discovery of cannibalism in New Zealand when he was at work on the project of charting the eastern coastline of the islands in 1768 and the following year. His *Journals* are a fascinating, and very revealing, record of what awaited explorers in the latter end of the eighteenth century, and he would doubtless have been astounded to find that even a hundred and more years later the conditions he had known had not so greatly changed. Parts of his *Journals* deal with his voyage in his ship *Endeavour*, in which he visited the Society Islands and Tahiti before sailing further south to chart the eastern coasts of New Zealand and Australia. Tahitians who had voyaged with him were as sickened as he was by what they found. . . .

Calm light airs from the north all day on the 23rd November hindered us from putting out to sea as intended. In the afternoon, some of the officers went on shore to amuse themselves among the natives, where they saw the head and bowels of a youth, who had been lately killed, lying on the beach, and the heart stuck on a forked stick which was fixed to the head of one of the largest canoes. One of the gentlemen bought the head and brought it on board, where a piece of the flesh was broiled and eaten by one of the natives, before all the officers and most of the men. I was on shore at this time, but soon after returning on board was informed of the above circumstances, and found the quarter-deck crowded with the natives, and the mangled head, or rather part of it (for the under-jaw and lips were wanting), lying on the taffrail. The skull had been broken on the left side, just above the temples, and the remains of the face had all the appearance of a youth under twenty.

The sight of the head, and the relation of the above circumstances, struck me with horror and filled my mind with indignation against these cannibals. Curiosity, however, got the better of my indignation, especially when I considered that it would avail but little, and being desirous of becoming an eye-witness of a fact which many doubted, I ordered a piece of the flesh to be broiled, and brought to the quarter-deck, where one of the cannibals ate it with surprising avidity. This had such an effect on some of our people as to make them sick. Oedidee, the native who had embarked with us some time before, was so affected with the sight as to become perfectly motionless, and seemed as if metamorphosed into a statue of horror. It is utterly impossible for art to describe that passion with half the force that it appeared in his countenance.

When roused from this state by some of us, he burst into tears, continued to weep and scold by turns, told them they were vile men and that he neither was nor would be any longer their friend. He even would not suffer them to touch him. He used the same language to one of the gentlemen who cut off the flesh, and refused to accept or even touch the knife with which it was done. Such was Oedidee's indignation against this vile custom; and worthy of imitation by every rational being.

At four o'clock in the morning of the 24th November, we unmoored with an intent to put to sea; but the wind being at north and north-east without, and blowing strong puffs into the cove, made it necessary for us to lie fast.   While we were unmooring, some of our old friends came aboard to take their leave of us, and afterwards left the cove with all their effects; but those who had been out on the late expedition remained; and some of the gentlemen having visited them found the heart still sticking on the canoe, and the intestines lying on the beach; but the liver and lungs were now wanting.   Probably they had eaten them after the carcass was all gone.

It would seem from this particular extract that Cook and his officers had got on to relatively easy terms with the 'gentlemen', as he so oddly refers to them, who gave these demonstrations of what was for them a normal practice.   But it was not always such an easy relationship.   Elsewhere in his *Journals* he recounts episodes where they were in very real danger.   Danger, incidentally, of two kinds; neither of them pleasant to contemplate. . . .

In this situation we were not above two cables' length from the rocks, and here we remained in the strength of the tide, from a little after seven till near midnight.   The sea broke in dreadful surf upon the rocks.   Our danger was imminent and our escape critical in the highest degree; from the situation of these rocks, so well adapted to catch unwary strangers, I call them 'The Traps'.

There was not a man aboard *Endeavour* who, in the event of the ship's breaking up, would not have preferred to drown rather than be left to the mercy of the Maoris.   For as *Endeavour* slowly circled the North Island, those few words spoken by the Maori boys—"Do not put us ashore there; it is inhabited by our enemies who will kill and eat us"—began to grow into a hideous reality.   Yet even as fresh evidence came to light that these people were indeed cannibals, the ship's company still refused to believe the truth their eyes told them.

Tupia inquired if it was their practice to eat men, to which they answered in the affirmative; but said that they ate only their enemies who were slain in battle.   We now began seriously to believe that this horrid custom prevailed amongst them, for what the boys had said we had considered as a mere hyperbolical expression of their fear.   But some days later some of our people found in the skirts of the wood, near a hole, or oven, three human hip-bones, which they brought on board: a further proof that these people eat human flesh.

Not long afterwards, Cook and his men were witnesses of the gruesome sight of human beings gnawing human bones with an absolute lust, their hands and faces, as he said, smeared with blood while they picked fragments of human gristle from between their sharply filed teeth.

> At this sight (he writes) we were struck with horror, though it was only confirmation of what we had heard many times since we arrived upon the coast. As we could have no doubt but that the bones were human, neither could we have any doubt but that the flesh which covered them had been eaten. They were found in a provision-basket: the flesh that remained appeared manifestly to have been dressed by fire; and in the gristles at the end were the marks of the teeth which had gnawed them.

Captain Cook was something more than a fine and courageous sailor and navigator: he was an observer with a scientific turn of mind. So, too, were some of his officers, men such as Banks and Solander, for instance. Sinking their own personal feelings, they availed themselves of every opportunity for studying the natives and their customs, and the result, as shown in Cook's carefully kept *Journals*, is a fine piece of reportage. The account of what they saw, in its detail and accuracy, has hardly been surpassed even by the anthropologists and others who came much later on the scene, here and elsewhere.

> This (Cook continues) was but a small Maori family, not more than a dozen at most. Yet, upon inquiry who the man was whose bones we had found, they told us that about five days before, a boat belonging to their enemies came into the bay, with many persons on board, and that this man was one of the *seven* whom they had killed.

Since only a basketful of bones was left by the time Cook and his officers came on the scene, less than a week later, the family had disposed of one whole carcass at least between them every day. Banks, apparently, risked a challenge: were they really cannibals, or were these just remnants of some bodies that had been disposed of otherwise? Cook adds, dispassionately: "One of the cannibals thereupon bit and gnawed the human arm which Banks had picked up, drawing it through his mouth and showing by signs that the flesh to him was a dainty bit.

Tupia carried on the conversation: 'Where are the heads?' he asked. 'Do you eat them, too?' 'Of the heads,' answered an old man, 'we eat only the brains.' Later he brought on board *Endeavour* four of the heads of the seven victims. The hair and flesh were entire, but we perceived that the brains had been extracted. The flesh was soft, but had by some method been preserved from putrefaction, for it had no disagreeable smell." Cook adds that, after a great deal of haggling as to price, the Maori were induced by Banks to sell them one of the heads; but they would part with no more than one.

Later, having had more than ample opportunity to investigate and draw his conclusions about the cannibalistic practices of the Maori, with whom his own relations were so unusual, Cook makes his statement:

> This custom of eating their enemies slain in battle (for I firmly believe they eat the flesh of no others) has undoubtedly been handed down to them from earliest times; and we know it is not an easy matter to wean a nation from their ancient customs, let them be ever so inhuman and savage; especially if that nation has no manner of connection or commerce with strangers. For it is by this that the greatest part of the human race has been civilised; an advantage which the New Zealanders, from their situation, never had.
>
> One of the arguments they made use of to Tupia, who frequently expostulated with them against this custom, was that there could be no harm in killing and eating the man who would do the same by them if it was in his power. For, said they, "Can there be any harm in eating our enemies, whom we have killed in battle? Would not those very enemies have done the same to us?" I have often seen them listen to Tupia with great attention, but I never found his arguments have any weight with them. When Oedidee and several of our people showed their abhorrence of it, they only laughed at them.

Captain Cook was writing in the '70's of the eighteenth century. Dr Felix Maynard, writing not much more then a hundred years ago, reports the case of Touai, a New Zealand chief who was brought to London in 1818 and resided there for a long time, becoming "almost civilised"; but—

> He confessed in his moments of nostalgia that what he most regretted in the country from which he was absent was the feast of human flesh, the feast of victory. He was weary of eating English beef; he claimed that there was a great analogy between

the flesh of the pig and that of man.   This last declaration he
made before a sumptuously served table.   The flesh of women
and children was to him and his fellow-countrymen the most
delicious, while certain Maoris prefer that of a man of fifty, and
that of a black rather than that of a white.   His countrymen,
Touai said, never ate the flesh raw, and preserved the fat of the
rump for the purpose of dressing their sweet potatoes.

Maynard adds a piece of gratuitous information.   Some
missionaries had expressed their fear of being eaten.   A New
Zealand chief to whom they were speaking sought to put their
minds at rest.   Maoris, he told them, if they were wanting a
taste of human flesh would be far more likely to seek it among
their foes in neighbouring tribes because black men had a far
more agreeable flavour than white men, when cooked.   This,
he said, was due to the fact that the whites seem to take a lot
of salt with the food they eat, while Maoris take practically
none at all.

> There is not a bay, not a cove, in New Zealand (Maynard
> reported) which has not witnessed horrible dramas, and woe to
> the white man who falls into the New Zealanders' hands.   When
> the victor eats his foe after the combat, he believes he eats not only
> his body but also his soul.   It is an outrage to eat the body; and
> it is an advantage to eat the *waidoua*—the soul of the vanquished—
> because this is then assimilated with one's own.   This superstition
> is all-powerful in wartime.   Usually, after a fight they commence
> by devouring the bodies of the oldest and most courageous war-
> riors, those most completely tattooed, leaving the corpses of the
> younger men aside, those that were novices in warfare, even
> though their flesh might be more appetising.   Thus, before all,
> the victors value the assimilation, the appropriation, of the life
> and courage of the most celebrated warriors, *however thin and
> fleshless they may be.*

Maynard adds a brief comment here;   one which we have
already seen made by other investigators: "Considered from
this point of view, cannibalism is almost excusable among
barbarous peoples."   He then goes on to describe the details of
the feasts:

> New Zealanders particularly esteem the brain, and reject the
> remainder of the head;   but an English missionary has reported
> that Pomare, a chief of the Bay of Islands, ate six entire heads.
> Chiefs' heads are usually dried and perfectly preserved by an
> ingenious process.   When a tribe wishes to make peace, it offers

the vanquished tribe, as proof of its good intentions, the heads of
the chiefs the others have lost.   These heads are also articles of
commerce in the neighbourhood of the Bay of Islands.

The bones of chiefs are very carefully gathered up, and from
them they construct knives, fish-hooks, arrow-points, and points
for lances and javelins, as well as ornaments for the toilet.   I
possess some fish-hooks pointed with very sharp fragments of
human bone.   Sometimes they detach the hand and the forearm
and dry them at a fire of aromatic herbs.   The muscles and
tendons of the fingers contract so that the whole forms a hook,
which they place in their huts for the suspension of baskets and
weapons.   I have seen several of these used as clothes-pegs.
They utilise the remnants of the corpse in this manner in order to
cause the family of the chief who is no more to feel that, even after
death, he is still the slave of the victor.   Before the feast of victory,
each warrior drinks the blood of the enemy he has killed with his
own hand.   The *atoua*, the god of the conquered, then becomes
subject to the *atoua* of the victors.   In the neighbourhood of
Hokianga, Hongi ate the left eye of a great chief.   According to
their belief, the left eye becomes a star in the firmament, and Hongi
considered that henceforth his star would be much the more
brilliant, and the strength of his sight would be augmented by all
that which was possessed by the defunct.

Maynard goes on to say that he believes the action of cutting
off an enemy's head, raising it by the hair above one's mouth in
order to drink the warm blood running from the arteries,
swallowing the left eye and chewing the muscles is all done in
order to inherit a star and a soul.   There were always, so far as
he could ascertain, human sacrifices following the death of a
chief.   Tradition and, for want of a better word, 'religion',
he says, demanded that the bodies of slaves should be placed
upon that of a chief, but very often the sacrificers chose to eat
them instead.

Though the New Zealanders do not conceal their cannibalism (he
ends), their chiefs sometimes endeavour to excuse themselves for
it.   "The fish of the sea eat one another," they say; "the large
fish eat the small ones, the small ones eat insects; dogs eat men
and men eat dogs, while dogs eat one another; the birds of the air
also prey upon one another; finally, the gods devour other gods.
Why, among enemies, should *we* not eat one another?"

There is usually a suspension of fighting after the death of the
first chief to fall in combat.   The party which has not lost that
leader claims the body of the defunct.   If the others are intimi-
dated, they yield it at once, and in addition, the chief's wife, who
is immediately put to death; she even voluntarily yields herself

up, if she loved her husband. The priests cut up the corpses, divide them into fragments, and eat some; offering the greater number to their idols, while consulting the gods upon the issue of the present war.

Maynard's observations were the result of investigation in the early part of the nineteenth century. Three-quarters of a century later, Edward Tregear did some investigating for the purpose of writing a book he subsequently called quite simply *The Maori Race*. His researches were widespread and comprehensive, and the results were to show, among other things, that the Maori could not be said to have changed much in the generations that had passed.

After battle (Tregear writes) comes the terrible and revolting episode of the cannibal feast. It is unfortunately impossible to pass it over without notice, for Maori history is too full of allusion and incident connected with the practice for us to avoid mention and description of some of its horrors.

Prisoners taken in the fight were slain in cold blood, except those reserved for slavery—a mark of still greater contempt than being killed for food. Sometimes after the battle a few of the defeated were thrust *alive* into large food-baskets and thus degraded for ever. As a general rule, however, they were slain for the oven.

In days near our own it is recorded that a chief named Wherowhero ordered 250 prisoners of the Taranaki people to be brought to him for slaughter. He sat on the ground and the prisoners were brought to him one by one to receive the blow of the chief's *mere*—a weapon till lately in the possession of his son, the late Maori 'King'. After he had killed the greater number of them he said, "I am tired. Let the rest live." So the remainder passed into slavery.

How numerous sometimes these war captives were may be judged by the fact that when Hongi returned from his raid on the southern tribes he brought back 2,000 prisoners to the Bay of Islands. One of the latest cannibal feasts of consequence was held at Ohariu, near Wellington, when 150 of the Muaupoko tribe went into the ovens. When the Maoris overcame the gentle Moriois of the Chatham Islands, not only did they keep the captives penned up like live-stock waiting to be killed and eaten, but one of the leading chiefs of the invaders ordered a meal of six children at once to be cooked to regale his friends.

I was shown a part of a beach on the Chatham Islands on which the bodies of eighty Moriori women were laid side by side, each with an impaling stake driven into the abdomen. It is difficult for one not accustomed to savage warfare to note how shockingly callous and heartless this desecration of the human body made the actors in these terrible scenes.

Tregear then gives a specific instance of this almost unbeliev-able callousness which struck him so forcibly.   Indeed, it is hard to parallel the behaviour recorded here, except perhaps in Fiji and in some parts of New Guinea.

A Maori relating an account of an expedition said, *incidentally*: "On the way I was speaking to a red-haired girl who had just been caught out in the open.   We were then on the eastern side of Maunga Whau, Auckland.   My companions remained with the girl whilst I went to see the man of Waikato who had been killed.   As we came back, I saw the head of the red-haired girl lying in the ferns by the side of the track.   Further on, we over-took one of the Waihou men carrying a back-load of the flesh, which he was taking to our camp to cook for food.   The arms of the girl were round his neck, whilst the body was on his back." If one can mentally picture the scene, with the man striding along, carrying the headless, disembowelled trunk of the naked girl, enough of this kind of horror will have been evoked.

Tregear mentions one odd point: odd because it is exactly the reverse of a practice we have already noted among the sorcerers of Papua who, Seligmann reported, made a practice of eating corpses for the purposes of their sorcery.   Certain families, notably those of the Papahurihia, a tribe of wizards, refused ever to touch human flesh because, they maintained, such food would entirely destroy their magical powers.

When the bodies could not all be eaten (Tregear continues), some of the flesh was stripped from the bones and dried in the sun, being hung on stages for that purpose.   The flesh was then gathered into baskets and oil was poured over it, the oil being rendered-down from the bodies; this was done to prevent it spoiling from damp.   Sometimes the flesh was potted into cala-bashes, as birds were potted.   The bones were broken up and burnt in the fire.   The body of a chief might be flayed, and the skin dried for covering hoops or boxes.   The heads of the inferior chiefs were smashed and burnt, but those of the great were pre-served by smoking.   Sometimes the bones were broken and knocked like nails into the posts of the storehouses—a great indignity.
Bones were also taken away to be made into fish-hooks, or as barbs for bird or eel spears.   The hands were dried with the fingers bent towards the palm, and the wrists were tied to a pole which was stuck into the ground, and baskets containing the

remains of a meal were hung upon the fingers.   Some of the Nga-
puhi tribe were treated this way early this century.   The hands
were fastened to the walls of a house, with the wrists upwards and
fingers turned up as hooks.   The hands had been roasted until
the outer skin had come off.   The palms were quite white inside.

It is curious how small, macabre details like these bring home
the full significance and horror of such practices even more
forcibly than descriptions of wholesale massacre and feasting.
The image of a basket of human flesh hanging from the rigid
fingers of a human hand severed at the wrist and fastened to a
pole in the hut is surely the apotheosis of the macabre.

If the deceased had been a great chief (Tregear continues), care
was taken to degrade every part of the skeleton.   The thigh-
bones were made into flutes, or cut into sections that could be
worked into rings for the legs of captive parrots.   From other
bones would be made pins for holding the dress-mats together, or
needles for sewing dogskin mats.   The skull might even be used as
a water-vessel for carrying water in, for wetting the ovens.   But
chiefs' heads were carried back to be erected on posts so that they
might be taunted, or fixed on the corner sticks of a loom to be
mocked by a woman as she sat weaving.   In fact, no method of
showing contempt, especially of defiling the remains of the defeated
by associating them with food, was spared.
    Sometimes the heart of the vanquished was roasted for cere-
monial purposes.   When the Kaiapoi stronghold was attacked by
the forces of Rauparaha, the heart of a chief of the defending party
was cut out and roasted in a fire, while all the attacking warriors
stood round it in a ring.   The priests chanted and the warriors
stretched out their arms towards the heart while it was cooking.
When the priests ended their chant, the warriors took up the song,
while the chief priest tore off a portion of the heart and threw it
among the enemy to weaken them.
    The heart of a victim of sacrifice was not always eaten for war
purposes.   Sometimes it was for other reasons.   Thus Uenuku
ate the heart of his wife, who had committed adultery.   The heart
of the human sacrifice was eaten at a house-building ceremony,
and also at the tattooing of the lips of a chief's daughter and at the
felling of a tree to be used for a great chief's canoe.

This last point gives a hint of contact between the Maori and
the Fijian Islanders, among whom this practice has already
been noted.   The anthropologist A. P. Rice records this also,
and adds that the custom of devouring a human heart might be
found also in the course of the ceremony of mourning the passing

of a chief, when the tribe was at the same time honouring his widow.

Rice goes on to comment on the element of heredity in regard to cannibalism, and quotes an anonymous French missionary, one of whose converts was a young Maori of, insisted the missionary, "a particularly gentle and lovable disposition, very shy—even timid, and extremely popular with everyone at the mission where he was employed." . . .

One day (said the missionary) he happened to meet a young girl who had run away for some reason from her home in a neighbouring village. The young Maori suddenly became possessed of an unaccustomed demon. He seized the young girl, took her to his hut, killed her in cold blood; cut up her body in the traditional manner, and then invited his friends to partake with him in a meal, the chief and most favoured dish of which consisted of this young Maori girl.

In his observations about cannibalism, particularly in regard to the practice in New Zealand, Rice makes one very unexpected and interesting point:

There is—though it sounds macabre—one redeeming feature in this matter of cannibalism: it makes those who participate in it well acquainted with the anatomy of the human frame. That is why a Maori is so frequently a master of surgery—surgery that may be rude, but is nevertheless extremely effective. He is fairly adept in the matter of dislocated joints and fractured bones, though of course owing to their lack of proper instruments—not to mention anaesthetics—any patient undergoing the amputation of, say, an arm or leg must evince an indifference to pain in order that the amateur surgeon may not be made nervous as he operates.

Rice's observation is reasonable; the comment that concludes it comes a little unexpectedly from an anthropologist!

It is, of course, the eye-witness account that remains longest in the memory, and our last reference to the cannibalism of the Maori shall be taken from the reports of white traders and others who came, wittingly or otherwise, to be involved in such incidents.

The first concerns the Master of the trading-brig *Elizabeth*, one Captain Stewart, who allowed himself to be persuaded by a Maori chief to smuggle him and a party of his tribesmen aboard the ship so that they might arrive unexpectedly at the shores of an island where their enemies lived. Te Rauparaha must have been a person of some plausibility, for Captain Stewart allowed a hundred and more natives to secrete themselves in part of his holds before he set sail for their mutual objective: the one to pick up a cargo of flax, the other with a very different end in view.

Between one and two in the morning, the *Elizabeth* dropped anchor off shore. At daylight, Stewart found canoes coming out to visit the ship, and one by one, the crews were allowed to come aboard, and were then battened down below hatches. As soon as sufficient canoes were available, the tribesmen from the other hold came up on deck, boarded the canoes, and paddled across the bay, to fight the depleted community and ultimately return with canoe-loads of victims, who were then thrown down into the holds where already their fellow-tribesmen were battened down.

> None of those taken prisoner were killed, nor were any of those killed on shore cooked on board, nor in the cooking-vessels belonging to the ship (says the report). All the bodies were cooked on shore in the primitive Maori fashion of the day. They dig a hole in the earth two feet deep, in which they make a quantity of round stones red-hot with dry wood, after which they take out all the stones except a few at the bottom, over which they lay several alternate tiers of leaves and flesh, until there is as much above the ground as below. They then throw about two or three quarts of water over all, and confine the steam with old mats and earth so completely that in 20 minutes the flesh is cooked; it is in this way that they cook and cure all their provisions.

The prisoners, the dead and alive flesh, were brought ashore and seated in rows on the beach, the preserved flesh being carried off in baskets to the place appointed for the cannibal feast. It was estimated that about one hundred baskets of flesh were landed, and that each basket contained the equivalent of one human body. Then commenced a dance which was described by an eye-witness:

> The warriors, entirely naked, their long black hair, although matted with human gore, yet flowing partially in the wind; in the left hand a human head and in the right hand a bayonetted musket held by the middle of the barrel. Thus, with a song, the terrible expression of which can only be imagined by being heard, did they dance round their wretched victims, every now and then

approaching them with gestures, threatening death under its most horrible forms of lingering torture.

The captives, with the exception of one old man and a boy who were sentenced to death, were apportioned amongst the conquering warriors as slaves. The tables were laid. About a hundred baskets of potatoes, a large supply of green vegetables, and equal quantities of whale-blubber and human flesh, constituted the awful menu. The old man, from whose neck suspended the head of his son, while the body formed part of the cannibal feast, was brought forth and subjected to torture from the women before the last scene of all.

The banquet went on to a finish, and, though it proved none the less attractive to the participants, was rendered all the more hideous to the onlookers by the fact that the midsummer season when it took place, added to the hasty and incomplete manner in which the human flesh had been prepared in the ovens, caused the human—yet unhuman—food to become putrid in a most revolting form before it was spread out for the banquet. Officers of the boat witnessed this frightful orgy, and some of them brought to Hobart Town mementoes of the scene, dissected from the bodies as they lay out for the repast.

The second report is from one of a group of white traders, and comes in the form of a letter from Daniel Henry Sheridan. The group of traders had become involved in a vendetta between two tribes, the Waikato and the Taranaki; but this time it would seem that they had not allowed themselves, as Captain Stewart did, to play some part in the proceedings. They were unwilling and horrified witnesses—which was bad enough:

The principal part of the prisoners that day were cripples, women and children; the remainder making their escapes as well as their weak state would allow them (they had been besieged for a considerable time). A party of the enemy were employed in despatching as many as would be sufficient for the evening's meal; their slaves getting the ovens ready, and the remainder went in search of more prey, which they found to the number of *twelve hundred*.

On the 23rd, they commenced the slaughter of the prisoners that were taken alive. They were crammed into huts, well guarded, the principal chief executioner, with a sharp tomahawk in his hand, ready to receive them. They were then called out one by one. Those that had well carved or tattooed heads had their heads cut off on a block, the body quartered and hung upon fences that were erected for the purpose. Those with indifferent heads received one blow, and were then dragged to a hole to bleed. The young children, and grown-up lads, were cut down the belly and then roasted on sticks before the fires.

I have, since this bloody deed was committed, paid a visit to the fatal spot to view the remains of this horrid carnage. Within several miles in all directions, are placed in the ground pieces of wood, painted red, as a memorial of the spot where those that were left behind had some friend or relative slain. On advancing nearer, is a heap of bones, since burned, as near as I can imagine of about 300 persons. Thence to about a quarter of a mile are skeletons, not burned, strewed about the place where the enemy had formed their settlements, and the ovens still remaining where they had been cooked.

I believe they did not eat any flesh inside the place where they butchered them, as I could not see any bones in it; it had not been disturbed since the savages left it to pay us a visit. The block they struck the fatal blow on was still remaining, the blood and the notches from the axe were still quite fresh. The trees were stripped of their leaves, and the branches thereof supplied, instead, with dead bodies, cleaned and ready for cooking.

On taking a general view of the place, I observed that the enemy had formed three different settlements, and in each of them was a heap of bones similar to the first I had seen, and also to each, a rack, placed along the spot where they eat their victuals; on it they place the heads of their unfortunate victims, that they may continually keep the objects of their revenge in their sight and mind, which is the continued bloodthirsty practice of this disgraceful race, whose constant study is meditating the death of their fellow-countrymen. . . .

Sheridan gives a number of descriptions of scenes that he has been obliged to witness, each more horrible than the last: episodes wherein, for example, a quarrel between two women in a tribe leads to mass-slaughter, with heads falling left and right, and the inevitable feasting and 'curing' of the heads as trophies and mementoes. The tribesmen took, he says, a perverse delight in casting the entrails of some of their victims into the only stream in the neighbourhood supplying water fit for white men to drink. This, he says, according to their superstition made the water sacred, so that he and his companions dared not drink from it from fear of something worse than the mere fact of possibly being poisoned by the pollution. He then gives one more incident which, as he says, "with horror I beheld":

To the gun I was stationed at, they dragged a man slightly wounded in the leg, and tied him hand and foot until the battle was over.   Then they loosed him and put some questions to him, which he could not answer, nor give them any satisfaction thereof, as he knew his doom. They then took the fatal tomahawk and put it between his teeth, while another pierced his throat for a chief to drink his blood. Others at the same time were cutting his arms and legs off. They then cut off his head, quartered him and sent his heart to a chief, it being a delicious morsel and they being generally favoured with such rarities after an engagement.

In the meantime, a fellow that had proved a traitor wished to come and see his wife and children. They seized him and served him in like manner. Oh, what a scene for a man of Christian feeling, to behold dead bodies strewed about the settlement in every direction, and hung up at every native's door, their entrails taken out and thrown aside and the women preparing ovens to cook them! By great persuasion, we prevailed on the savages not to cook any inside the fence, or to come into our houses during the time they were regaling themselves on what they termed sumptuous food—far sweeter, they said, than pork.

On our side, there were eight men killed, three children, and two women, during the siege. They got sixteen bodies, besides a great number that were half roasted, and dug several up out of the graves, half decayed, which they also ate. Another instance of their depravity was to make a musket ramrod red hot, enter it in the lower part of the victim's belly and let it run upwards, and then make a slight incision in a vein to let his blood run gradually, for them to drink. . . .

Sheridan ends his letter, in which he has recounted such hideous incidents with such a wealth of detail: "I must here conclude, being very scanty of paper; for which reason, columns of the disgraceful conduct of these cannibals remain unpenned

by

Daniel Henry Sheridan."

At their worst—indeed, at their average level—the cannibalistic practices of the Maori were hardly surpassed even among the tribes occupying territories on the Equator; but it must be borne in mind that in recent years these aborigines of New Zealand have revealed an extraordinary capacity for absorbing much of what is best in so-called civilisation. Today, though the number of pure Maori is steadily decreasing as a result of inter-marriage with other inhabitants of the islands, some thousands of them yet remain: men and women of fine potentialities. It is in this respect that they differ so fundamentally from the Blackfellow of Australia with whom, by unthinking people, they are all too often confused.

Cannibalism, in the sense in which it has been discussed in the past chapters, can hardly be said to exist in the world of today. There *may* be isolated pockets of survival in the heart of New Guinea and among some of the tribes in the remotest corners of South American or African jungles; but they will be no more than the rarest of phenomena.

To find examples other than these it would be necessary to investigate the reports of survivors of shipwreck in such areas as the Indian Ocean, where rafts have been known to float for days and even weeks, with their occupants dying one by one of thirst and sunstroke till only one was left—one who in despair overcame the innate repugnance of contemporary man to touch human flesh, and drove himself to taste blood, to swallow a morsel of flesh in order to survive another hour or day and thus increase his chances of eventual rescue. There are such tales; but to quote from them in such a context as this seems hardly justifiable.

The Second World War is not yet so far behind us that the names Belsen, Buchenwald and Auschwitz mean nothing to us today. In concentration camps such as those, the ultimate in degradation was reached; and the ultimate in degradation, as we have seen, implies a complete disregard for the sanctity of the human being. The endless volumes of reports on the Proceedings at the so-called Nuremberg Trials afford evidence of practices which, even in cold print, carry the odour of the charnel-house.

In his revelatory book, *The Scourge of the Swastika,* Lord Russell of Liverpool wrote with the support not only of a wide range of official sources of information, but with the authority behind him of Anthony Somerhough, Q.C., formerly Head of the British War Crimes Group in Germany.

There were no gas chambers in Belsen (Russell writes), but thousands were nevertheless exterminated by disease and starvation.

During the last few months of the camp's existence the shortage of food was so acute that the prisoners (the camp staff were still well fed) resorted to cannibalism, and one former British internee gave evidence at the trial of the Commandant and some of his staff that when engaged in clearing away dead bodies, as many as one in ten had a piece cut from the thigh or other part of the body, which had been taken and eaten, and that he had seen people in the act of doing this. To such lengths had they been brought by the pangs of hunger.

This witness said: "I noticed on many occasions a very strange wound at the back of the thigh of many of the dead. First of all I dismissed it as a gunshot wound at close quarters, but after seeing a few more I asked a friend and he told me that many of the prisoners were cutting chunks out of the bodies to eat. On my very next visit to the mortuary I actually saw a prisoner whip out a knife, cut a portion out of the leg of a dead body and put it quickly into his mouth, naturally frightened of being seen in the act of doing so. I leave it to your imagination to realise to what state the prisoners were reduced, for men to risk eating bits of flesh cut from corpses."

Incidents such as these can, of course, be multiplied almost indefinitely. Whether the word 'cannibalism' can fairly be applied to them is a different matter. Meaning, as it originally did, 'man-eating', of course the word is just; but over the passage of time the word has acquired other, and subtler, connotations.

The distinguished Swedish criminologist, Söderman, who died recently after the greater part of a lifetime devoted to police work in many European countries, towards the end of which he revived the famous International Police Commission, has one strange tale—and a true tale at that—to tell of Germany in the present century. It is not the Germany of the concentration camps but that of the between-the-wars period when food was scarce. . . .

In the early twenties there was a hot-dog vendor plying his trade at one of the railroad stations in Berlin. His name was Grossmann and he had once been a butcher. Grossmann was about fifty years old, a thin, insignificant little man with a haggard face and a sloping moustache. About twice a month he used to spend a day on the platform where long-distance, slow trains with cheap fourth-class carriages stopped. If he saw getting out of one of these carriages a girl who looked as if she were coming to the city to hunt for a job as a housemaid, he would approach her (provided she was fat enough), politely lift his cap and inquire

whether he could be of any assistance.   During the conversation
he would drop a remark that he was in need of a housekeeper for
his bachelor household and that she could have the job if she
wanted.   He paid well, he used to say, and there was not much
work.   Often a girl accepted, and any who did would not be
seen again.

Grossmann kept each of these girls for a couple of days, then
murdered her.   He cut up the bodies with a butcher's skill, kept
the flesh and disposed of the balance in some sewer.   Then he
pickled the meat, ground it and put it into his sausages, which he
later sold at the railway station.   This constant stream of girls
into his flat finally alerted some neighbours, who put the police
on his track.   Bundles of female clothes were discovered in the
closets, and finally Grossmann confessed.

Söderman has other stories of the same kind to tell, culled
from his case-book, but there is little point in duplicating anything at once so macabre and so near our own times.

The nearest we come to cannibalism in the sense in which it
has been treated throughout these chapters—closely associated
with, or occasionally divorced from ceremonial and sacrifice—
is in connection with the activities of the Mau Mau.   It is very
clear from such books as L. S. B. Leakey's *Mau Mau and the
Kikuyu* that cannibalism in the East African areas where these
tribesmen operate either never wholly died, or has been
secretly revived in order to give strength and urgency to an
illicit movement.   There is no doubt that some form of
cannibalism is practised in connection with the initiation
ceremonies that take place.

The organisation generally referred to as 'Mau Mau' is
considered to be merely a new name for the old Kenya Central
Association, which was an organisation devoted to the obstruc-
tion of the white man's activities in monopolising more and
more of the territories looked upon as belonging to the native.
It became necessary to enlist all the support available, and such
support as was enlisted had to be established as utterly and
finally loyal, against no matter what temptation to default.
Thus the oaths binding the members of the organisation had
to be made as rigid and unbreakable as possible.   And just as,
where cannibalism was associated with religio-magical ceremony, each successive generation of tribal priest or chief
strengthened and elaborated the ritual, so among the Mau Mau

each successive oath-taking ceremony became more and more violent in its control over the participants.

Writing in 1954, Ione Leigh stated that there were then eight degrees of oath-taking, each with a different ritual. . . .

The first oath, which is the mildest, is taken in a darkened room where an arch of sugar-cane or banana-leaves has been erected. In an atmosphere of gloom, the candidate divests himself of all European articles such as watches, shoes and clothing. Rings of Igoka grass are then placed over his head and wrists, and standing naked before the arch he takes the oath. Seven *sodum* apples are included in the ritual to bring misfortune to him if he breaks the oath; the eyes of a slaughtered sheep, pierced with *mugai* thorns, also denote the fate of those who break their vows.

A 'banana-bell', which has been hollowed out and filled with a mixture of blood and earth, is rotated seven times round his head, after which a stick of wild hibiscus is dipped into the blood and put to his lips. He licks the blood, and bites the chest of the slaughtered sheep seven times. Blood is then drawn from his arm and mixed with the sheep's blood, which all initiates must drink. This forms the 'blood-brotherhood'. Live cats and dogs and certain parts of human bodies are sometimes nailed to Mau Mau altars.

Leigh writes that the oaths and rituals increase in bestiality. Among the pledges that the initiate must give is one stating that whenever he kills a European he will cut off the head, extract the eyeballs, and then drink the liquid from them.

For the fourth oath (Leigh continues), which is usually taken before an African becomes a Captain in the Mau Mau army, a dead body has to be provided. At the ceremony the fingers of the dead man are bent seven times, and his eyes pricked seven times. A Major takes the fifth oath. He is required to bite the brain of a dead African seven times. For a Brigadier, the brain of a *white* man has to be provided. The candidate proceeds to eat seven pieces of it. A General, who takes the seventh oath, is required to eat, besides the brain, the wrist-bones of a white man, broken up and mixed with his excrement and blood.

For the last oath, a man and a child must first be killed. The heart of the child is cut from its body, and pricked seven times with a nail; the brains and blood of the dead man are then mixed with the blood of the oath-takers, and all members are required to drink the draught.

In order to intensify the 'atmosphere' of these oath-taking ceremonies, they were usually accompanied by sexual orgies and perversions involving many animals—rams, dogs, sheep and so on. These orgies are so disgusting that the authenticated reports on them are not available for general study. They may be consulted on the premises of the Colonial or Commonwealth Relations Office Library, and in one or two of the major libraries; to turn the pages of these documents is a more brutalising experience than any resulting from a perusal of the reports of travellers and missionaries in the cannibal territories of the South Sea Islands, Central South America, Equatorial Africa, or the North Island of New Zealand.

The final word on cannibalism may perhaps be left to A. I. Hopkins, whose comments on the customs of the Solomon Islanders have already been quoted. Writing in more general terms, he has this to say:

> It is noticeable how people who have never been cannibals despise the horrible thing; and how quickly it disappears when a cannibal tribe comes into contact with a wider world than that merely of their own bush villages. Directly daylight falls on the habit, it withers away. This is remarkable when we remember the sanctity of it in primitive man's eyes. The cannibal is *not* necessarily a hopelessly degraded brute, but a man who has not yet lived out of the dark obscurity of bush tribalism, and so has blindly followed a practice deep-rooted in the sacrificial ideas common to man the world over from his earliest days.

BIBLIOGRAPHY

Among the authors and works consulted, the most important are the following:

Basden, G. T., *Among the Ibos of Nigeria* (Seeley Service, 1921)

Bates, H. W., *The Naturalist on the Amazons* (John Murray, 1863)

Benedick, Ruth, *Patterns of Culture* (Routledge, 1935)

Bentley, Rev. W. Holman, *Pioneering on the Congo* (R.T.S. two vols., 1900)

Berry, R. G., *The Sierra Leone Cannibals* (Proceedings of the Royal Irish Academy, vol. xxx, section C., no. 2, 1912)

Bjerre, Jens, *The Last Cannibals* (Michael Joseph, 1956)

Boas, Franz, *The Social Organisation and Secret Societies of the Kwakiutl* (Report of the U.S. National Museum, 1895)

Brown, Rev. G., *Melanesians and Polynesians* (Macmillan, 1910)

Chalmers, Rev. J., *Life and Work in New Guinea* (R.T.S., 1895)

Codrington, R. H., *The Melanesians* (Oxford University Press, 1891)

Coombe, Florence, *Islands of Enchantment: Many-sided Melanesia* (Macmillan, 1911)

Cotlow, L., *Zanzabuku* (Robert Hale, 1957)

Dennis, Rev. J., *Social Evils of the Non-Christian World* (London, 1899)

Elkin, A. P., *The Australian Aborigines* (Angus & Robertson, 1938)

Evans-Pritchard, E.E., Article in *Africa*, vol. 26 (The African Institute, 1956)

Fox, C. E., *The Threshold of the Pacific* (Kegan Paul, 1924)

Frazer, Sir James G., *The Golden Bough* (Macmillan, twelve vols., 1890–1915)

Grubb, W. B., *A Church in the Wilds* (Seeley Service, 1925)

Gwyther, J., *Captain Cook and the South Pacific* (Houghton, Mifflin, Boston, 1954)

Hinde, S. L., *The Fall of the Congo Arabs* (Methuen, 1897)

Hopkins, A. I., *In the Isles of King Solomon* (Seeley Service, 1928)

Horne, G., and Aiston, G., *Savage Life in Central Australia* (Macmillan, 1924)

James, E. O., *Origins of Sacrifice* (John Murray, 1933)

Johnson, Martin, *Cannibal-Land* (Boston and New York, 1922)

Johnston, Sir Harry, *George Grenfell and the Congo* (Hutchinson, two vols., 1908)

Kapen, E. W., *Sociological Progress in Mission Lands* (Fleming Revell, New York, 1914)

Keane, A. H., *South America* (London, 1909)

Kyle-Little, Syd., *Whispering Wind* (Hutchinson, 1957)

Lange, Algot, *In the Amazon Jungle* (Putnam, New York, 1912)

Leakey, L. S. B., *Mau Mau and the Kikuyu* (Methuen, 1952)

Leigh, Ione, *In the Shadow of the Mau Mau* (W. H. Allen, 1954)

Mariner, W., and Martin, J., *An Account of the Natives of Tonga Islands* (Constable, Edinburgh, 1827)

Maynard, F., and Dumas, A., *The Whalers* (Hutchinson, 1937)

McNab, Robert, *The Old Whaling Days* (Whitcombe & Tombs, New Zealand, 1913)

Meek, C. K., *The Northern Tribes of Nigeria* (Clarendon Press, Oxford, two vols., 1925)

Meek, C. K., *Tribal Studies in Northern Nigeria* (Routledge & Kegan Paul, Ltd., two vols., 1931)

Memorandum on the Mau Mau Oath Ceremonies (Report to the Secretary of State for the Colonies by the Parliamentary Delegation to Kenya, January, 1954) (H.M.S.O., 1954)

Métraux, A., *Easter Island* (André Deutsch, 1957)

Michelsen, Rev. Oscar, *Cannibals Won for Christ* (London, 1894)

Murray, J. H. P., *Papua, or British New Guinea* (Fisher Unwin, 1912)

Perry, W. J., *The Children of the Sun* (Methuen, 1923)

Purves, D. L. (Editor), *Cook's Voyages Round the World* (Nimmo, Hay & Mitchell, Edinburgh, c. 1880)

Reed, A. H. and A. W. (Editors), *The Journals of Captain Cook* (New Zealand, 1951)

Rice, A. P., Article in *The American Antiquarian*, vol. xxxii (1910)

Romilly, H. H., *The Western Pacific and New Guinea* (John Murray, 1886)

Roscoe, John, *The Bagesu and Other Tribes of the Uganda Protectorate* (The Royal Society, 1924)

Roth, H. Ling, *The Natives of Sarawak* (London, two vols., 1896)

Russell of Liverpool, Lord, *The Scourge of the Swastika* (Cassell, 1954)

Seligmann, C. G., *The Melanesians of British New Guinea* (Cambridge University Press, 1910)

Simpson, Colin, *Adam in Ochre* (Angus & Robertson, 1938)

Spence, Basil, Article in *Sudan Notes and Records*, vol. III, no. 4 (Dec. 1920)

Spencer, B., and Gillen, F. J., *The Arunta* (Macmillan, two vols., 1927)

St Johnston, A., *Camping Among Cannibals* (Macmillan, 1883)

Talbot, P. A., *Southern Nigeria* (Clarendon Press, Oxford, three vols., 1926)

Tregear, E., *The Maori Race* (New Zealand, 1904)

Walker, H. W., *Wanderings among South Sea Savages* (Witherby, 1909)

Wallace, A. R., *Travels on the Amazon* (Ward Lock, 1853)

Ward, Herbert, *A Voice from the Congo* (Heinemann, 1910)

Williams, F. E., *Orokaiva Society* (Clarendon Press, Oxford, 1930)

Williams, F. E., *The Natives of the Purari Delta* (Port Moresby, 1924)

INDEX

INDEX